EDEXCEL
A LEVEL
HISTORY

*Active*Book included

Paper 3:

Industrialisation and social change in Britain, 1759–1928: forging a new society

Chris Shelley | Adam Kidson
Series editor: Rosemary Rees

ALWAYS LEARNING

PEARSON

Published by Pearson Education Limited, 80 Strand, London, WC2R 0RL

www.pearsonschoolsandfecolleges.co.uk

Copies of official specifications for all Edexcel qualifications may be found on the website:
www.edexcel.com

Text © Pearson Education Limited 2016

Designed by Elizabeth Arnoux for Pearson

Typeset and illustrated by Phoenix Photosetting, Chatham, Kent

Produced by Out of House Publishing

Original illustrations © Pearson Education Limited 2016

Cover design by Malena Wilson-Max for Pearson

Cover photo © Getty Images: Science and Society Picture Library

The rights of Chris Shelley and Adam Kidson to be identified as authors of this work have been asserted
by them in accordance with the Copyright, Designs and Patents Act 1988

First published 2016

19 18 17 16

10 9 8 7 6 5 4 3 2

British Library Cataloguing in Publication Data

A catalogue record for this book is available from the British Library

ISBN 978 1 447 985372

Copyright notice

Printed in the UK by CPI

Websites

Pearson Education Limited is not responsible for the content of any external internet sites. It is essential
for tutors to preview each website before using it in class so as to ensure that the URL is still accurate,
relevant and appropriate. We suggest that tutors bookmark useful websites and consider enabling
students to access them through the school/college intranet.

A note from the publisher

In order to ensure that this resource offers high-quality support for the associated Pearson
qualification, it has been through a review process by the awarding body. This process confirms
that this resource fully covers the teaching and learning content of the specification or part of
a specification at which it is aimed. It also confirms that it demonstrates an appropriate balance
between the development of subject skills, knowledge and understanding, in addition to preparation
for assessment.

Endorsement does not cover any guidance on assessment activities or processes (e.g. practice
questions or advice on how to answer assessment questions) included in the resource, nor does it
prescribe any particular approach to the teaching or delivery of a related course.

While the publishers have made every attempt to ensure that advice on the qualification and its
assessment is accurate, the official specification and associated assessment guidance materials are the
only authoritative source of information and should always be referred to for definitive guidance.

Pearson examiners have not contributed to any sections in this resource relevant to examination
papers for which they have responsibility.

Examiners will not use endorsed resources as a source of material for any assessment set by Pearson.

Endorsement of a resource does not mean that the resource is required to achieve this Pearson
qualification, nor does it mean that it is the only suitable material available to support the qualification,
and any resource lists produced by the awarding body shall include this and other appropriate
resources.

Contents

Aspects in breadth: from wool combers to bus conductresses – a mobile society, 1759–1928

Aspects in depth: towards prosperity

How to use this book

STRUCTURE

This book covers Paper 3, Option 34.1: Industrialisation and social change in Britain, 1759–1928: forging a new society, of the Edexcel A Level qualification.

You will also need to study a Paper 1 and a Paper 2 option and produce coursework in order to complete your qualification. All Paper 1/2 options are covered by other textbooks in this series.

EXAM SUPPORT

The examined assessment for Paper 3 requires you to answer questions from three sections. Throughout this book there are exam-style questions in all three section styles for you to practise your examination skills.

Section A contains a compulsory question that will assess your source analysis and evaluation skills.

A Level Exam-Style Question Section A

Study Source 15 before you answer this question.

Assess the value of the source for revealing the benefits of Greg's apprentice system for the apprentices themselves and the impact of the system on the working of the mill at Styal.

Explain your answer, using the source, the information about its origin and your own knowledge about the historical context. (20 marks)

Tip
When answering this question you should consider the different people who stood to benefit from the system – does the source offer a broad idea as to who benefited?

Section B contains a choice of essay questions that will look at your understanding of the studied period in depth.

A Level Exam-Style Question Section B

How far were Wedgwood's innovative designs responsible for the success of Josiah Wedgwood's business? (20 marks)

Tip
Reflect on how far Wedgwood's designs were key to his success, balanced against, for example, his ability to target specific wealthy patrons.

Section C will again give you a choice of essay questions but these will assess your understanding of the period in breadth.

A Level Exam-Style Question Section C

How far do you agree that the establishment of Titus Salt's model village Saltaire was the most significant event that influenced the conditions of workers in the years 1759–1928? (20 marks)

Tip
When answering this question you should look for key phrases given in the question. Here the phrase 'most significant' is used – was the creation of Saltaire the most significant influence upon working conditions in the timeframe given?

The Preparing for your exams section at the end of this book contains sample answers of different standards, with comments on how they could be improved.

FEATURES
Extend your knowledge

These features contain additional information that will help you gain a deeper understanding of the topic. This could be a short biography of an important person, extra background information about an event, an alternative interpretation, or even a research idea that you could follow up. Information in these boxes is not essential to your exam success, but still provides insights of value.

EXTEND YOUR KNOWLEDGE

The origins of the British car trade
The first British car company was started in 1896 by group of investors who had speculated unsuccessfully in the Coventry cycle industry. That venture had failed due to the recession in cycle manufacturing and it was decided to attempt to produce cars using imported components from France, which had already developed a car industry, and so was born the Lanchester Car Company. Between 1900 and 1914, 393 motor manufacturing companies were founded in Britain. However, only 113 were still trading in 1914. Despite an increasing demand for automobiles the market remained relatively small.

Knowledge check activities

These activities are designed to check that you have understood the material that you have just studied. They might also ask you questions about the sources and extracts in the section to check that you have studied and analysed them thoroughly.

ACTIVITY
KNOWLEDGE CHECK

Improving education

1 Having considered the changes that were made to education during the 19th century, plot a line graph depicting the progress made by these reforms. The *x*-axis should be the reforms and the *y*-axis the extent of progress (1 – lowest to 10 – highest).

2 Briefly justify the choices you have made and comment upon the shape of your graph. What does it suggest about the overall trend?

3 Write down your ideas as to what might have influenced the introduction of these reforms during the years before 1870.

Summary activities

At the end of each chapter, you will find summary activities. These are tasks designed to help you think about the key topic you have just studied as a whole. They may involve selecting and organising key information or analysing how things changed over time. You might want to keep your answers to these questions safe – they are handy for revision.

ACTIVITY
SUMMARY

Improving working conditions?

1 How did the Industrial Revolution affect working conditions in Britain?

2 What motivated government legislation in Britain's factories?

3 How much did reforms change workers' conditions?

4 What impact did New Model Unionism have for industrial relations?

5 How important was technological advancement for the lives of British workers?

Thinking Historically activities

These activities are found throughout the book, and are designed to develop your understanding of history, especially around the key concepts of evidence, interpretations, causation and change. Each activity is designed to challenge a conceptual barrier that might be holding you back. This is linked to a map of conceptual barriers developed by experts. You can look up the map and find out which barrier each activity challenges by downloading the progression map from this website: www.pearsonschools.co.uk/historyprogressionsapproach.

progression map reference

THINKING HISTORICALLY Cause and consequence (6c)

Connections

Extracts 3–5 show some typical aspects of mercantilism.

Work in groups or individually and answer the following:

Read Extract 3.

1 How might this be seen as similar to Greg's determination to be more successful than his rivals?

Read Extract 4.

2 What did Greg believe about the importance of exportation?

3 How is this similar to LaHaye's ideas about mercantilism?

Read Extract 5.

4 How did Greg's actions reflect this description?

5 Make a list of other similarities between mercantilism and the activities of Samuel Greg. How did millowners' understanding of mercantilism affect their actions during the 19th century?

6 Why it is important for historians to see these links across time and be able to explain how causal factors can influence situations much later in time?

Getting the most from your online ActiveBook

This book comes with three years' access to ActiveBook* – an online, digital version of your textbook. Follow the instructions printed on the inside front cover to start using your ActiveBook.

Your ActiveBook is the perfect way to personalise your learning as you progress through your A Level History course. You can:

- access your content online, anytime, anywhere
- use the inbuilt highlighting and annotation tools to personalise the content and make it really relevant to you.

Highlight tool – use this to pick out key terms or topics so you are ready and prepared for revision.

Annotations tool – use this to add your own notes, for example links to your wider reading, such as websites or other files. Or, make a note to remind yourself about work that you need to do.

*For new purchases only. If the access code has already been revealed, it may no longer be valid. If you have bought this textbook secondhand, the code may already have been used by the first owner of the book.

Introduction
A Level History

WHY HISTORY MATTERS

History is about people and people are complex, fascinating, frustrating and a whole lot of other things besides. This is why history is probably the most comprehensive and certainly one of the most intriguing subjects there is. History can also be inspiring and alarming, heartening and disturbing, a story of progress and civilisation and of catastrophe and inhumanity.

History's importance goes beyond the subject's intrinsic interest and appeal. Our beliefs and actions, our cultures, institutions and ways of living, our languages and means of making sense of ourselves are all shaped by the past. If we want to fully understand ourselves now, and to understand our possible futures, we have no alternative but to think about history.

History is a discipline as well as a subject matter. Making sense of the past develops qualities of mind that are valuable to anyone who wants to seek the truth and think clearly and intelligently about the most interesting and challenging intellectual problem of all: other people. Learning history is learning a powerful way of knowing.

WHAT IS HISTORY?

History is a way of constructing knowledge about the world through research, interpretation, argument and debate.

Building historical knowledge involves identifying the traces of the past that exist in the present – in people's memories, in old documents, photographs and other remains, and in objects and artefacts ranging from bullets and lipsticks, to field systems and cities. Historians interrogate these traces and *ask questions* that transform traces into *sources of evidence* for knowledge claims about the past.

Historians aim to understand what happened in the past by *explaining why* things happened as they did. Explaining why involves trying to understand past people and their beliefs, intentions and actions. It also involves explaining the causes and evaluating the effects of large-scale changes in the past and exploring relationships between what people aimed to do, the contexts that shaped what was possible and the outcomes and consequences of actions.

Historians also aim to *understand change* in the past. People, states of affairs, ideas, movements and civilisations come into being in time, grow, develop, and ultimately decline and disappear. Historians aim to identify and compare change and continuity in the past, to measure the rate at which things change and to identify the types of change that take place. Change can be slow or sudden. It can also be understood as progressive or regressive – leading to the improvement or worsening of a situation or state of affairs. How things change and whether changes are changes for the better are two key issues that historians frequently debate.

Figure 1 Fragment of a black granite statue possibly portraying the Roman politician Mark Antony.

Debate is the essence of history. Historians write arguments to support their knowledge claims and historians argue with each other to test and evaluate interpretations of the past. Historical knowledge itself changes and develops. On the one hand, new sources of knowledge and new methods of research cause *historical interpretations* to change. On the other hand, the questions that historians ask change with time and new questions produce new answers. Although the past is dead and gone, the interpretation of the past has a past, present and future.

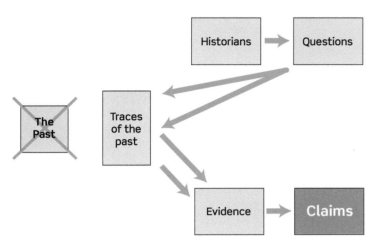

Figure 2 Constructing knowledge about the past.

THE CHALLENGES OF LEARNING HISTORY

Like all other Advanced Level subjects, A Level history is difficult – that is why it is called 'advanced'. Your Advanced Level studies will build on knowledge and understanding of history that you developed at GCSE and at Key Stage 3 – ideas like 'historical sources', 'historical evidence' and 'cause', for example. You will need to do a lot of reading and writing to progress in history. Most importantly, you will need to do a lot of thinking, and thinking about your thinking. This book aims to support you in developing both your knowledge and your understanding.

History is challenging in many ways. On the one hand, it is challenging to build up the range and depth of knowledge that you need to understand the past at an advanced level. Learning

about the past involves mastering new and unfamiliar concepts arising from the past itself (such as the Inquisition, Laudianism, *Volksgemeinschaft*) and building up levels of knowledge that are both detailed and well organised. This book covers the key content of the topics that you are studying for your examination and provides a number of features to help you build and organise what you know – for example, diagrams, timelines and definitions of key terms. You will need to help yourself too, of course, adding to your knowledge through further reading, building on the foundations provided by this book.

Another challenge is to develop understandings of the discipline of history. You will have to learn to think historically about evidence, cause, change and interpretations and also to write historically, in a way that develops clear and supported argument.

Historians think with evidence in ways that differ from how we often think in everyday life. In history, as Figure 2 shows, we cannot go and 'see for ourselves' because the past no longer exists. Neither can we normally rely on 'credible witnesses' to tell us 'the truth' about 'what happened'. People in the past did not write down 'the truth' for our benefit. They often had clear agendas when creating the traces that remain and, as often as not, did not themselves know 'the truth' about complex historical events.

A root of the word 'history' is the Latin word *historia*, one of whose meanings is 'enquiry' or 'finding out'. Learning history means learning to ask questions and interrogate traces, and then to reason about what the new knowledge you have gained means. This book draws on historical scholarship for its narrative and contents. It also draws on research on the nature of historical thinking and on the challenges that learning history can present for students. Throughout the book you will find 'Thinking Historically' activities designed to support the development of your thinking.

You will also find – as you would expect given the nature of history – that the book is full of questions. This book aims to help you build your understandings of the content, contexts and concepts that you will need to advance both your historical knowledge and your historical understanding, and to lay strong foundations for the future development of both.

Dr Arthur Chapman
Institute of Education
University College London

Industrialisation and social change in Britain, 1759–1928: forging a new society

The Industrial Revolution was a momentous period in British history. Not only did it transform Britain into the world's foremost industrial power, it also motivated a great shift in both the working practices of the labouring population and also society itself. Prior to the mid-1700s, Britain had developed a small but prominent economy and this was reflected in the actions that the country took upon the world stage: conservative and small-scale, but with ambitions to enhance it further in the slowly expanding world markets, first by empire building and then through industrial dominance. During the years 1759–1928, these ambitions were realised as Britain became a dominant power and, with newfound confidence, took centre stage during the emerging industrial era. This transition would not have been possible without the working people who provided the energy and physical manpower that allowed Britain to take advantage of technical innovation and industrial methods. In the process of fuelling this growth, the experiences of workers underwent a significant transformation: moving first from a domestic-style of industry to that of a factory-based system, and from hand power to electrification. In each case, the results had a tremendous impact upon workers' lives.

SOURCE 1

An exterior view of Richard Arkwright's first water-powered mill at Cromford in Derbyshire, c1771. Owned by Arkwright, Cromford Mill is usually regarded as the birthplace of the Industrial Revolution.

ARKWRIGHT'S COTTON MILL.

1759 – Josiah Wedgwood founds china factory in Burslem

1769 – Wedgwood factory at Etruria is opened

1780 – Sunday schools are established

1796 – Boulton and Watt open their Soho Foundry

1802 – Heath and Morals of Apprentices Act is passed

1833 – Factory Act is passed Government grant for education is offered

1847 – Factory Act is passed, limiting the working day to ten hours

1870 – Education Act is passed John Starley patents the all-metal Ariel bicycle

1891 – Education Act is passed

1911 – J.M. Barrie's *Peter Pan* is published

1919 – Triple Alliance ends

1927 – Trade Disputes Act is passed

1759
1769
1780
1796
1802
1833
1847
1870
1891
1911
1919
1927

1762	**1762** – Wedgwood appointed royal potter
1771	**1771** – Cromford Mill in Derbyshire is opened
1790	**1790** – Samuel Greg builds the Apprentice House at Styal
1799	**1799** – Combination Act is passed
1831	**1831** – Work begins on the Clifton Suspension Bridge
1843	**1843** – Charles Dickens' *A Christmas Carol* is published
1863	**1863** – Charles Kingsley's *The Water-Babies* is published
1888	**1888** – Matchgirls' strike
1908	**1908** – Children's Act is passed
1914	**1914** – Austin Motor Company produces armaments
1926	**1926** – General strike

This option explores first how the process of industrialisation was able to take place. It considers key technical innovations and innovators who helped to bring about a new way of working: Josiah Wedgwood, Samuel Greg, Isambard Kingdom Brunel, John Starley and Herbert Austin. The contributions of each of these men can be seen in the weathered face of industrialised Britain today – in the railways and bridges of Brunel most clearly perhaps, but looking more closely they can also be seen in the mass production techniques and professionalised workings that were first pioneered in this country by Wedgwood and Austin.

Just as the country developed economically, so did it grow socially, albeit perhaps in an unintended manner; this development is the second theme for attention. Industrial expansion encouraged a more confident workforce that increasingly demanded improvements to both its working and living conditions, and as the period wore on it gradually achieved these demands. Not only was legislation passed, but individuals, enriched by the burgeoning economy, undertook private social experiments to find new ways of working and living – Titus Salt's now famous Saltaire model village and factory is perhaps the best known of these. Collectively these developments helped to promote a more inclusive society – one that did not simply view workers as there to be worked excessively for the benefit of employers, but rather a more collaborative relationship whereby the importance of workers was acknowledged and acted upon. This more sympathetic attitude developed over the course of the 19th century and was perhaps the result of spreading affluence, which itself encouraged a more reflective approach to the world and personal relationships.

In focusing upon each of these themes during the industrial age, this option encourages the same sense of reflection and allows for a closer look at how the country grew up, and how our current working and living practices came to be established.

3.1 Changing patterns of adult work and working conditions

KEY QUESTIONS

- What drove the changes to working patterns and conditions in the years 1759–1928?
- What impact did workers' unions have on changes to working conditions in the years 1759–1928?

INTRODUCTION

The history of Britain in the years 1759–1928 is very much a history of transformation. Within this period, the country underwent incredible changes, not least within its economy. These changes reshaped society and recast the nation from that of a small island-based economy into the world's largest industrial power by the end of the 19th century. The cause of this transformation was twofold: first, the introduction of machinery driven by power into Britain's industries, initially by water and then steam; and secondly, the organisation of this industry into factories. Each of these developments allowed the existing commercial enterprises – weaving and glass-making for example – to grow substantially. The advent of water-powered machines in particular encouraged the transition of Britain's industry from its traditional, small-scale, domestic base to a more professional and industrialised **factory system**. It was this shift more than any other that dramatically transformed the economic and social structures in Britain. It did this by raising productivity and also reducing manufacturing costs, precipitating both a rapidly expanding economy and also the creation of a more urban working and middle class.

The industrialisation of Britain during this time had a profound effect upon the lives of the country's growing population. The shift towards more urban living based around the new factory system encouraged challenging working conditions, as new enterprises sought to maximise their profits and exploit the growing demand for work among a rapidly expanding population. In this regard, the industrialisation of Britain not only generated employment and substantial profits, it also created difficult social and economic problems. These problems helped to characterise the interactions between the emergent working class and new middle class – a relationship that would be fraught with tension as the two demographics each jostled for the enhancement of their respective positions.

KEY TERM

Factory system
A method of mass manufacturing using machinery held in a central location and operated by employed labour.

1769 – James Watt patents his steam engine

1799 – Combination Act is passed

| 1760 | 1770 | 1780 | 1790 | 1800 | 1810 | 1820 | 1830 | 1840 |

1771 – Richard Arkwright opens Cromford Mill

1802 – Health and Morals of Apprentices Act is passed

WHAT DROVE THE CHANGES TO WORKING PATTERNS AND CONDITIONS IN THE YEARS 1759–1928?

Industry and work before 1759

At the start of the 18th century, Britain was already an important industrial nation both in terms of its domestic economy and also its growing export markets. The basis of British commerce and its domestic economic prosperity lay primarily in three distinct fields: textiles, mining and metalwork. Each of these had been thriving industries in their own right. However, by the early 18th century some of them began to decline – mining in particular. Mining had been important in Cornwall and the north. However, it had primarily been **opencast** mining and by the mid-1700s the resources they could extract were all but depleted. As such, the enterprise began to contract – tin mining on Dartmoor, for example, had almost vanished by 1730.

Britain's other main industries were able to survive in part because of new developments in their fields. Abraham Darby established the country's first coke-fuelled blast furnace at Coalbrookdale in Shropshire in 1709, which allowed for the creation of high-quality iron by burning with much more purity and heat than the charcoal that was traditionally used. This helped to invigorate the iron industry, while further afield Sheffield was able to produce quality steel used for cutlery that is still well known today.

However, it was textile manufacturing in the West Country, East Anglia and West Yorkshire that saw the most significant changes, and would transform the mode of working in Britain. Employing thousands of weavers and spinners, these industries were arguably the backbone of the national economy, but they were largely unsophisticated and decidedly localised in their organisation. British industry in the early 1700s was very much a domestic enterprise, with small-scale **cottage industries** producing goods usually on a part-time basis – particularly in the West Country where agricultural workers often supplemented their income by weaving and spinning in the evenings and winter months. These individuals would usually be subcontracted by merchants who had bought up raw materials and required them to be fashioned into sellable goods. The families of those contracted would then work together to fulfil the order. As a system of production, cottage industries had several benefits – not least the conditions of work, which could be decided by the workers themselves – but it was also impractical and often very slow.

Before 1759, therefore, British industry was varied but not without its problems. It had the potential for growth, although some fundamental changes were necessary before it could become the powerhouse of the nation that it did in the century that followed.

KEY TERM

Opencast
A type of mining used to extract minerals close to the surface by digging large pits known as quarries in the earth.

KEY TERM

Cottage industry
Also known as the 'domestic system'. The practice of manufacturing goods on a small scale within individual homes and often on a part-time basis.

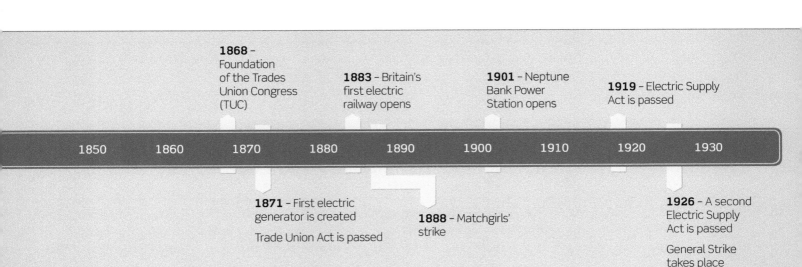

1868 – Foundation of the Trades Union Congress (TUC)

1883 – Britain's first electric railway opens

1901 – Neptune Bank Power Station opens

1919 – Electric Supply Act is passed

1850   1860   1870   1880   1890   1900   1910   1920   1930

1871 – First electric generator is created

Trade Union Act is passed

1888 – Matchgirls' strike

1926 – A second Electric Supply Act is passed

General Strike takes place

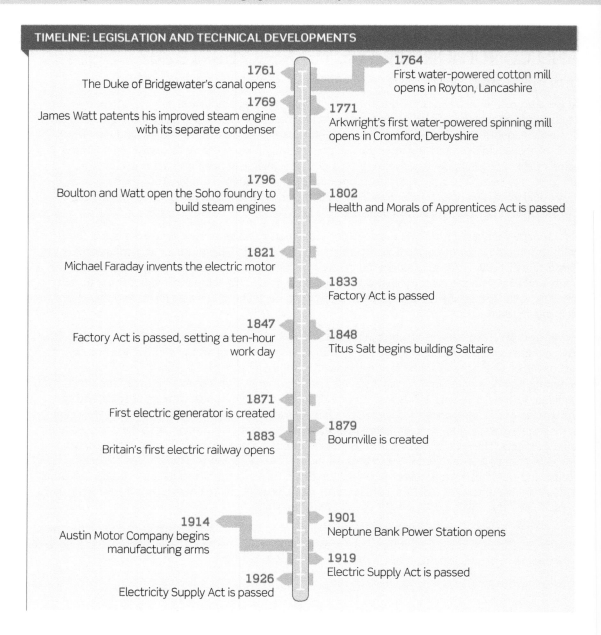

TIMELINE: LEGISLATION AND TECHNICAL DEVELOPMENTS

1761
The Duke of Bridgewater's canal opens

1764
First water-powered cotton mill opens in Royton, Lancashire

1769
James Watt patents his improved steam engine with its separate condenser

1771
Arkwright's first water-powered spinning mill opens in Cromford, Derbyshire

1796
Boulton and Watt open the Soho foundry to build steam engines

1802
Health and Morals of Apprentices Act is passed

1821
Michael Faraday invents the electric motor

1833
Factory Act is passed

1847
Factory Act is passed, setting a ten-hour work day

1848
Titus Salt begins building Saltaire

1871
First electric generator is created

1879
Bournville is created

1883
Britain's first electric railway opens

1914
Austin Motor Company begins manufacturing arms

1901
Neptune Bank Power Station opens

1919
Electric Supply Act is passed

1926
Electricity Supply Act is passed

The impact of technology

In the mid-1700s, Britain began a dramatic period of economic and industrial development that made the small island nation the single biggest economic power in the world during the next century. This development became known as the Industrial Revolution and it was motivated by a number of factors, not least technological innovations that allowed British employers to more efficiently manufacture their goods and, in combination with an expanding empire, take a dominant lead in the world economy.

The transition from cottage industry to the factory system from the mid-18th century

As the basis of British prosperity, it is perhaps fitting that what could perhaps be regarded as the most significant industrial development of the 18th century took place in the country's cotton industry. This was Britain's most prominent industry – in Manchester alone there were 30,000 people employed in it by 1774. It was in this industry that a former wigmaker by the name of Richard Arkwright created a water-powered spinning frame in 1768 that could be continuously worked and required few people to maintain it. Patented the following year, it directly challenged the position of the more traditional hand-spinning methods that were currently employed within the homes of Britain's textile cottage industry. Not only was this new machine capable of working around the clock, but it was also possible for it to be handled by unskilled workers. This had the added benefit of cheaper wages, since there would be no need to pay skilled rates as had been the custom when seeking out those spinners and weavers who worked in the traditional ways. The introduction of this 'water frame', as it became known, revolutionised the cotton industry and helped to establish a new method of production that was both more efficient and cheaper: the factory system.

EXTEND YOUR KNOWLEDGE

Richard Arkwright (1732–92)

Arkwright was born in Preston to a tailor, and was himself apprenticed to a barber in nearby Kirkham. In the early 1750s, he set up his own shop in Bolton and there developed a waterproof dye that could be used to colour wigs. After the death of his first wife, in 1761 Arkwright married Margaret Biggins and from this time began to fashion himself as an entrepreneur. Using the proceeds from his wig dye, he began to take an interest in cotton machinery. In 1768 he returned to Preston with John Kay, a clockmaker by profession, and together they designed and built a spinning frame that mechanically spun cotton thread into yarn. This invention challenged the traditional methods of hand-spinning and was powered by water – consequently it was known as a 'water frame'. Arkwright took out a patent on this invention in 1769, and in 1771 opened his first factory in Cromford, Derbyshire. By 1782 he had made £200,000 and employed 5,000 workers in his various factories across the north of England. In 1786 he was knighted.

SOURCE

1 A colour engraving of Richard Arkwright's 1768 water-powered spinning frame. This was a semi-mechanical machine designed to spin cotton.

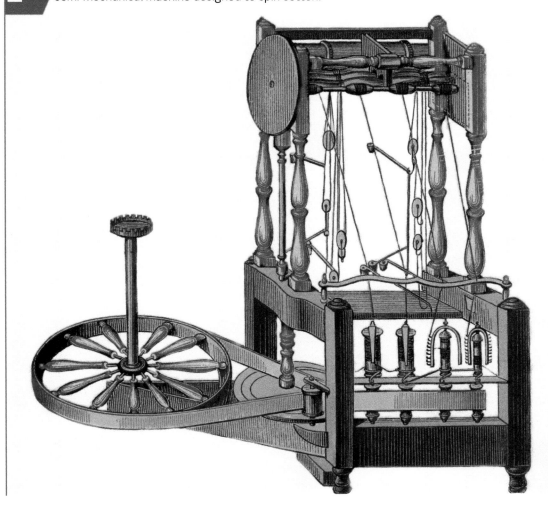

KEY TERM

Carding
A process for preparing fibres for spinning. It disentangles and cleans the fibres by passing them between rough surfaces that are moving in different directions.

The first water-powered mill opened in Royton in Lancashire in 1764 and was a **carding** mill. Arkwright's own spinning mill in Cromford, Derbyshire, opened seven years later and employed 300 workers to operate his frames. The opening of these mills began the transition from the domestic system of cottage industry to a more centralised and concentrated factory system that then became the dominant model for all of Britain's developing industries for the next 150 years. This model was based upon the expensive machines being housed in a single place of work and employees coming to work at them, rather than in their homes as under the old system. This was beneficial for two specific reasons: first, it created a more organised and efficient way of working, since raw materials went only to one place where many spinners and weavers operated; and second, it allowed the owners of these new 'factories' to maintain better control over their employees and therefore extract more production from them. In this regard, the new system was an advance towards more formally organised industrial and commercial practices, which offered a greater opportunity for both personal profit and national prosperity. It is for the creation of this new system that Arkwright has broadly been heralded as the 'father of the Industrial Revolution', having established the means by which Britain would flourish in the newly developing industrial era.

EXTRACT 1

From Joel Mokyr 'The rise and fall of the factory system: technology, forms and households since the Industrial Revolution', a paper delivered to the Carnegie-Rochester Conference on macroeconomics, Pittsburgh, in November 2000.

The Industrial Revolution brought about factories where none were before. The transition was relentless but gradual. Most firms did not switch abruptly from the domestic system to a factory system, but continued to farm out some processes to domestic workers, until mechanization and technological complexity had sufficiently expanded to make it worthwhile to bring the workers under one roof. The cotton industry provides the best example of this mixed factory system. In 1760, this industry was overwhelmingly a domestic industry. The water frame spinning machine changed all that. Richard Arkwright's works in Cromford employed about 300 workers; he also helped found the New Lanark mills in Scotland, which employed a workforce of 1600 in 1815 (most of which were indoor). Such huge firms were unusual, perhaps, but by 1800, there were in Britain around 900 cotton-spinning factories, of which a third were 'mills' employing over 50 workers and the rest small sheds and workshops, with a handful of workers – though even those by that time were larger than households…

From water to steam power from the late-18th century

Richard Arkwright not only transformed industrial practices but he also relocated industry to places where water was readily available and could be easily harnessed to power his new machines. This meant fast-flowing rivers were needed, and mills began to appear along the banks of England's waterways – notably the Styal Mill belonging to Samuel Greg, established on the river Bollin in Cheshire in 1784, and the Tonedale Woollen Mills on the River Tone outside the town of Wellington in Somerset. The latter was established in the 1790s and would later create the khaki dye that would colour the uniforms of the British Army during the Second Boer War. The requirement for an abundant water supply forced British workers out of their homes and into the new factories and mills, and in this sense Arkwright can also be credited with directly contributing to the literal demise of the old cottage-based industry.

Despite the importance of Arkwright, he was not the only figure to noticeably contribute to the start of Britain's Industrial

Revolution. It is certainly fair to suggest that he informed the adoption of the factory system, but it was also men such as Matthew Boulton and James Watt who coaxed Britain into the industrial age through their equally bold inventions and entrepreneurial guile. James Watt developed and patented an improved version of Thomas Newcomen's steam engine in 1769 – one which had a separate condenser that consequently allowed for more efficient use of its fuel and which would therefore be cheaper to run. Matthew Boulton was a manufacturer of metal goods whose business sense helped Watt to extend his patent until 1800 and also funded his refinement of the engine. Collectively, they began to build steam engines, first onsite at the purchaser's premises, and then themselves at their Soho Foundry after 1796. These machines were initially used to support Cornish tin mining, but after 1800 Boulton and Watt engines could be found throughout the country powering the factories through their efficient use of steam pressure.

The real significance of the Boulton and Watt engines was the freedom they gave to manufacturing interests in Britain. Until the development of these engines, machines were powered by water, which necessitated a water wheel and usually horses to work them. The introduction of steam-powered engines meant that this geographical restriction was no longer applicable – mechanised factories and mills could be placed wherever the owner desired, generally into urban areas. Since these steam engines were powered by coal, factories could be moved from riversides and into towns where canals, and later trains, could bring the coal. This particular development arguably fuelled the explosion in Britain's industrial output. In the 19th century factories sprang up throughout the country and new towns and cities grew up around them as people flocked to these areas in search of work.

Canal building

With the immediately noticeable impact of inventions such as the steam engine and water frame, it is necessary to also highlight the importance of canals for industrial growth. Although canals had been in existence in Roman times, these had often been following natural rivers and, therefore, did not necessarily link up newly developing industrial areas. However, in July 1761 the 3rd Duke of Bridgewater opened his first canal, which linked his Worsley coal mines in the north-west of England with Manchester. This was intended to allow the more efficient transportation of his coal to the growing city which, it was expected, would enhance the profits of his businesses. Profit was certainly achieved by the duke, but a more long-term benefit to the nation was that his canal helped to make Manchester one of the most industrialised cities in Britain. It provided an effective means for transporting fuel for the growing number of steam engines that were increasingly being used to power the new factories and mills setting the industrial pace.

From steam to electricity in the early 20th century

The cornerstone of industrial development was the introduction of machines. They could work continuously and could often do the work of many men and women. With the subsequent transition from domestic-based to factory-based machine working, power became the next significant step forward, first from water to steam, and then, towards the end of the 19th and into the early 20th century, the introduction of electrical power.

The development of electricity had an equally profound impact upon the national economy and on the working lives of its population. Just as the factory system transformed the nature of working, the advent of electricity reinvented it by allowing increased automation and potential around-the-clock shift work because of the better lighting that electricity afforded. In this sense, both the factory system and electrification dramatically transformed the working lives of the British population and set the basis for the patterns of work employed today.

The world had been aware of electricity since the 1600s, but it was not until the English scientist Michael Faraday invented the first electric motor in 1821 that the potential of electricity as a form of power really became a practical reality. Having established the basic principles, Faraday's motor was developed and became commercially viable in 1871 when Belgian electrical engineer Zenobe Gramme created an electrical generator that could convert mechanical energy into electrical power. The benefits of electricity over steam primarily lay in the greater efficiency that electricity provided. Electrical generators required far less maintenance than steam-powered motors, which relied on belts and shafts that often needed replacing. After the 1890s, when factories began to install electrical generators, many of these establishments saw a 30 percent increase in their productivity. Such were the benefits of this new technology that by the turn of the century factory electrification began in earnest, and between 1900 and 1930 the majority of Britain's industrial centres had made the conversion.

This process was supported by the creation of central power stations for the purpose of supplying electricity to local areas and businesses. The first such central power station was Neptune Bank, which was opened in June 1901 by the Newcastle upon Tyne Electric Supply Company (NESC). NESC purchased the construction from the Walker and Wallsend Gas Union Company after they had obtained parliamentary approval for the supply of electricity in that area two years earlier and had subsequently begun the project. The opening of Neptune Bank arguably heralded a new era for British industry, as it allowed for a consistent and reliable source of electricity, which was essential for production. Such was the power demand placed upon this station that a second was commissioned in 1904 – Carville Power Station. This station eventually superseded Neptune Bank with a much greater capacity: in 1907 it could produce 25,000 kilowatts (kW) compared with Neptune Bank's 3,000 kW.

The creation of centralised power stations also encouraged the development of a national system of power supply, as increasingly people and businesses began to rely upon electricity. In the early 20th century, Britain's 600 power stations often employed different voltages, which made it difficult to integrate a national system. In 1905, Charles Merz, a partner in the firm Merz and McLellan, which had helped to construct Neptune Bank, recognised the benefits of unifying the voltages of power in Britain as this would mean a more efficient supply. In 1916, Merz successfully encouraged parliament to see the benefits of a unified national system that could take advantage of the country's small size and provide a dense network of electricity provision, which would in turn efficiently supply both domestic homes and, more importantly, allow for better production in industry. The

outcome of this was the establishment of a committee in 1917 to investigate the possibility of such a network under the Liberal politician Archibald Williamson.

The subsequent report from this committee, which came out in 1918, stated that the existing variety of small stations meant that costs to consumers were far greater than if their supply could be centralised in fewer, larger facilities. This formed the basis of the 1919 Electricity Supply Act, which provided for the creation of five electricity commissioners to act as regulators for the growing sector. The powers of this body were later increased by the 1926 Electricity Supply Act, which established the Central Electricity Board and paved the way for the creation of Britain's National Grid, which came into service in 1938.

SOURCE

2 From Lord Kelvin's speech at the opening of the Neptune Bank Power Station in Newcastle upon Tyne in June 1901. Kelvin was the first British scientist to be elevated to the House of Lords and had achieved this honour in recognition of his work in thermodynamics – Kelvin accurately proved the temperature of absolute zero.

We have seen at work what many have not seen before – a system realised in which a central station generates power by steam engines and delivers electricity to consumers at distances varying, I think, from a quarter of a mile to over three and a half miles... A larger station is in prospect, larger work is contemplated. This admirable but comparatively small station at Neptune Bank makes a splendid beginning... What I am seeing today is the dream of my life realised. I do not know the limits of electricity, but it will go beyond anything we can conceive of today...

ACTIVITY
KNOWLEDGE CHECK

The importance of technology

1 Using the material you have read and your own knowledge, produce a line graph that illustrates the development and impact of technology. Along the x-axis (base) you should write the development and year, and along the y-axis (height) you should score the impact from 1 to 10, with 10 being most significant.

2 What shape is your graph, and what might you interpret from it about the impact of technological development?

The impact of legislation

The technological advancements between 1759 and 1928 were undoubtedly great and had a profound impact upon the working lives of Britain's population. The introduction of the factory system in particular was a fundamental shift in working practices that greatly compromised the conditions and style of work adopted by British workers. Prior to the development of this system, people had been employed in their own homes – work would often be undertaken on a **piecework** basis and therefore workers and their families could set the pace of their working day, choosing when to work and for how long. Under the new, more regimented, factory regime, however, these conditions were radically changed, as employers sought to extract as much productivity from their employees as possible. This was in part due to the desire for profit, but also because the new machinery they bought was expensive and, therefore, they sought to maximise its potential in the increasingly competitive commercial markets that were developing.

> **KEY TERM**
>
> Piecework
> Work paid for per item produced by the worker, rather than paying them a wage or salary.

In the race for greater profits and market share, working conditions and patterns for those employed in the new factories and mills were far bleaker than previously encountered working within the domestic system. Rather than setting their own working day, employees were required to work hours determined by their employer, often reaching 14 hours and, in some cases, 18 hours a day. The impact of these long days was compounded by the conditions in which people worked – factories and mills were noisy and poorly ventilated, conditions that had significant health consequences in addition to the immediate dangers of operating moving machinery when very tired. Given these hazards, accidents were frequent and mortality was high. The average age to which a factory worker in Manchester lived was only 17 years during the early 1840s, according to the social reformer Edwin Chadwick, whose *Report on the Sanitary Condition of the Labouring Population of Great Britain* was published in 1842. Given this low age, the government periodically passed legislation to regulate working conditions after pressure from reform-minded MPs, who themselves were often motivated by working-class movements desirous to improve their workplace experiences (see page 25).

The Combination Acts of 1799 and 1800

To suggest that all the legislation passed by the British government was always intended to improve the conditions of the country's working people would be misleading. Certainly, laws were passed that achieved this aim, but this was not the immediate intention of the government. As industrialisation got underway, there was first a sympathy with employers rather than the workers themselves. This was principally because of the economic benefits that these businesses brought the nation: they produced the goods that allowed merchants to export abroad and which consequently promoted economic growth. This commercial mindset was the product of **laissez-faire** thinking that had dominated government policy since the late 17th century. Under this theory, economic development was achieved by leaving employers and the markets to themselves; therefore for government to intervene in living and working conditions would not be expected. Consequently, in the newly emerging industrial world, early legislation sought to protect employers and to break down any barriers that might affect their ability to produce and, more importantly, prosper.

> **KEY TERM**
>
> Laissez-faire
> An economic concept promoting the right of people to manage their own affairs with limited intervention from the state, in the belief that leaving things to naturally take their course is always the best policy. It is particularly dominant as a theory under which governments leave businesses to manage their own affairs within the economic market. This is often referred to as 'free trade'.

Given the very different nature of working within the new factory system that was developing, one of the greatest barriers encountered by employers was the workforce itself. Faced with challenging working conditions such as long hours in noisy and dangerous environments, in the late 18th century workers had begun to form themselves into **trade unions** as a way to extract better wages and working conditions – using the threat of combined strike action should their demands not be met. These unions were often extensions of existing **craft guilds**, which artisans had developed as a means of ensuring the quality of their products and as a means of controlling entry into their craft. In the challenging circumstances of the late 18th century, this development of unions was viewed with some distress in Britain, as their emphasis upon workers' rights was seen as having the potential to encourage **Jacobinism** – a radical attitude that had encouraged revolution in France and was arguably central to the outbreak of war that Britain waged against that nation at the time. In response to the perceived threat of unions, the government passed Combination Acts in 1799 and 1800 that made it illegal for workers to join together against their employer. These Acts carried a prison sentence of up to three months for anyone who contravened the legislation, and as such the opportunity for workers to help themselves was taken from them. In 1824, these Acts were repealed and replaced with the Combinations of Workmen Act in 1825, which made combining for the express purpose of demanding either wage increases or changes to working hours illegal.

> **KEY TERMS**
>
> Trade union
> An association of workers from a trade who bind together to protect and improve working conditions by collective bargaining and action.
>
> Craft guild
> An association of craftsmen who bind together in order to protect their particular craft. They developed in the medieval period.
>
> Jacobinism
> The practices of Jacobins, the members of the Jacobin Club, which was a revolutionary political club in France.

SOURCE 3

From the Combination Act 1800. It was introduced by William Pitt the Younger's administration after fears that striking workers might promote Jacobinism and undermine the national economy. At the turn of the century Britain was engaged in war with France.

I. Whereas it is expedient to explain and amend an Act [39 Geo. III, c. 81]... to prevent unlawful combinations of workmen... be it enacted... that from... the passing of this Act, the said Act shall be repealed; and that all contracts, covenants and agreements whatsoever... at any time... heretofore made... between any journeymen manufacturers or other persons... for obtaining an advance of wages of them or any of them, or any other journeymen manufacturers or workmen, or other persons in any manufacture, trade or business, or for lessening or altering their or any of their usual hours or nine of working, or for decreasing the quantity of work (save and except any contract made or to be made between any master and his journeyman or manufacturer, for or on account of the work or service of such journeyman or manufacturer with whom such contract may be made), or for preventing or hindering any person or persons from employing whomsoever he, she, or they shall think proper to employ... or for controlling or anyway affecting any person or persons carrying on any manufacture, trade or business, in the conduct or management thereof, shall be... illegal, null and void...

II.... No journeyman, workman or other person shall at any time after the passing of this Act make or enter into, or be concerned in the making of or entering into any such contract, covenant or agreement, in writing or not in writing... and every... workman... who, after the passing of this Act, shall be guilty of any of the said offences, being thereof lawfully convicted, upon his own confession, or the oath or oaths of one or more credible witness or witnesses, before any two justices of the Peace... within three calendar months next after the offence shall have been committed, shall, by order of such justices, be committed to and confined in the common gaol, within his or their jurisdiction, for any time not exceeding 3 calendar months, or at the discretion of such justices shall be committed to some House of Correction within the same jurisdiction, there to remain and to be kept to hard labour for any time not exceeding 2 calendar months.

Early factory reforms

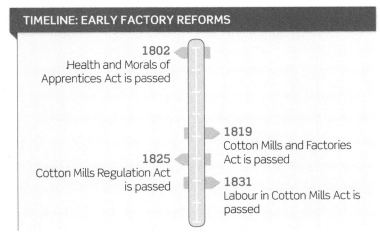

TIMELINE: EARLY FACTORY REFORMS

1802
Health and Morals of Apprentices Act is passed

1819
Cotton Mills and Factories Act is passed

1825
Cotton Mills Regulation Act is passed

1831
Labour in Cotton Mills Act is passed

As industrialisation continued and factories grew apace, increasingly the government felt bound to address some of the emerging problems within the country's urban workplaces – especially concerning the employment of children and their working conditions. What motivated this interest in particular

was a medical report published in 1784 about an outbreak of fever in one of the mills in Radcliffe, Manchester, which belonged to the future prime minister Sir Robert Peel. Concerned by the conditions laid out in the report, in 1802 Peel introduced the Health and Morals of Apprentices Act, which required that mills and factories be adequately ventilated and that the children working in them work no more than 12 hours a day and no longer at night. It also set out demands for child apprentices to receive a basic education and to attend church at least twice a month. The Act was the first attempt by a British government to improve working conditions. However, it was poorly enforced and it only applied to apprentices and not the broader workforce of children who were not apprenticed. In this regard, the Act was insubstantial at achieving wholesale improvements, although it did pave the way for further reforms. These included the Cotton Mills and Factories Act in 1819, which set an age restriction for children's employment. Under this Act, child workers had to be over nine years of age and, if under 16, were also restricted to 12-hour working days. This Act only applied to the cotton industry, but it covered all child workers and not just apprentices as the earlier Act had done. In this respect, legislation was gradually being extended to regulate working practises for the very young, but it was still being balanced with the economic demands of the country and with some awareness of the impact of such legislation for employers. The impact of this legislation became evident when an amendment to the Act was introduced in 1825 by John Cam Hobhouse, who proposed allowing magistrates to take their own initiative when upholding the law. Many employers evaded the Act and allowed underage children to work in their mills, since this was both good for them and also the children's families, who often relied on the extra income they brought home. This left the employer exposed to potential legal action and, as was argued by critics of the legislation, gave greater power to the workers themselves, who could consequently extract concessions for their silence.

Despite opposition – usually from mill-owning MPs themselves – the issue of child labour was a growing concern for parliament, and subsequent legislation sought to reduce the working day even further. In 1831, Hobhouse introduced further successful legislation that forbade night working for anyone under 21 years of age, while the 12-hour working day was extended to those under 18. Like earlier legislation, it was only applicable to cotton. This was because by the 1820s the cotton industry was Britain's most successful enterprise, thanks in the main to the cheap supply of raw materials, the fact that cotton yarns were more suited to mechanical handling and also travelled more easily than their woollen rivals. That the legislation only applied to this industry was a significant limitation given the diversity of Britain's industrial economy by the 1830s, and as such social reform-minded MPs were resolved to extend protections across more industries.

The Factory Act 1833

The most noteworthy of legislation was perhaps that introduced by Michael Sadler and Lord Ashley in 1833, which proposed regulating the working day for those working in the textile industry. This objective had been attempted with previous legislation. However, its enforcement had been minimal; under the 1819 Act, for example, only two cases had been effectively brought to trial and this was largely the result of the dominance of support for **free trade**, which insisted that government leave employers to manage their own affairs. The context by 1833 had arguably shifted in favour of greater regulation of factories, since there had developed a reforming zeal in Britain: first, following political changes with the passage of the **Great Reform Act** in 1832 and then the push for the abolition of slavery, which finally came with the Abolition of Slavery Act in 1833. These events created a groundswell of support for factory reform, since many people had begun to liken the working conditions in them to slavery itself – particularly in regard to the hours worked by children and young adults. Given this criticism, the enthusiasm for factory reform was quite substantial and in consequence the passage of the proposed legislation was quite straightforward. The resultant Factory Act set out the following.

- There would be no child workers under nine years of age.
- Employers must have a certification of age for their child workers.
- Children between the ages of 9 and 13 were only allowed to work a maximum of nine hours a day.
- Children between the ages of 13 and 18 could only work up to 12 hours each day.
- There would be no night working for any children.
- Children should receive at least two hours of schooling each day.
- Four inspectors were appointed as part of a Factory Commission to enforce the law.

SOURCE

 From a speech made by Michael Sadler MP in 1832.

Even, at this moment, while I am thus speaking on behalf of these oppressed children, what numbers of them are still at their toil, confined to heated rooms, bathed in perspiration, stunned with the roar of revolving wheels, poisoned with the noxious effluvia of grease and gas, till at last, weary and exhausted, they turn out almost naked, plunge into the inclement air, and creep shivering to beds from which a relay of their young work-fellows have just risen; and such is the fate of many of them at the best while in numbers of instances, they are diseased, stunted, crippled, depraved, destroyed.

The impact of the 1833 Act was mixed. In one sense, it did not immediately improve the working conditions for the young because it was still significantly limited. The legislation only applied to the textile industry and, perhaps more importantly, the four inspectors appointed could not effectively inspect Britain's 4,000 mills by themselves. In this respect, it offered a framework for future improvements and perhaps signalled the intention to address the labour issue in factories, rather than have any immediate positive effect. Indeed, the restriction of children's labour was often ignored by employers – many children continued to work long hours and also at night. Such action was often freely entered into, since the families of working children usually relied upon the additional income provided by their offspring. By not considering the financial impact upon working families' lives, the Act arguably forced their non-compliance and as such its motivation, however laudable, was therefore undermined by the very people whom it was intending to help. Despite these limitations, it did nonetheless establish a more determined attitude and at least a basis for better regulation. The creation of a Factory Commission was a significant step forward because for the first time there was now a permanent regulatory body to inspect Britain's factories and enforce the new legislation – albeit in need of better resourcing.

SOURCE

 From a factory inspector's report in 1836 that records the continuing practice of employing children for long hours and night work despite the passage of the 1833 Factory Act, which prohibited such conditions.

My Lord, in the case of Taylor, Ibbotson & Co. I took the evidence from the mouths of the boys themselves. They stated to me that they commenced working on Friday morning, the 27th of May last, at six A.M., and that, with the exception of meal hours and one hour at midnight extra, they did not cease working till four o'clock on Saturday evening, having been two days and a night thus engaged. Believing the case scarcely possible, I asked every boy the same questions, and from each received the same answers. I then went into the house to look at the time book, and in the presence of one of the masters, referred to the cruelty of the case, and stated that I should certainly punish it with all the severity in my power. Mr Rayner, the certificating surgeon of Bastile, was with me at the time.

Factory reform after 1833

The 1833 reform was a prominent moment in the lives of British workers since it was achieved as a result of increasing concern about the conditions in which they worked. In the late 18th and early 19th centuries, this sympathy had been limited by economic incentives but, as industrialisation continued and more people became employed in factories, a more responsible attitude developed in regard to the nature of employment. In the years following the legislation, further reforms were introduced to extend similar protections to other industries.

The most notable of these reforms was the Factory Act 1844, which restricted the working day to 12 hours and, perhaps most significantly, introduced several clauses that amounted to health and safety requirements in the workplace. These included the requirement that machines with especially dangerous moving parts, which children in particular worked near, should be fenced off; and that mill owners wash their premises every 14 months. These provisions were very progressive and were perhaps the first real attempt to introduce some measure of health and safety into the workplace. They were introduced as part of a broader interest in the well-being of Britain's workers – a consequence of an increasingly affluent middle class that began to seek improvements to the workplace after periodic outbreaks of disease, notably cholera in the 1830s. By setting down certain requirements to enhance the safety of working, the Factory Act 1844 was very well intended. However, its ultimate impact was slow to be seen. This was in part down to the limited number of factory inspectors provided by the commission to ensure compliance, but also the need for workers to remain employed. Therefore, factories where sufficient safety measures were not carried out were often able to continue without action against them. In this deficiency, it would be reasonable to suggest that the Act was very limited. However, it marked a growing awareness of the need for safety and, more particularly, the value of workers to a factory. In this last regard, the impact was more subtly felt, as over subsequent years workers were gradually able to acquire more power over their working experiences (see page 25).

The 1844 Act was followed up with the Factory Act 1847, which limited the working day to ten hours – a demand that had been first issued more than a decade earlier with the Ten Hours Movement. The immediate impact of this particular legislation saw workers being granted a long-held demand that not only improved their working experience but, more importantly, offered the chance to gain further improvements. Over the course of the next ten years, working practices were gradually regulated in terms of the hours in the day that people could work. For example, an 1850 Act stated that women and children were only to work between the hours of 6 a.m. and 6 p.m. in summer and 7 a.m. and 7 p.m. in winter. This was added to in 1878 with the Factory and Workshop Act, which limited women to working 56 hours a week and also raised the minimum working age to ten years old. In 1901, the working age was subsequently raised to 12 years. These reforms were fundamental to promoting a better working experience as they helped to make the working day more manageable and realistic. In addition, they also marked a more progressive attitude towards work within wider society; excessively long hours, especially for children, were increasingly looked upon with concern, and the legislation reflects this more sympathetic attitude. As a marker for social change, the legislation is therefore very significant and tangibly made the experiences of workers more manageable and slowly established something like the pattern of work enjoyed today.

EXTEND YOUR KNOWLEDGE

The Ten Hours Movement

This was a workers' movement that developed in the Pennines during 1830. It was organised by Richard Oastler, a factory manager, who increasingly felt that the length of the working day was tantamount to slavery. In September 1830, he wrote a letter to the *Leeds Mercury* where he set out his criticisms very clearly. This encouraged the creation of short-term committees to work with the growing number of trade unions to achieve a reduction of working hours. His cause won the sympathy of politicians such as Michael Sadler and Lord Ashley, who then periodically introduced legislation to effect the necessary changes. In 1847, an Act was finally passed achieving the ten-hour limit.

ACTIVITY
KNOWLEDGE CHECK

The significance of legislation

Having read about the legislation introduced by the British government, produce and complete a table with the following headings: 'Key legislation', 'Circumstances motivating its creation' and 'Impact on workers'.

The initiatives of Titus Salt and other employers

The improvements to the lives of Britain's working class were not only dependent upon acts of legislation by the government, but also the initiatives of several pioneering employers who looked beyond their balance sheets and profit margins. Individuals such as Titus Salt – influenced to an extent by the earlier work of Robert Owen (see Chapter 2, page 48) – was not only a man of industry, but also a social reformer who saw the developing Industrial Revolution as an opportunity to experiment with his own ideas for the nation's progress.

Titus Salt was in every sense a pioneer. As a mill owner from Bradford who first worked for his father's firm, Daniel Salt and Son, and who, upon his father's retirement in 1833, took over the **worsted cloth** mill directly, Salt used his position to promote not only his own business, but also the lives of his workers. Between 1833 and 1851, his mills became the biggest employer in Bradford, a city that leapt from a population of 13,000 at the turn of the century to 104,000 by 1851. A consequence of this rapid growth was the pollution that was subsequently generated – with more than 200 smokestacks in the city, the air was unpleasant to breathe and often caused respiratory problems. Furthermore, the sewage generated by the increasing population was emptied into the Bradford Beck (the city's main source of water), which resulted in the spread of disease, with regular outbreaks of cholera and typhoid. Bradford was, therefore, one of the most unhealthy places to live in Britain and in the mid-19th century it had one of the country's lowest average age expectancies for unskilled workers – just 18 years.

SOURCE

From Georg Weerth, a German writer who visited Bradford in 1846, commenting upon the condition of that city.

> Every other factory town in England is a paradise in comparison to this hole. In Manchester the air lies like lead upon you; in Birmingham it is just as if you were sitting with your nose in a stove pipe; in Leeds you have to cough with the dust and the stink as if you had swallowed a pound of Cayenne pepper in one go – but you can put up with all that. In Bradford, however, you think you have been lodged with the devil incarnate. If anyone wants to feel how a poor sinner is tormented in Purgatory, let him travel to Bradford.

As one of the largest employers, Salt was unusual in that he took a great interest in the health problems of the city and was actively concerned about the well-being of the inhabitants of Bradford. His concern encouraged him to try to address the issue of air pollution within his own mills and he experimented with ways of reducing the amount of pollutants his chimneys produced. He settled on using a **Rodda smoke burner**, which was designed to reduce the amount of fuel used in burning and employed a closed shell that trapped the smoke and consumed much of it within the burning process. This design reduced the amount being expelled through the mills' chimneys and in 1842 Salt made arrangements for these burners to be used in all of his mills.

The concern he exhibited for improved conditions in the city also extended to his own workforce, to whom he was careful to pay good wages and take care of during times of economic slump. Here, traditional practice was often to lay off workers as contracts declined. However, Salt preferred to keep his workers during these downturns since that bred loyalty and a reliable labour force. This was a costly endeavour but the luxury cloth that Salt's mills produced – made from Peruvian **alpaca wool** – remained a popular commodity and the mills reaped substantial profits that consequently allowed Salt to retain his employees during difficult times.

Saltaire model factory and village

In 1848 Salt was elected Mayor of Bradford and, in this position, he endeavoured to encourage his fellow mill owners to employ the use of the Rodda smoke burner to help reduce the pollution in their city. However, there was little enthusiasm for the idea. Salt was confronted with a general unwillingness by the city's other manufacturers to address local working conditions at the expense of personal profit – these individuals refused to accept that the smoke their chimneys produced had a harmful effect upon their workers. In the face of such resistance, Salt decided to leave Bradford and establish his business three miles outside of the city on the banks of the River Aire. His intention here was to create a new community for his large workforce, one that was not only conducive to industry but also provided a better standard of working conditions for those he employed.

The heart of this new community was a new mill. Construction began in 1850 and took 20 years to finally complete. When it was finished, it was the largest and most modern in Europe, and it was also designed with significantly more sympathy towards its workforce. To reduce noise levels for example, the loud shafting that drove the machines was placed underground, while large flues allowed dust from the wool working to easily escape from the buildings. Furthermore, the entire mill was fitted with Rodda smoke burners to limit the air pollution that was generated. As a construction, the Saltaire Mill, as it became known, was a very progressive building and this reflected the attitude of Titus Salt who was motivated by a sense of humanity as well as profit.

This greater sense of human motivation was further exemplified in the development of Saltaire. Initially, the 3,500 employees of the mill travelled from Bradford; however, part of the construction also involved building 850 homes for employees, as well as additional facilities for the improvement of their quality of life. Saltaire had its own park, church, school, library and selection of shops. Furthermore, Salt's employees were encouraged to participate in recreational activities – the park had its own cricket facilities, while a gymnasium was also created to promote fitness. In effect, Salt had created a new town around his mill – one that was significantly healthier than Bradford. Each of the houses that were constructed was supplied with fresh water from the community's own 500,000 gallon reservoir and public baths and wash houses were also created to encourage workers to keep themselves clean.

These were very evident improvements from the squalor of Bradford. However, as progressive as Saltaire was, to suggest it was entirely Utopian would be misleading. The motivation behind the experiment was not simply humanitarian but also moralistic and designed to promote profit. As such, both the model village and mills were subject to restrictions intended to promote both of these requirements. This was made very clear by a series of laws that Salt himself created and by which the community would be governed. For example, there were 20 rules governing the use of the public park in the village and these included the following.

- No admittance to anyone who is intoxicated.

- Children to be accompanied by an adult.

- The use of the playgrounds is not permitted on Sundays.

- No disorderly conduct, including gambling, will be allowed in the park.

- Public discussion and religious meetings will only be permitted with the written permission of the Firm.

These were typical of the broader rules that Salt imposed and exemplify a desire to encourage good behaviour and a moral attitude. In addition to such regulation, the use of Saltaire's 45 **almshouses** would only be awarded to people of 'good character', while loitering in the community hospital was also forbidden. Perhaps most tellingly, however, was the absence of public houses in the village – instead Salt encouraged more constructive ways to spend free time: fishing, reading and chess were encouraged diversions.

KEY TERM

Almshouse
Charitable housing usually given to the elderly who could no longer work to pay rent.

The rules imposed by Salt denote a sense of regularity and order – common traits in Victorian morality – and this was carried through into the overall structure of both the village and mill. For example, the village was constructed on a grid pattern, with streets named after the royal family: Victoria Road, Albert Terrace and Albert Road, to name a few. These streets contained different types of home dependent upon who was intended to occupy them. Families of millworkers were able to rent houses with two bedrooms, while single workers were given rooms in boarding houses or lodgings within family homes. Reflecting Salt's progressive attitude, these houses were not the back-to-back variety found in other northern cities, but rather had backyards that allowed for good ventilation and space.

The community that Salt created at Saltaire was in a narrow sense just a personal endeavour – the ambition of one man to improve the condition of those who were dependent upon him. As a motivation, this is in itself laudable, but it also helped to pioneer a broader awareness of the need to improve working conditions, and the experiment at Saltaire stood as a model in its strictest sense for the future of factory reform.

A steel engraving of Salt's textile mill, Saltaire, West Yorkshire, 1869 by W.M. Lizars.

John Rylands (1801–88) and George Cadbury (1839–1922)

Titus Salt was not the only employer who was motivated to improve the lives of his employees. His pioneering efforts were added to by other similarly minded individuals such as John Rylands and George Cadbury – both of whom had made personal fortunes in manufacturing: Rylands through textiles and as a merchant in Manchester, and George Cadbury through his family's chocolate production business in Birmingham.

John Rylands was the owner of the country's largest cotton business, which was based in St Helens in Lancashire. He was Manchester's first multimillionaire, having successfully expanded the factory he opened with his brothers and merged with their father's retail firm to create Rylands & Sons in 1819. At its peak, the firm employed 15,000 workers and produced 35 tonnes of cloth each day across the 17 mills that made up the enterprise. In 1847, John Rylands became the sole owner of the business upon the death of his father (his brothers had retired eight years earlier).

Like Salt, Rylands also had a social conscience that he was prepared to act upon. An early example of his philanthropy was his support for the building of the Manchester Ship Canal, for which he invested £50,000 when it was feared that its construction would not be completed. Although this canal undoubtedly benefited his own business, the level of investment he made when it was evident the project might fail is still indicative of his public-spiritedness, since many other businesses in the area would also benefit. Among the many charitable causes to which he gave funds were orphanages and almshouses for aged women. He also built two chapels and a library in Stretford and donated substantial funds to the poor.

George Cadbury was the third son of John Cadbury, the founder of Cadbury's chocolate, and, together with his brothers, was concerned with the quality of life enjoyed by his employees. The family were **Quakers** – a religious group that were well known for their humanitarian and sympathetic attitudes. George and his brothers were aware of the dirty and polluted environment in which many of their workers worked and lived in the industrial centre of Birmingham and wanted to improve these conditions. Having taken over their father's business in 1861, they sought to establish a cleaner environment in which they could work. To this end, like Salt, they sought to create a new model factory town away from the grimy city centre. In 1879 they created Bournville, a new town four miles south of Birmingham that was intended to provide a healthier and cleaner environment

KEY TERM

Quaker
A member of the Religious Society of Friends, a religious movement established in the mid-17th century by George Fox. It maintains that God is an 'inner light' that resides within each person. This belief subsequently encourages a more sympathetic and compassionate attitude towards every individual.

for their workers. By 1900, Bournville had 313 houses and they included large gardens – unusual for workers in other towns, where homes were built as compactly as possible in order to minimise costs and make the most efficient use of space possible.

In addition to improved housing, the factory at Bournville paid above-average wages and also provided the opportunity for paying into a pension scheme, as well as other employment benefits such as medical provision and joint committees to discuss the progression of the business. These were progressive steps for workers and the adoption of these practices at Bournville was arguably instrumental in promoting the wider provision of such benefits by the end of the century.

The efforts of Rylands, Cadbury and especially Salt evidenced a growing concern among many employers for the well-being of their workforce. The development of this awareness is perhaps the consequence of several factors: firstly, a social-spiritedness that recognised that employees are fundamentally no different from themselves and as such deserved decent opportunities for a better standard of living, and secondly, an increasing sense of the value of a loyal workforce. Having become wealthy from the labours of these people, there was perhaps an awareness among employers of the value of their workforce – an idea that became much more apparent as industrialisation quickly became the backbone of the British economy and dependence on a reliable workforce increased. This realisation was fundamental to the improved conditions that workers began to enjoy and was arguably the foundation of the better conditions that employees benefit from now. In this sense, the significance of individuals such as Salt, Cadbury and Rylands lies in their pioneering actions – establishing a model for future development that ensured both a loyal workforce that would itself promote greater profit and greater benefits for the workers themselves.

The impact of the First World War on patterns of work

By the beginning of the 20th century, the nature of working in Britain had changed dramatically from that of the late 18th century. During this period, workers had moved from working in their homes to large factory-based employment, where they endured difficult working conditions, mitigated by limited protections before the middle of the century because of the pursuit of profit. Despite improvements over the course of the second half of the 19th century, working conditions generally remained challenging for the majority of those employed – long hours remained a common difficulty for male adults especially, with the current eight-hour day not being achieved until 1935.

Women and work

Further to these long hours, employment was also male-dominated. This was partly the result of government legislation limiting the working hours of women and children more robustly than male adults, but it was also the consequence of conservative attitudes that felt men and women had different roles; men were the breadwinners while women were the homemakers. Though very much a middle-class idea, since working-class women had long been employed in factories and mines, this concept began to flourish towards the end of the 19th century. This belief – known as '**separate spheres**' – developed in the 19th century and increasingly influenced employment practices as preference was given to male applicants. The most common employment opportunities that women found tended to be alongside those men working in domestic service as butlers and footmen, only they worked as maids, housekeepers and nannies – roles that were deemed unthinkable for men. By the turn of the century, there were 1,740,800 women employed in domestic service, while the next largest employer of women was teaching, with only 124,000.

KEY TERM

Separate spheres
An idea that maintained that men and women had separate functions in society. It was the function of men to work outside of the home in paid employment, while women remained in the home and kept it in order for their returning men.

The workplace, outside of domestic service, was therefore heavily male-dominated. However, the start of the First World War transformed this arrangement. With men being called up for active service after 1914, out of necessity women were provided the opportunity to step into previously male roles. More women entered the factories as munitions workers; they also became agricultural labourers, bus conductors, ambulance drivers and performed a host of other roles that had previously been denied to them. Although many of these would only be temporary – munitions work, for example, declined after the end of war – the opportunity had arguably raised the issue, which could now no longer be ignored. In the case of munitions work, more than 700,000 women were employed in this dangerous industry by the end of the war – accounting for around 40 percent of the jobs women were performing during this period (with the exclusion of domestic service). In this regard, the war, though brutal and unforgiving, also provided opportunity for women to break down gender employment barriers. In the years following 1918, this was to greatly inform the future of not only Britain's workplaces, but also social attitudes towards gender discrimination.

SOURCE
8

From the magazine *Punch* in June 1916. *Punch* was a politically satirical publication that addressed significant issues of the day.

It is quite impossible to keep pace with all the new incarnations of women in war-time – 'bus-conductress, ticket-collector, lift-girl, club waitress, post-woman, bank clerk, motor-driver, farm-labourer, guide, munition maker. There is nothing new in the function of ministering angel: the myriad nurses in hospital here or abroad are only carrying out, though in greater numbers than ever before, what has always been woman's mission. But whenever he sees one of these new citizens, or hears fresh stories of their address and ability, Mr Punch is proud and delighted. Perhaps in the past, even in the present, he may have been, or even still is, a little given to chaff Englishwomen for some of their foibles, and even their aspirations. But he never doubted how splendid they were at heart; he never for a moment supposed they would be anything but ready and keen when the hour of need struck.

The entry of women into male work roles was perhaps the most noticeable impact of the First World War upon British workplaces, but there was also a shift in work patterns specifically. The urgency of war meant that hours of work were reformed to maximise the productivity of those working on the home front. One way this was achieved in Britain was the adoption of British Summer Time (BST) in May 1916, which extended daylight hours so that factories could open for longer. In addition to extended hours, the increasing reliance upon women raised the issue of wage discrepancies between the sexes. Prior to the war, women in work were paid on average less than half that of their male counterparts – men received on average 26 shillings a week and women only 11 shillings. With the rise in the number of women workers, and in particular of women doing the exact same work as men, the question of wages became a significant issue. In mid-August 1918, the women employees of the London's bus and tram services went on a strike that quickly spread to the south-east of England and also to the London Underground, making the issue an acute one that the British government could not ignore. The strike eventually came to an end towards the end of August when women were conceded their war bonus of five shillings, which had been withheld. However, the principle of equal pay was not agreed.

The consequence of the strike was that the government appointed a committee to investigate the possibility of equal pay for women. The report published after the war in 1919 endorsed the principle of equal pay for equal work, but also acknowledged that women would be less likely to be as productive as men on the grounds of lesser strength and personal health requirements. Although this report did not produce a tangible benefit for women, it did present a clear undertaking by the government to at least recognise the value that women had in the workplace, and this was arguably a definite stride towards diluting the male concentration in Britain's workplaces.

A Level Exam-Style Question Section C

How far do you agree that the establishment of Titus Salt's model village, Saltaire, was the most significant event that influenced the conditions of workers in the years 1759–1928? (20 marks)

Tip

When answering this question you should look for key phrases given in the question. Here the phrase 'most significant' is used – was the creation of Saltaire the most significant influence upon working conditions in the timeframe given?

ACTIVITY
KNOWLEDGE CHECK

The role of individuals

1 What motivated Titus Salt to set up Saltaire?

2 How did this experiment attempt to improve living and working conditions for his workers?

3 What do you think is the significance of Titus Salt and his model factory?

WHAT IMPACT DID WORKERS' UNIONS HAVE ON CHANGES TO WORKING CONDITIONS IN THE YEARS 1759–1928?

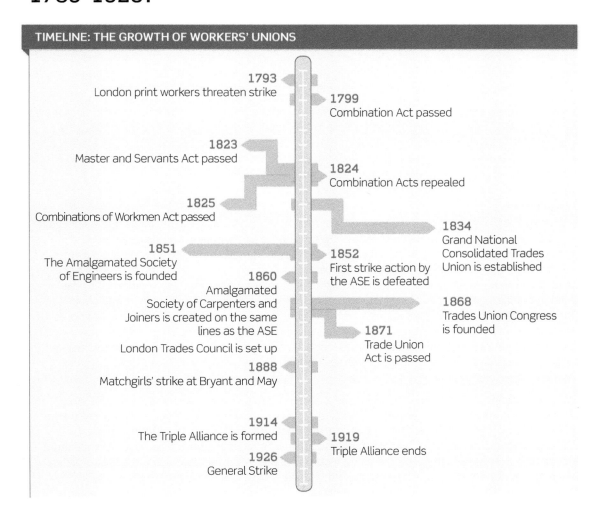

TIMELINE: THE GROWTH OF WORKERS' UNIONS

1793
London print workers threaten strike

1799
Combination Act passed

1823
Master and Servants Act passed

1824
Combination Acts repealed

1825
Combinations of Workmen Act passed

1834
Grand National Consolidated Trades Union is established

1851
The Amalgamated Society of Engineers is founded

1852
First strike action by the ASE is defeated

1860
Amalgamated Society of Carpenters and Joiners is created on the same lines as the ASE

1868
Trades Union Congress is founded

London Trades Council is set up

1871
Trade Union Act is passed

1888
Matchgirls' strike at Bryant and May

1914
The Triple Alliance is formed

1919
Triple Alliance ends

1926
General Strike

The influence and limitations of workers' associations and unions to 1851

Workers' associations

With the expansion of Britain's industry after 1759 and a subsequent growth in urban working, the nature of the factory setting encouraged workers to bind together in common interest. Long hours, dangerous conditions and low wages presented sufficient motive to seek improvements. As employers became increasingly reliant on their workforce, that workforce sought to extract more favourable conditions through a united front, manifested by first the establishment of trade associations and then more formal unions. These groups were initially organised by skilled tradesmen such as printers, cobblers and mechanics, who sought to protect both their trade and their bargaining hand from being weakened by the growing number of unskilled interlopers that industrialisation attracted.

These early associations had the potential to give workers the opportunity to improve their conditions at work. However, in reality they exhibited a more introverted and self-interested motivation. Having been established by skilled tradesmen, they tended to focus on their own trades within their immediate working area rather than any universal sense of loyalty to a broader class, and as such they remained small, locally focused organisations with little interest outside their own districts. Emphasis was placed upon securing benefits within their profession and this mostly involved setting values on skilled labour above that of unskilled, and particularly ensuring that entry to their

Closed shop
The practice of only employing individuals who are members of a trade union or who are in good standing with that union.

skilled professions was carefully monitored to avoid dilution. Therefore, they tended to operate as regulators for appointing apprentices and they embarked upon early forms of **closed shop** practices. In undertaking these actions, in effect these associations sought to protect their own interest in the face of changing economic structures in Britain. Among the most prominent of these groups were the London printers, who in 1793 petitioned their masters for an increase in their fees given the rising cost of living. They obtained 539 signatures in support of their demands and this degree of unity was able to generate sufficient concern by their employers that led to a successful outcome for the printers. They enjoyed this success because printing was a skill and therefore employers could not easily replace them in the event of a strike. For the growing number of unskilled workers in the textile mills and factories, however, the same opportunity was less effective and decidedly bleak.

Early associations were generally well supported by those in the trade and, because of the skills they had, they could usually command significant improvements as their positions could not easily be replaced in the event of a strike. Consequently, from the late 18th century onwards, there existed a reasonably effective mechanism for workers to unite in common protection. However, it was very selective – unskilled workers did not enjoy the same level of protection.

Trade unions

Unlike the early associations, trade unions were more formal, and organised workers into a collective and united body with the intention of achieving a common aim for the group, usually better working conditions or wages. In binding together, the intention was to create a more forceful voice with which to seek protection. They grew in response to the excessive hours and low wages that employers sought to impose in the pursuit of greater profit, practices that were reinforced by the rapid population growth that made labour cheap. Between 1750 and 1850, Britain's population rose from 6 million to over 17 million, and such prolific growth reinforced the freedom of employers to set whatever conditions they wanted, on the grounds that if workers were not happy with their working conditions then new workers could easily be found. Under these conditions, isolated action enjoyed limited success and it became necessary to seek other ways of securing the interests of general workers.

Two events helped the growth of unionism in Britain. The first was war with France in 1793 and the second was the relentless growth of mechanised working, which demanded less-skilled workers and which therefore threatened the interests of the existing associations. Initially, the outbreak of war was fundamental to the growth of trade unionism in Britain because it created the environment for economic discontent to grow. The rising food prices that war generated made the cost of living much greater for the working population and this brought the issue of wages more roundly into focus for all workers, regardless of skill or industry. By 1799, weavers in Wigan, for example, had organised themselves into a union to strengthen their hand in seeking a stop to wage reductions, and this practice quickly spread throughout the region. The Association of Weavers had 14 branches in Lancashire by May 1799 and, using this strength, they sought to put pressure upon parliament for redress of their concerns. This particular group is a good example of the growing sense of solidarity, as weavers were a well-regarded workforce who had commanded above-average wages and yet were motivated towards trade unionism because of the worsening economic situation brought on by war.

SOURCE

From an address issued to the general public by the Bolton committee of the Association of Weavers, dated 13 May 1799. It was an address that was intended to be printed and distributed in every town in England.

The present existing Laws that should protect Weavers, etc., from imposition, being trampled underfoot, for want of a union amongst them, they are come to a determination to support each other in their just and legal rights, and to apply to the Legislature of the country for such further regulations, as it may in its wisdom deem fit to make, when the real state of the cotton manufactory shall have been laid before it... [we seek] candid consideration how every necessary of life has increased in price, while the price of labour has undergone a continual decrease.

In addition to a broader awareness among traditionally secure industries, the emergence of the factory system encouraged further growth of unionism. Before the emergence of factories, work was primarily conducted within the home by small units of labour – usually family members or apprentices. In this system, there was a degree of autonomy with regard to working conditions, but this was removed under the factory system and everyone was required to work to the masters' agenda, creating the opportunity for increased resentment and discontent. In this sense the factory created an environment where mutual progress was replaced by a conflicting set of values: fair wages and respect for one, profit and productivity for the other. Under this scheme, the only way for workers to balance these demands, given the power of the masters, was to bind together in the hope that such action would get themselves heard and even elicit some positive response. This was not an easy thing to achieve, however, since Combination Acts (see page 16) banned such unions and these Acts were not repealed until 1824.

Despite this hurdle, the first effort at creating a broader union interest came in 1818 with the Philanthropic Hercules in London and the Philanthropic Society in Lancashire. These organisations sought to unite the working class from across all trades. However, they could not overcome the realities of trade interests among the existing unions. Unable to establish a core group, these efforts were short-lived. A more successful endeavour came from John Doherty in 1829 when he created the Grand General Union of the Operative Spinners of Great Britain and Ireland, and then the National Association for the Protection of Labour. Although these organisations each lasted less than two years, they demonstrated a growing focus towards organising an effective trade unionism along broader lines than ever before so as to promote a larger platform for worker rights.

EXTEND YOUR KNOWLEDGE

John Doherty (1798–1854)
John Doherty became a cotton spinner in 1808 and moved from Ireland to Manchester in 1816. Arrested in 1818 for his involvement in the Lancashire spinners' strike, he spent two years in prison. He was elected leader of the Manchester Spinners Union in 1828 and then championed a general union to win worker rights. He was successful in establishing the Grand General Union of the Operative Spinners of Great Britain and Ireland in 1829.

Despite these early failures, in 1834 a general trades union was finally established, which represented a high point in the history of labour organisation. The Grand National Consolidated Trades Union was the most successful of the networked unions before 1851, and it claimed to have more than one million members, although this figure is difficult to confirm. The impact of the Grand National was twofold. Firstly, it presented itself as a united organisation of workers that conveyed the effect of working-class solidarity. Secondly, it encouraged the widespread use of 'the Document' by employers. Unfortunately, in both instances the impact was mostly a negative one for workers' rights and evidenced the long way they still had to go.

In terms of working-class solidarity, the Grand National only presented a united movement on the surface. In reality, it remained a diffuse body of independent unions that remained focused on their own trade interests rather than the wider concerns of all workers. This was down to the strength of traditional thinking and also because of the failure of the organisation to effectively support its members when they went out on strike. The reason for this failure was the meagre funds available – it relied upon subscription fees from affiliated members, but often these were not paid. Of the claimed one million members, only 16,000 had actually paid their fee and this was not enough to maintain the organisation, nor fund those members who went on strike. The precarious nature of this situation was exposed in 1834 when 1,500 mill workers in Derby were locked out of their place of work for failing to abandon their union. Despite the strike lasting for four months, even these committed union men eventually renounced the union and went back to work.

The death knell for the Grand National sounded with the increased use of what became known as 'the Document', a form denouncing union membership that employers demanded their employees sign. It became a prerequisite for employment in many areas of the country, and if existing employees refused to sign it then they would usually find themselves locked out of their workplace, as was the case in Derby. The 'Document' essentially gave employers the power to sift out union members and secure obedience to their own demands on the threat of unemployment. So effective was this practice that by 1835 the Grand National collapsed under the twin financial burden of having to support loyal members who were locked out for their union commitment and the loss of fees from those who renounced their affiliation.

SOURCE

An example of 'the Document' used by employers to stop employees from joining trade unions. This one was used in the building trade in 1833.

> We, the undersigned... do hereby declare that we are not in any way connected with the General Union of the Building Trades and that we do not and will not contribute to the support of such members of the said union as are or may be out of work in consequence of belonging to such union.

Government restrictions to unionism

The effectiveness of early trade unionism was therefore very limited, both because of internal difficulties and also employers' opposition. It was further compounded by the actions of the government, which increasingly saw unionism as a threat to economic progress and also as a political threat once war with France broke out in 1793. This immediate challenge was met with the passage of the Combination Acts (page 16), which made the formation of unions illegal. Although these Acts were eventually repealed in 1824, the government remained a strong advocate for employers' rights – an attitude that was well evidenced by the passage of the Master and Servant Act in 1823. This legislation provided for a three-month prison term for anyone deemed to have broken their contract of work before it was completed. In effect, this made striking illegal and there were on average 10,000 prosecutions a year under this Act between 1857 and 1875. Once more, the opportunity for workers to improve their conditions by their own efforts was restricted.

Despite the evident growth of trade unionism between 1759 and 1851, there was no equal discussion between employers and employees. The balance of power remained firmly located with the employers, who were able to exploit the financial vulnerability of the working class and maintain a tight grip on working practices. However, the trade unions did not help themselves either. Loyalty to individual trades continued to undermine the creation of a genuinely national body that might have been able to co-ordinate an effective challenge to the dominance of employers. At the beginning of the 19th century, trade unionism had generated a significant amount of promise but by 1851 had failed to deliver on those expectations.

The role of new model trade unions from 1851

The challenges facing workers in their pursuit of better working conditions saw the development of a new approach to unionism. Rather than retain single trade-specific groups, there grew larger organisations that bound individual unions into broader, united groupings with the intention of using their size to better advantage. The most important of these to develop after 1850 was the Amalgamated Society of Engineers (ASE), which was established in 1851. This organisation was created by binding together three smaller independent unions – the Old Mechanics, the Steam Engine Maker's Society and the General Smiths – and as a result heralded a **New Model Unionism** that would significantly influence the expansion of unionism and, by extension, the opportunities for redressing worker grievances in regard to conditions.

The creation of the ASE was a reaction to industrialisation and, specifically, the growth in unskilled labour that it generated, which, in the eyes of skilled workers, was drowning industry and dragging down wages. In this sense, the motivation was no different from that of earlier associations and as such it created a divide among the workers themselves – 'skilled' and 'unskilled'. This division did little for the overall improvement of conditions because it maintained existing self-interests and allowed employers to exploit these differences. Indeed, the creation of these new models created what Sydney and Beatrice Webb described as an aristocracy of labour that encouraged lingering resentments and suspicion among other workers who felt their interests were not being as well considered.

KEY TERM

New Model Unionism
The development of larger unions by skilled workers who used more conservative methods such as negotiation rather than militancy to achieve their aims. The basis of this model was that by acting respectfully and moderately workers would be able to exercise more influence over employers.

SOURCE 11

A trade union scroll representing the Amalgamated Society of Engineers, created by the union in January 1851. The vignette on the plinth represents Samuel Crompton, James Watt and Richard Arkwright – notable engineers who pioneered industrial development in Britain.

Organised labour

Despite this lingering focus on the skilled trades, the emergence of the New Model Unions, for example the ASE, did offer a better chance of forcing changes because of the strength they commanded. These new groups were more organised and could raise significant funds for their objectives than previous organisations such as the Grand National. Under the direction of their general secretary, William Allan, the ASE also adopted a rigid administrative system: an elected executive council was formally in charge, while the paid general secretary managed the day-to-day affairs of the union and also the co-ordination of the local branches. Part of the obligation of membership was a tax on its members for the specific purpose of securing adequate strike pay, rather than the more traditional reliance on voluntary donations. Given the better financial position that members of the ASE were in as skilled working men, this particular policy generated substantial sums of money, which amounted to more than £12,000 in 1852. With such funds, the union became the most prominent in the country and was even able to support other unions in their battles for employment rights for workers.

The most influential action the ASE took was in 1859–60 when builders in London were out on strike seeking a reduction in their working day. Their demand for a nine-hour day became the arena in which the engineers were able to exhibit the advantages of their organisation by contributing three separate donations of £1,000 to the builders' strike fund, which enabled them to hold out for six months. More importantly, the ASE's support helped the builders to force a concession from their employers. By using their own resources to support other union actions, New Model Unionism was directly promoting working-class interests. Given the evident success that it yielded, it encouraged other unions to consider why the ASE was so successful, which subsequently inspired a reappraisal of the traditional model of localised, industry-specific unionisation among other organisations.

SOURCE

12 From A.W. Humphrey, *Robert Applegarth: Trade Unionist, Educationalist, Reformer*, published in 1891. Robert Applegarth, general secretary of the Amalgamated Society of Carpenters and Joiners after 1862, explains the origins of the society in a speech made to the organisation c1870.

No fewer than 225 building establishments were closed and 24,000 men were deprived of employment. It was a pitched battle between Labour and Capital. Its brightest feature was the magnificent way in which Trade Unionists all over the country rallied to the support of their fellow Unionists in London. The great Amalgamated Society of Engineers made three contributions of £1,000. Applegarth, like hundreds of others, was busy collecting subscriptions for the war-chest.

Faced with such an attack, unions dropped the demand for nine hours and held out for the right of combination, and in February, 1860, the 'Document' was unconditionally withdrawn and, as a substitute, a statement relating to the law concerning trade combinations was hung up in all workshops. But for the aid from other Unions, the men would have been hopelessly beaten. The carpenters and joiners had learned their lesson. Speaking nearly ten years afterwards, at a gathering of the Carpenters and Joiners in the Free-masons' Tavern, when he presented an address to Professor E.S. Beesly, Applegarth touched on the starting of the Amalgamated Society. 'The London lock-out,' he said, 'induced a number of their trade to hold an inquest on the system of "localism", and their verdict was, "the thing won't do". They then decided to follow the example set by the Amalgamated Engineers, and a start was effected with 11 branches and about 350 members; but as for funds, he feared they were like many a young couple starting in life, full of hope and promise, but with very limited means – in fact they started without funds.' The new society was set on its feet in June, 1860. At the end of the year it had 20 branches and 618 members, and the only branches outside London were those at Kidderminster and Devonport. The following year, Applegarth led the organisation to which he belonged in Sheffield into the Amalgamated Society. It became the Sheffield No. 1 Branch.

Respectable methods

The basis of New Model Unionism's success, as seen by the ASE, not only lay in the national structure of the union that it developed, but also the manner in which it conducted itself. Despite the early use of strike action in 1852, which took place in opposition to the use of piecework and excessive overtime, the ASE actively promoted a more moderate approach to dealing with employers. In the eyes of its leaders, particularly William Allan, respectability was a better way to achieve their goals rather than strike action. He felt that using rational negotiation based on their sought-after skills and strength in numbers to persuade employer's to agree to their demands, would be more likely to achieve results. This was a new departure for trade unionism, which had up to this point always adopted a more combative stance towards employers, and it was successful for three reasons.

- The rapidly industrialising economy had made Britain the 'workshop of the world' by the 1850s and this development relied heavily on the growth of technical industries and therefore more skilled labour. Given this context, skilled unions like the ASE acquired significant leverage because their skills were in great demand.

- In the increasingly moderate and respectable climate of mid-Victorian Britain, peaceful negotiations attracted more favourable responses from those with influence.

- It found favour with the general public, whose lives were often inconvenienced by industrial disputes. In appealing to the public in particular, the New Model Unions were able to enhance their powers of negotiation with both employers, and especially politicians, who were increasingly responsive to the wishes of the broader population by the later 1860s. The ASE was able to use this influence to form a relationship with the Liberal Party, which was both attracted to and reasonably sympathetic to the moderate activities of the union. In return, the Liberals could tap into the support of the large membership that the ASE commanded.

The ASE model was a very successful one but it was by no means universally adopted. The strength of the union lay primarily with the profession of its members. Skilled labour was increasingly in demand after 1850 and those unions that safeguarded these skills were granted a little more latitude when it came to negotiations. In this sense, the ASE had a distinct advantage over the less-skilled organisations, which could not command the same respect from employers and consequently relied more heavily upon traditional methods of strike action, which tended to result in workers losing out rather than gaining substantial benefits. By offering alternative modes of action, the ASE also presented a clear divide in the trade union movement; skilled professions could adopt the 'new model' offered by the ASE, while the semi-skilled and unskilled professions remained reliant upon the 'old model'.

The creation of the ASE was a watershed in union history because it transformed the nature of the entire movement. Although localised unions continued, with the success of the ASE as the first example of New Model Unionism the trend was set for larger, national unions that could access more funds and wield greater influence. Such was the popularity and success of this trend that by the end of 1874 the British trade union movement counted more than one million members – a figure that could not be ignored by employers. This development was arguably one of the reasons that worker's rights slowly improved in the second half of the 19th century, with a seemingly systematic reduction in the working day, improved education for younger workers and improvements to safety in the workplace. New Model Unionism had finally given skilled workers an effective opportunity to promote their interests and a strong voice with which to comment on their place in the growing British economy.

ACTIVITY
KNOWLEDGE CHECK

The significance of New Model Unionism

1 How did New Model Unionism differ from the early trade associations?

2 According to Source 12, what was the motivation for the creation of the Amalgamated Society of Carpenters and Joiners in 1860?

3 What does Source 12 suggest was the reason for the success enjoyed by the ASE and the London builders?

The influence of unskilled workers' unions from 1888

The development of New Model Unionism and its expansion after 1860 saw unionism generally become more acceptable in Britain. Although employers continued to resist the advances of this perceived menace, the government began to recognise the benefits of such organisations – especially during elections, when the network of organised labour could be especially useful in drawing out voters. In 1871 it passed the country's first Trade Union Act, which gave the unions legal status and protected their funds. The passage of the legislation publically acknowledged the right of workers to form unions for the purpose of engaging employers in discussion for improvements to their conditions of work. In terms of workers' experiences this was perhaps a very progressive step, since it finally granted them the legal means to protect themselves and, as such, after this date the relationship between them and their employers began to equalise to a certain extent. The days of master dominance were drifting into the past as employees now had legal support for their cause.

Despite this improvement, unskilled workers still did not enjoy the same real protections as the larger New Model Unions of the skilled workers. For these individuals, therefore, there was a need to form themselves into similarly large groups as the skilled crafts so as to be able to take full advantage of the legal status now enjoyed by unionism. The move by Britain's unskilled professions into larger organisations became known as **New Unionism** and it began in the mid-1880s.

New Unionism

This movement developed from 1886 onwards, following a minor economic depression that raised unemployment during that year and saw riots in London. As such, there grew an increased sense of determination to assert the rights of workers and to ensure adequate protection for themselves. The cause was stirred by Tom Mann, a member of the ASE who had found himself out of work on several occasions and who felt that unionism, as it currently existed, had become too soft and timid in the face of Britain's employers. His pamphlet *What a Compulsory Eight-Hour Working Day Means to the Workers* demanded a more dynamic approach to be set by these unions.

SOURCE 13 From Tom Mann's pamphlet *What a Compulsory Eight-Hour Day Means to the Workers*, published in 1886.

To Trade Unionists, I desire to make a special appeal. How long, *how long* will you be content with the present half-hearted policy of your unions? I readily grant that good work has been done in the past by unions, but, in Heaven's name, what good purpose are they serving now? All of them have large numbers out of employment even when their particular trade is busy. None of the important societies have any policy other than of endeavouring to keep wages from falling. The true unionist policy of *aggression* seems entirely lost sight of; in fact the average unionist of today is a man with a fossilized intellect, either hopelessly apathetic, or supporting a policy that plays directly into the hands of the capitalist exploiter.

In the difficult economic circumstances of that year, Mann's criticism resonated among the working class, and in subsequent years existing unions began to adopt more strident actions, while New Unions for unskilled and semi-skilled workers emerged that embraced a more proactive militant stance against employers that previously had been stamped out by the dominance of the skilled, moderate New Model Unions.

The matchgirls' strike, 1888

Perhaps the earliest example of this new-found interest in militant trade unionism can be seen in the small strike that was undertaken by female match workers from the Bryant and May factory in London in 1888. The basis of this strike was the unpleasant conditions in which these women and young girls – most over the age of 14 – were required to work. Not only were their days long, as they often had to be in the factory from 6 a.m. to 6 p.m. with only two breaks daily, their wages were also very low and amounted to an average of 4 shillings a day. Adding to this poor rate of renumeration was the existence of a very unforgiving punishment system that docked the girls' pay for breaking rules such as:

- dropping a match on the floor

- talking to one another

- sitting down

- being late to work

- going to the bathroom without permission.

Given these excessive demands, many of the girls often went home without any payment at all.

As bad as the employment conditions were, the health of these girls was especially poor, partly owing to the nature of their work. The majority of them were employed to dip the match heads into phosphorous, which served as the means of igniting the match. This chemical is particularly toxic and the girls would regularly inhale its fumes as they worked. The consequence of this was that they often developed what was colloquially termed 'phossy jaw', a cancer of the jawbone that gradually disintegrated the jaw and was fatal for the unfortunate worker.

The conditions of employment at Bryant and May were publicised by Clementina Black, a member of the Women's Trade Union Association, at a meeting of the **Fabian Society** in June 1888. In the audience to hear of the experiences of the matchgirls was Annie Besant – a social reformer with an interest in women's rights. The next day Besant went to the factory to speak to the girls themselves, and, having discovered the true extent of their condition, wrote an article about their plight in her newspaper, *The Link*. The article was provocatively entitled 'White slavery in London' and it drew significant interest from the public and from Bryant and May itself, who then tried to force its workers to sign a document saying that they were happy with their conditions. When several girls refused to do so, they were sacked, and by the end of the week 1,400 women went out on strike as a result – encouraged by Annie Besant, who quickly undertook to organise a Matchmakers' Union.

EXTEND YOUR KNOWLEDGE

Annie Besant (1847–1933)
Annie Besant was a social reformer and prominent socialist. She was married in 1867 to a clergyman with whom she had two children, but the marriage ended in 1873 because of her secular views. In 1877 she, along with Charles Bradlaugh, editor of the secular newspaper *The National Reformer,* was prosecuted for publishing a book advocating birth control that had been written by Charles Knowlton. A keen supporter of women's rights, she became active in trade unionism in 1888 and helped to organise the matchgirls' strike of that year. In 1898, she travelled to India. She supported home rule there by organising a home rule league, which sought to achieve greater powers for Indians through peaceful means in 1915. She died in India in 1933.

SOURCE 14

From Annie Besant's article 'White slavery in London', published in her newspaper *The Link*, 23 June 1888.

The hour for commencing work is 6.30 in summer and 8 in winter; work concludes at 6p.m. Half-an-hour is allowed for breakfast and an hour for dinner. This long day of work is performed by young girls, who have to stand the whole of the time. A typical case is that of a girl of 16, a piece-worker; she earns 4s a week, and lives with a sister, employed by the same firm, who 'earns good money, as much as 8s or 9s per week'. Out of the earnings 2s is paid for the rent of one room; the child lives on only bread-and-butter and tea, alike for breakfast and dinner, but related with dancing eyes that once a month she went to a meal where 'you get coffee, and bread and butter, and jam, and marmalade, and lots of it'; now and then she goes to the Paragon, someone 'stands treat, you know', and that appeared to be the solitary bit of colour in her life. The splendid salary of 4s is subject to deductions in the shape of fines; if the feet are dirty, or the ground under the bench is left untidy, a fine of 3d is inflicted; for putting 'burnts' – matches that have caught fire during the work – on the bench 1s has been forfeited, and one unhappy girl was once fined 2s. 6d for some unknown crime. If a girl leaves four or five matches on her bench when she goes for a fresh 'frame' she is fined 3d, and in some departments a fine of 3d is inflicted for talking. If a girl is late she is shut out for 'half the day', that is for the morning six hours, and 5d is deducted out of her day's 8d. One girl was fined 1s. for letting the web twist round a machine in the endeavour to save her fingers from being cut, and was sharply told to take care of the machine, 'never mind your fingers'. Another, who carried out the instructions and lost a finger thereby, was left unsupported while she was helpless. The wage covers the duty of submitting to an occasional blow from a foreman; one, who appears to be a gentleman of variable temper, 'clouts' them 'when he is mad'.

The strike lasted for more than three weeks and attracted the attention of not only Besant's newspaper, but also the *Pall Mall Gazette,* the *Labour Elector* and even *The Times,* although the latter was more critical of Besant and her socialist supporters than the actual conditions at Bryant and May. By early July, the proprietors of Bryant and May agreed to end the fines system and allow the dismissed women to return to work. In this regard, the events of June 1888 were very significant for the future of worker–employer relations, since it was the first occasion where an unorganised body of workers successfully gained public attention and were able to force an employer to improve their conditions of work.

SOURCE 15

The matchgirl strikers in London, June 1888. The strike itself gained quite significant attention at the time since it involved a prominent local business and, more interestingly, was action being taken by women.

MEMBERS OF THE MATCHMAKERS' UNION.

A Level Exam-Style Question Section C

How far can workers' unions be regarded as the main cause for the improvement to working conditions in the years 1759–1928? (20 marks)

Tip

When answering this question you should also consider the events that allowed for the creation of workers' unions.

The Triple Alliance

The matchgirls' strike was arguably the start of a much broader unionist movement that sought to extend the protection of unionisation to unskilled and semi-skilled workers. The success of the Bryant and May workers consequently ushered in New Unionism, which created a more dynamic relationship between workers and employers as the former increasingly found a louder voice with which to demand improvements to their working conditions.

After 1888, this voice only increased in volume as an array of unions developed for unskilled professions – the National Union of Dock Labourers in Glasgow the following year for example was particularly notable – while a trend towards general unions also emerged later, in the 1920s. The result of this expansion was that towards the end of the 19th century and into the early 20th, union activity increased at a significant rate, which promised to advance workers' interests and culminated in the General Strike in 1926, when employers tried to resist this newfound confidence.

Perhaps the best example of this greater assertiveness was the alliance made between the Miners' Federation of Great Britain, the National Union of Railwaymen and the Transport Workers' Federation in June 1914. This was a tremendous co-ordination of unions, since each of the three were themselves an existing amalgamation. The National Union of Railwayman was made up of the United Pointsmen and Signalmen's Society, the Society of Railway Servants and the General Railway Workers' Union. The Transport Workers' Federation, founded in 1910, consisted of the National Sailors' and Firemen's Union, the Dock Labourers Union and the Dock, Wharf, Riverside General Workers Union. Each of these organisations was a large body in its own right, but in unison they became a monolithic body that had the potential to wield significant might should they choose to strike. The intention of this alliance was to co-ordinate members' activities for mutual benefit. This idea had its origins in labour discontent that began in 1910 and ignited a sustained period of industrial unrest that saw more than 10 million days lost to strike action between 1910 and 1914. By comparison, the 1900–1909 period saw an average of only 2.5 million days lost.

This level of unrest had its foundations in the late 19th century, when industry underwent rapid expansion as new markets were opened in Asia and competition grew with other nations such as the USA. The implication of this increased competition was a tightening up of British industrial practices as businesses sought to meet the economic challenges from abroad, and this often brought them into direct conflict with their workers. In 1910, for example, miners in Durham and Northumberland had been subjected to a three-shift system that upset their home life and they opposed the changed work pattern, lasting three months on strike before returning to work without any concessions. This was but one of the many strikes that took place in the next few years, reaching a high point in 1912 when 41 million days were lost to strike action.

The main reason for this heightened degree of activity was the development of the New Unionism model of broader, more militant, unions for unskilled labour that had grown after 1888. These unions were deliberately organised along more militant lines as their organisers embraced a markedly more socialist agenda than the earlier New Model Unions, which had embraced conservative methods to negotiate with employers. Those methods and their in-demand skills gave the New Model Unions a better bargaining hand when dealing with employers, but the unskilled professions did not enjoy the same luxury. As such, they embraced a more radical ideology called **syndicalism**, which proposed organising industry into syndicates run by the workers themselves. This would give workers greater freedom to produce and, in the opinion of syndicalist leaders, this would be more beneficial for both the economy and the workers.

KEY TERM

Syndicalism
An economic concept deriving from socialism for organising industry into confederates or groups run by the workers themselves.

On the basis of this radical alternative to the existing mode of production – the employer/employee hierarchy – workers' unions were naturally more militant and sought to take every opportunity to promote their vision and improve their experiences.

It was in this environment that the Triple Alliance was formed, with the express intention of maximising the strength of its membership to promote their mutual interest. In this sense, the arrangement was a deliberate attempt to take advantage of a worsening industrial environment. However, it was not directly taken up because of the outbreak of war in August 1914. Nor was the revolutionary nature of syndicalism the main agenda for this alliance – perhaps for a few radical members it had some appeal, but the rank and file were mostly interested in the more tangible issues of wage and condition improvements.

The failure of the Triple Alliance by 1919

In the post-war years, the Triple Alliance was finally brought to life and brought pressure on the British government when demobilised soldiers returned and wartime workers faced unemployment. In Belfast and Glasgow, this unrest was exemplified by a 40-hour strike by munitions workers. In Glasgow, this turned violent on 31 January 1919 when police used batons on some of the 60,000 picketers. The consequences of the increasing unrest were that moves were made to use the Triple Alliance to assert and protect the interests of their members. On 16 October 1919, the Railwaymen and Transport Workers unions threatened to strike over their demand for increased wages and in support of the Miners' Federation, which had already gone out.

The government was forced to take swift action to maintain the essential services that these unions provided. In addition, they also negotiated a six-month wage increase for the miners, which enabled their strike to be called off within two weeks of its commencement. The fact that the government took such an approach is testament to the perceived power of the Alliance and the new awareness of the strength that certain British unions enjoyed in the early 20th century. The agreement was therefore received as a positive development. However, it merely delayed conflict for half a year as depression set in 1920 and once more the issue of wages sprang up as employers began to make cuts. The employers of the miners instigated a **lockout** on 31 March and the Alliance was once more instituted, with the Railwaymen and Transport Workers unions agreeing to come out in sympathy with them in April. Before the start of the sympathy strike, negotiations began with the government but they were broken off by the miners very quickly. When their allies requested that the miners rejoin the negotiations, this was rejected too, and the sympathy strikes were called off. In this moment, the Triple Alliance came to an end.

KEY TERM

Lockout
A technique used by employers to force workers to accede to their demands. In essence employers would lock their employees out so they could not physically work and therefore earn their wages.

The failure of the Alliance was the result not so much of the conditions in which they were operating, but rather the traditional problem of mobilising wide support from diffuse groups in a crisis. This was an issue of logistics, but more specifically of individual interests, which often came to influence decision-making on such pressured occasions. In this sense, the Alliance was perhaps a noble experiment that had the potential for success but was ultimately compromised by traditional interests and agendas when the time for collective action arrived.

The end of the Alliance signalled an important moment in industrial relations, since the power of the unions was significantly weakened by the loss of unity that the movement had created. Without this protection, employers were better placed to set the parameters of any discussion with their employees. This was borne out in subsequent years when, on 30 June 1925, mine owners sought to cut wages and add one hour to the working day. In part this was a reaction to a slump in the economy following the end of war and was arguably an attempt to become more competitive, however it was not well received. The impact of this action by the mine owners was that the working conditions faced by the miners were further reduced, and as such it was loudly challenged by the unions, who sought to recreate the Triple Alliance. It also received the support of the Trades Union Congress in the event of any strike action they undertook.

Such action was averted by the timely intervention of the Conservative government, which agreed to subsidise mine owners so that no wage cuts would be necessary. This action acknowledged the challenging circumstances under which the miners were placed, however it was only a temporary measure, lasting at most nine months. In effect, this was an attempt to buy time for the government, since the economy was struggling to grow during the early 1920s. These challenging times were intensified by Britain's return to the gold standard, which raised the price of exports. Within this difficult environment there was no easy fix for industrial relations, so a Royal Commission was established to find a solution. Under Sir Herbert Samuel the Commission made the very unwelcome recommendations of a 13.5 percent wage cut with no extension of hours and the removal of the government subsidy. This led to new industrial action. Mining unions declared for strike action on 4 May 1926 – an event that started with the miners but quickly expanded into a general strike as other unions joined the fight for better conditions.

EXTEND YOUR KNOWLEDGE

General Strike, 1926
The British economy, like others across the world, slumped in the early 1920s as new markets opened up and competition began to affect pricing and industrial performance. During these years, employers sought to safeguard their businesses by reducing wages and trying to increase productivity, both to compensate for reduced prices and to gain market share. Because of these actions employees found themselves facing reduced wages and also increased competition for jobs as unemployment rose. These circumstances led to unions becoming more active in attempting to protect the interests of their members. Following the decision by mine owners to reduce wages and extend working hours, the National Union of Mineworkers voted for strike action on 4 May 1926. They were supported by the Trades Union Congress, which planned to call out workers from key industries in support, such as transport and builders. This amounted to one-fifth of the adult male population (approximately 3 million men) and constituted a General Strike – the biggest that Britain had ever seen.

A Level Exam-Style Question Section C

How far do you agree that the key turning point in the improvement of workers' rights in the years 1759–1928 was the matchgirls' strike of 1888? (20 marks)

Tip
When answering this question, you should consider what might be meant by the phrase 'key turning point' – was the matchgirls' strike the most influential event that changed the nature of workers' rights?

ACTIVITY
KNOWLEDGE CHECK

The growth of unskilled unions

1 Why did unskilled unions develop after 1888?

2 How did unskilled unions differ from skilled unions?

3 What was the significance of the Triple Alliance?

4 How effective was unionism in Britain by 1928?

Conclusion

The Industrial Revolution had a profound effect upon the people of Britain. The technological inventiveness of British entrepreneurs not only gave the nation a means to make great economic strides over other countries for the benefit of many, it also transformed the lives of those who worked in the new centres of industry that were created. This was both a blessing and curse. It promoted employment opportunities and offered the growing population a means to sustain itself through labour. However, the conditions in which people toiled were often very challenging. This encouraged a more forceful effort by the British people to assert their right to decent standards in their workplaces. Over the course of the 19th century and into the 20th century when industrialisation had become the backbone of the British economy, these voices became increasingly heard, and over time significant improvements were made. But despite this development, the demands of the market still governed employers' actions and as such, when the occasion demanded, conditions were often compromised so as to ensure profitability. This was a constant pattern throughout 1759–1928 and one that still continues today.

THINKING HISTORICALLY Change (7a)

Convergence and divergence

Technological change in Britain, 1761–1901

1761	1769	1821	1881	1901
Duke of Bridgewater's canal opened	James Watt patented his improved steam engine	Michael Faraday invented the electric motor	Britain's first electric railway is opened	First central power station is built in Britain

Economic change in Britain, 1761–1901

1764	1796	1799	1833	1847
First cotton mill is set up in Royton	Boulton and Watt open their Soho Foundry	First Combination Act is passed	Factory Act is passed	The ten-hour working day is introduced

1 Draw a timeline across the middle of a landscape piece of A3 paper. Cut out ten small rectangular cards and write the above changes on them. Then place them on the timeline with technological events above the line and economic below. Make sure there is a lot of space between the changes and the line.

2 Draw a line and write a link between each change within each strand, so that you have four links that join up the changes in the technological part of the timeline and four that join the economic changes. You will then have two strands of change: technological and economic.

3 Now make as many links as possible across the timeline between technological change and economic change. Think about how they are affected by one another and think about how things can link across long periods of time.

You should end up with something like this:

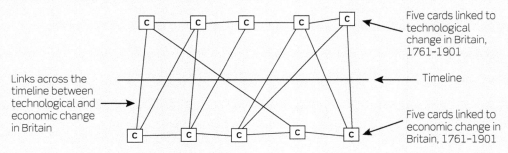

Answer the following:

4 How far do different strands of history interact with one another? Illustrate your answer with two well-explained examples.

5 At what point do the two strands of development converge (i.e. when do the changes have the biggest impact on one another)?

6 How useful are the strands in understanding the development of British industry during the 18th and 19th centuries?

ACTIVITY
SUMMARY

Improving working conditions?

1 How did the Industrial Revolution affect working conditions in Britain?

2 What motivated government legislation in Britain's factories?

3 How much did reforms change workers' conditions?

4 What impact did New Model Unionism have for industrial relations?

5 How important was technological advancement for the lives of British workers?

WIDER READING

Evans, E.J. *The Shaping of Modern Britain 1780–1914*, Pearson (2011)

Fraser, W.H. *A History of British Trade Unionism 1700–1998*, Macmillan (1999)

Griffin, E. *A Short History of the British Industrial Revolution*, Palgrave Macmillan (2010)

Murphy, D., Staton, R., Walsh-Atkins, P. and Whiskerd, N. *Britain 1783–1918*, Collins Educational (2003)

Pelling, H. *A History of British Trade Unionism*, Penguin (1963)

Scott-Baumann, M. *The Condition of England 1815–53*, Hodder (2008)

3.2 The world of childhood

KEY QUESTIONS

- What were the reasons for the changes to children's lives in the years 1759–1928?
- Why did attitudes towards children change in the years 1759–1928?

INTRODUCTION

The Industrial Revolution was one of the most formative periods in British history, transforming both the landscape and economic practices of the nation. It also had a significant social impact upon the lives of those living in Britain, not least in terms of how they conducted themselves in the workplace, but also in terms of how they interacted with one another and viewed each other's roles in the new industrial age.

The Industrial Revolution began a process of societal evolution that gradually saw attitudes towards particular demographics in Britain transform as the country developed and began to reassess many of its traditionally held values and practices. Most tangibly, this can be seen in the attitudes towards children in the workplace. In the late 18th century, the existence of labouring children was commonplace, with many occupying positions in the country's economy, usually acting as secondary support for adults – drawing carts in the mines for example – but they also performed some primary roles such as shepherding. The practice of using child labour was, therefore, not new to the industrial age. However, it did reach its peak during this period; as the demand for labour increased with the growth of factories, the use of children steadily rose with it. Children became significant contributors to the prospering economy, continuing to perform supporting roles in addition to undertaking essential jobs that their size and cheaper cost made them invaluable for, **scavengers** in the new textile mills being perhaps the most notable example of child work.

The role of children in the workplace was, therefore, well established but, as the nation modernised its working practices, it also developed a more progressive attitude toward its child labourers. As the Victorian period developed, opinion began to shift towards a more critical stance on child labour, as a new middle-class idea of childhood became established, one that celebrated innocence and wholesomeness – a vision that was far removed from the existing realities of the young labouring classes. This vision increasingly informed British social attitudes, and by the end of the 19th century the presence of children in the workplace had been scaled back considerably.

KEY TERM

Scavenger
A child in a textile mill whose job was to pick up any loose bits of yarn or wool from under and within the machinery so as to avoid wastage.

1788 – Sir Joshua Reynolds paints *The Age of Innocence*

1818 – John Pounds starts to provide free education for destitute children in Portsmouth

1837 – Charles Dickens's *Oliver Twist* is published

| 1780 | 1790 | 1800 | 1810 | 1820 | 1830 | 1840 |

1802 – Health and Morals of Apprentices Act is passed

1833 – Factory Act is passed

Government grant is given for education

WHAT WERE THE REASONS FOR THE CHANGES TO CHILDREN'S LIVES IN THE YEARS 1759–1928?

The impact of government action

The benefits of using child labour made it an acceptable practice in Britain and, given this acceptability, there was little government involvement to address the issue – regulation was almost non-existent in 1759. This freedom was partially the consequence of a broader policy of laissez-faire that British governments adopted during the 18th century. Fundamentally, this was a liberal belief in allowing markets to regulate themselves and the idea that economic success came from allowing business free rein to pursue profits. This had been the backbone of Britain's economic growth and the same concept continued to inform government policy into the 19th century as industrialisation took hold.

While the overriding principle of free trade governed British policy overall, the onset of industrial development did encourage some discussion of working practices – particularly given the growing number of children entering the workplace and the often challenging conditions under which they were required to labour. Accurate statistics for the 1700s are not available, but by 1821 49 percent of Britain's workforce was under the age of 20, suggesting that children were without doubt a prominent feature in the country's economic structure. The age at which children were admitted to the workplace varied from region to region, with those in the countryside starting contracted work at ten years old and those living in industrial areas such as Manchester and Birmingham starting at an average of eight-and-a-half. The reason for this variance was predominantly the availability of meaningful employment; in the new towns and cities there was often plenty of jobs to be undertaken, while in the countryside, because regular work was a little more scarce, children generally started later. This is not to say there was no significant employment available in the rural areas, since there were pockets of younger children still employed in domestic service by 1821, but rather that the overall trend pointed towards greater opportunities in urban environments. The number of such young children spending long hours in factories, often working 12-hour days, became a growing concern for members of parliament, since these factories were often poorly maintained and therefore attracted health problems to which younger children were more susceptible. This was usually because they were often weak when they arrived and the long days made them weaker, a situation that was further compounded by poor diet and unsanitary living conditions.

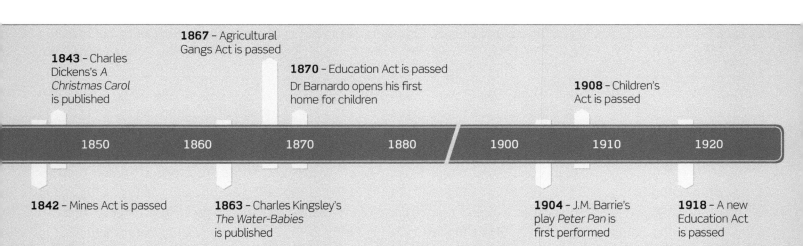

1867 – Agricultural Gangs Act is passed

1843 – Charles Dickens's *A Christmas Carol* is published

1870 – Education Act is passed

Dr Barnardo opens his first home for children

1908 – Children's Act is passed

| 1850 | 1860 | 1870 | 1880 | 1900 | 1910 | 1920 |

1842 – Mines Act is passed

1863 – Charles Kingsley's *The Water-Babies* is published

1904 – J.M. Barrie's play *Peter Pan* is first performed

1918 – A new Education Act is passed

The Factory Act 1802

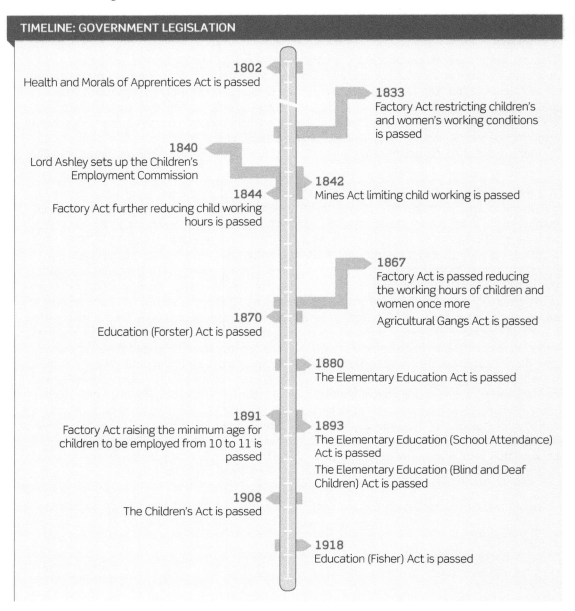

TIMELINE: GOVERNMENT LEGISLATION

1802
Health and Morals of Apprentices Act is passed

1833
Factory Act restricting children's and women's working conditions is passed

1840
Lord Ashley sets up the Children's Employment Commission

1842
Mines Act limiting child working is passed

1844
Factory Act further reducing child working hours is passed

1867
Factory Act is passed reducing the working hours of children and women once more
Agricultural Gangs Act is passed

1870
Education (Forster) Act is passed

1880
The Elementary Education Act is passed

1891
Factory Act raising the minimum age for children to be employed from 10 to 11 is passed

1893
The Elementary Education (School Attendance) Act is passed
The Elementary Education (Blind and Deaf Children) Act is passed

1908
The Children's Act is passed

1918
Education (Fisher) Act is passed

The first attempt by government to improve the experiences of children came in the cotton mills during 1802 following the passage of the Health and Morals of Apprentices Act, also called the Factory Act. It was introduced by Robert Peel after an outbreak of fever in one of his cotton mills near Radcliffe, in the Greater Manchester area, in 1784. Fever itself was not uncommon given the unsanitary conditions of Britain's towns in the late 18th century, but what allowed the fever to affect so many people in Radcliffe was the manner in which the local mills operated. These cotton mills employed **pauper** children as a means of cheap labour and apprenticed them. As apprentices, they would learn a trade but, in return for this opportunity, they worked long hours, often through the night, adopting the practice of 'hot bedding', where one child coming off shift would sleep in the bed of one about to start his or her shift. These apprentices were generally weak and underfed even before they entered the workplace, and then the long hours and exhausting work would make them more vulnerable to disease. In 1800, there were more than 20,000 of these parish paupers in Britain's mills and many were present in Peel's mill when fever broke out.

The outbreak of fever resulted in one of the country's first investigations into factory conditions, led by Dr Thomas Percival, who would later develop the field of occupational health. The findings of the report, published in 1784, made several recommendations that the later Factory Act incorporated.

This included the following.

- The owner of the factory was responsible for ensuring the Act as enforced in his factories.

- All rooms in a factory should be lime-washed twice a year and ventilated.

- Every apprentice should have two complete suits of clothing.

- Working hours of apprentices should not exceed 12 a day, nor start before 6 a.m., nor end after 9 p.m.

- Children should receive instruction in reading, writing and arithmetic every day for the first four years of their apprenticeship.

- Male and female apprentices should be provided with separate sleeping quarters, and not more than two to sleep in one bed.

- On Sundays the apprentices should receive Christian religious instruction.

As an attempt to improve the conditions of child workers, this Act was a very progressive step, since it sought to address both the issue of hygiene and also education for children – despite only applying to cotton mills. By ensuring the child workers received clean clothes and living quarters, there was a clear attempt, albeit a small one, to consider their physical well-being, while the requirement for some basic schooling also offered the opportunity for better job prospects in the future.

Enforcement of the Act

As progressive as this legislation was, it did retain fundamental limitations that prevented it from being as effective as it might have been. Its particular weakness lay in its application; it only applied to apprentices, which meant that the 'free children' (those who were directly employed rather than as apprentices) were not bound by the measure. In this regard, the wider effect of the legislation was therefore minimised. However, it was nonetheless a positive step forward for improving children's working conditions.

By seeking to regulate the experiences of apprentices, the Act ran counter to the popular principle of laissez-faire and as such there was a belief that the government was intervening excessively in the workplace – an environment where the employer should be allowed to operate unencumbered as per free-market thinking. It could be suggested that the final Act was deliberately restricted so as to reflect the continued strong belief in this idea. Indeed, such was the extent of its ongoing appeal that the enforcement of the Act was equally limited, since no inspectors were appointed to enforce this new law. In the absence of such figures, employers were able to avoid many of their new obligations, and the immediate experiences of children did not improve much beyond that which employers were willing to concede. Given these limitations – legislative weakness and employer's reluctance – it would require further, more substantial legislation in 1833 (see page 17) before any tangible progress would really be made.

The Mines Act 1842

The 1802 Factory Act was limited because it only applied to Britain's cotton and woollen mills. These were certainly in need of reforming, but in terms of child labour there was perhaps a greater need to offer regulation in the mining industry, which was also a significant employer of children. Children as young as six or seven were employed in a variety of roles that supported the older workers underground. Though generally supportive, these roles were equally burdensome and often just as dangerous as those performed by adults. Of particular notoriety was the role of 'hurrier', which involved children of between 10 and 14 wearing a harness over their shoulder and having to pull carts filled with coal through narrow passages up to the surface as many times as they could within their 12-hour shift. Equally challenging was the position of 'thrusters' – occupied by the youngest children, which involved pushing the carts, being pulled by hurriers, with their heads (see Source 2) – usually resulting in premature balding. These roles were among many others performed by children in the unforgiving and dangerous mines in Britain.

SOURCE

1 From the testimony of James Pearce, a child labourer in the mines, given to the Parliamentary Commission established in 1842 to investigate the conditions endured by children in British mines.

I am 12 years of age. I went down to the pits about 7 years and a half to open doors. I had a candle and a fire beside me to show me light. There was one door. The horse coming with empty basket and skip could open it with his head, but when he returned with his load I opened it then. I was 12 hours a-day, and got 6d [pennies] a day. I attended and got the money. When I was paid I took it home to my mother. I was a year and a half at this work. I once fell asleep and was well threshed by a driver. The horse was fast. It was down-hill and the horse could not draw back. He laid well into me; I cried out, but nobody would come and help me. I did not tell my father. I never thought anything about it afterwards.

About a year and half I went to walk with a candle before the horses, and pick the coals off the road; I had 8d a day. About a year and a half ago I took to the girdle and chain; I do not like it; it hurts me; it rubs my skin off; I often feel pain. I get 15d a day. I do not go to the Sunday-school. I go to chapel sometimes. I cannot say the Lord's Prayer, nor the Creed, nor the Ten Commandments. I cannot read. I never heard of Liverpool, nor of Manchester, nor of Bristol, nor of Birmingham. I have heard of London.

I had not time to eat a bit of meat from morning till night. I have often had blisters on my side; but when I was more used to it it would not blister, but it smarted very badly. The chain was made of the same stuff as the rope that goes down the pit. I crawled on hands and feet. I often knocked my back against the top of the pit, and it hurt it very sore. There was not room to stand to that height.

It was with increasing knowledge of these conditions, and specifically public awareness of half-naked women (due to the heat of working and poor ventilation) working alongside men underground, that the British government was being encouraged to reform legislation to improve working conditions in the mining industry by the early 1840s. The notion of men and women working in such undress upset the increasingly conservative sense of morality that pervaded Victorian society and it was this public disapproval that helped to fuel the drive for reform. This morality had emerged from the royal family's own sense of propriety and both Queen Victoria and Prince Albert's feeling that the excesses of George IV – whose activities had resulted in several scandals – had undermined both the reputation of the monarchy and embedded vulgarity within British society. As such Victoria and Albert's more conservative stance sought to re-establish a higher standard in society that would enhance not only their own standing but also that of the nation itself.

The main figure pushing for changes was Lord Ashley, who headed a Royal Commission set up in 1840 following an accident at Huskar Colliery near Barnsley that killed 26 children. The Commission was tasked with investigating the employment conditions in mines and more particularly the conditions endured by children. This body interviewed children and women who worked in the mines and after hearing of the excessive conditions they worked in (see Source 1), the Commission made recommendations for reform. The report of the Commission served as the basis of new legislation, introduced by Ashley later that year, which became known as the Mines Act 1842. The provisions set out in this legislation were as follows.

- No female was to be employed underground.

- No child under ten years old was to be employed underground.

- Parish apprentices between the ages of ten and 18 could continue to work in the mines.

EXTEND YOUR KNOWLEDGE

Lord Ashley (1801–85)

Lord Anthony Ashley Cooper, 7th Earl of Shaftesbury, was elected to parliament as a Conservative MP in 1826 and became a regular committee appointee. His fourth committee was to investigate pauper lunatics and the provision made for them in Middlesex and his involvement in this investigation led him to sponsor a bill in favour of reform in parliament. After this introduction to social reform, Ashley became an advocate of improving conditions for Britain's vulnerable persons, and in 1833 he introduced a bill to reduce the working day to ten hours, which eventually passed in 1847. The Mines Act was passed based upon the findings of a commission that Ashley led into the conditions of employment in the mining industry. He also served as president of the Ragged School Union, which sought to provide education to the poorest children in Britain. He died in Kent in 1885.

SOURCE
2
An illustration from 'The condition and treatment of the children employed in the mines and collieries of Britain', produced by the commissioners investigating those conditions as part of the Royal Commission. It was published in 1842.

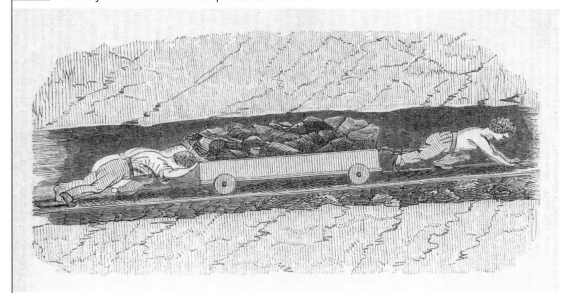

The Mines Act was a prominent step forward in the attempt to improve child working conditions since it effectively declared that children working underground was illegal. Although this was limited to those below the age of ten, it also banned women and girls entirely and at least started to restrict the age at which young boys could work. These limitations provide perhaps the real motive for the legislation – a Victorian sense of conservative morality rather than a necessarily sympathetic attitude towards child labour, or indeed the accident at Huskar. Certainly much of society was shocked by the working conditions, but the main reason for the initial investigation was the suggestion that women and men worked alongside one another, often half-naked because of the heat and poor ventilation. In this regard, the Act ensured that this scandalous practice would not continue.

If the Mines Act had the approval of the general public, it was not as well received by the mining companies themselves as it had implications for the effective running of their businesses. Children were a cheap source of labour, costing less than half that of an adult male worker, and the limitations placed upon their usage was potentially expensive. To this effect, there had been substantial opposition to the bill, headed by Peter Ainsworth, a colliery owner and also the MP for Bolton, and E.B. Denison, MP for West Riding. Each of these opponents suggested that the proposed legislation would have a negative impact upon the workers themselves, especially in its exclusion of women, whose livelihoods depended on their income from the mines. Such was the level of opposition from parliamentary colleagues (which included Hedworth Lambton, brother of Lord Durham and perhaps the most powerful coal mine owner in the north-east of England, and the Duke of Wellington) that Ashley had to concede much of his original intentions. For example, the age restrictions in his first proposal had been 13 years, but this had elicited substantial disapproval in both the Lords and Commons so that, to achieve the necessary votes, he relented to accept the ten years that was eventually applied to the employment of boys underground.

Given the level of opposition to the Mines Act, its passage suggests that the growing morality of wider British society was becoming a dominant feature of the Victorian period, despite the economic arguments proffered by the Act's opponents. In this regard, it is consequently quite reasonable to suggest that Britain was undergoing something of a social transformation. However, such changes also brought unintended consequences – for example, the argument that females would lose out did become something of a reality. In Scotland, more than 1,000 women lost their employment, while in South Wales, despite women still being able to work on the surface, many mining families with only daughters who had worked underground had to enter the workhouse because of the loss of female employment. Though perhaps well-meaning in terms of improving working experiences, the Act did little to actually improve the living conditions of children, many of whom came from mining families that relied on an income from each member.

ACTIVITY
KNOWLEDGE CHECK

Early legislative change in the years 1802–42

1 What motivated early reforms to child working?

2 How extensive were the reforms introduced?

3 How do you think these changes would affect the chances of further legislation?

Agricultural Gangs Act 1867

The majority of legislation affecting the working experiences of children was naturally weighted towards urban environments, as they were where poor conditions were clearly visible. Industrialisation had seen an explosion in new urban centres as factories multiplied and mines grew to accommodate the unrelenting demand for coal. These industries had become substantial employers of the young and were quick to attract the attention of social reformers intent on improving the lives of the country's children.

Despite this focus on towns and cities, agriculture continued to be a significant employer. Prior to the onset of the Industrial Revolution, this had been the mainstay of the British economy and had retained large numbers of labourers, despite a general shift towards urban centres. In 1841, just over 1 in 5, 22 percent of the country's workforce, worked on the land. Many were young children since they, along with women, were significantly cheaper to employ than men – often between a half and a third of the price. Just as legislation began to focus more keenly upon child workers in factories and mines, the position of children in the countryside also became the subject of parliamentary attention, and in the 1860s this resulted in a new agricultural Act.

The motivation behind this particular legislation was the manner in which children were employed in the rural areas. Since the 17th century, a common means of employment was to join an **agricultural gang**, which would then be employed on a piecework basis to complete a particular contract. Since children were much cheaper than adults, these agricultural gangs were often made up primarily of children, or women who were equally cheap to employ. These gangs travelled about the countryside in search of contract work and only remained in areas for the duration of the contract before moving on to another area in search of further employment. They were raised by a 'gangmaster', usually an out-of-work labourer who recruited members, between 10 and 40 in number, and then contracted with farmers to undertake work at a set level of pay. The nature of these gangs means that it is difficult to know with any accuracy how many people worked in this way, but in 1866 records in East Anglia and the East Midlands recorded the use of 6,399 people within such public gangs. These individuals

KEY TERM

Agricultural gang
A collection of individuals employed as a group to complete a given task. Often they would remain as a group and travel about the countryside offering themselves up for employment.

lived a nomadic existence that was not particularly conducive to a healthy lifestyle, and for children it was often especially damaging, both in terms of physical tiredness and also moral attitudes. Without a regular home life and by constantly moving from place to place, the children often grew up in temporary accommodation or public inns where they were left to fend for themselves and had every chance of developing uncivilised behaviours or falling into bad company.

Such a way of living was increasingly felt to be undesirable in mid-Victorian England, which was developing a more sympathetic attitude to childhood and certainly to establishing a greater sense of morality as to the manner in which children should behave. Such sentiments ensured that the nature of agricultural gang work became the focus of a new investigation into children's labour that took place in 1865. This investigation, introduced by Lord Ashley and entitled the Children's Employment Commission, heard evidence from 500 witnesses who spoke of unruly behaviour and also the exploitation of several young women by their gangmasters. The resultant report formed the bedrock of new legislation that was brought to parliament in 1867 and became the Agricultural Gangs Act. Its provisions stipulated the following.

- No child under the age of eight could be employed in a public gang – these were gangs that were created by the labourers themselves, who then travelled about seeking work as opposed to 'private' gangs, which were raised by the particular farmer needing work to be carried out.

- No women could be employed in a public gang with men.

- No women could be employed under a male gangmaster unless a female gangmaster was also present.

- Gangmasters had to be licensed.

- No licences were to be given to gangmasters who ran public houses.

- If in breach of any of these laws, the gangmaster could be penalised 20 shillings per person employed.

These provisions clearly endorse a growing Victorian interest in morality and the new legislation's focus upon the female–male divide reflects a growing awareness of the potential for improper relations, or indeed overt exploitation, in the nomadic lifestyle of the gangs.

By regulating the manner of these gangs' organisation, legislators such as Lord Ashley hoped to reduce the possibility of exploitation and also help to ensure that young children were able to receive a degree of education, since they were now unable to join a gang until at least the age of eight. This particular restriction formed part of a broader motivation towards improving the education of children, first in the interest of promoting skills, but also as part of a growing focus upon the importance of education to the development of future moral adults. Prior to this limitation, many children would miss schooling for the opportunity to earn money working in a gang.

The provisions of the legislation were quite far-reaching and were certainly intended to promote the welfare of both women and children. However, they were difficult to actually enforce since they only applied to public gangs – anyone working a private gang was able to conduct themselves as they pleased. Therefore, a consequence of the legislation was actually an increase in private gangs, circumventing the Act. Because of this, it could be suggested that the reform actually made it more challenging for children and women, since private gangs were arguably more variable and less regulated.

The passage of the Agricultural Gangs Act, and its broader attempt to safeguard the morality of children, was in one sense a marker of a widening concern for children. Prior to this legislation, the majority of reforms had been centred around the workplace generally and were concerned mostly with the length of working hours and lack of education. The 1867 Act, however, attempted a much broader reform of children's experiences by trying to regulate them – not only in the workplace, but in their private lives also. Much of the motivation behind focusing on children under eight working in gangs was the nomadic lifestyle that accompanied such work and the consequent absence of a suitable familial guide.

The Children's Act 1908

Given the broader focus of the 1867 Act, it is reasonable to suggest that after the mid-1800s there began a more determined effort to both increase the opportunities of children in Britain and establish some founding principles on which they could be afforded some protection. This paternalism was arguably a feature of the nation's growing affluence and particularly the increasingly conservative attitudes to social behaviours that developed as a result. As Britain developed economically, there also emerged a raft of social reformers who sought to help society evolve as a mirror to the country's economic prosperity. These individuals were often motivated by a strong sense of morality but also, in some cases, a genuine sympathy for the misfortunes of those trapped in difficult circumstances while others around them were able to prosper. Among the numbers of social reform-minded individuals were Charles Booth and Seebohm Rowntree, who sought to identify new ways and means of addressing this problem of poverty. In undertaking this challenge, their work would highlight the ongoing privations faced by children and encourage further legislation that would endeavour to not only improve their experiences, but also safeguard their well-being more robustly.

A study undertaken by Booth after 1886 was intended to better quantify the statistics on poverty. During the course of his team's investigations in London, which involved interviewing doctors, priests and members of the poorest people in the city, they discovered that more than 30 percent of the population there lived in abject poverty. Having initially undertaken the research because he doubted the claims of the **Social Democratic Federation** that a quarter of the city lived in poverty, the results were quite compelling.

An investigation similar to Booth's took place in York between 1899 and 1901 by Seebohm Rowntree – a member of the confectionery manufacturing family. His research, published as *Poverty: A Town Life,* echoed that of Booth and also found that 30 percent of the population of York was living in poverty (see Source 3). This number was calculated as being those who earned less than the estimated 21 shillings a week required to live a basic existence – what Rowntree called the 'poverty line'. Collectively, these studies recognised that the cause of such extreme poverty was illness, unemployment and age and that it was the very old, who were more infirm, and the very young, who could not command particularly good wages, who were most at risk.

The impact of these seminal investigations was a growing commitment from political parties to reform the social provisions in Britain – to improve the conditions of that country's poorest inhabitants and specifically those of children, who had been singled out as being most at risk. This commitment was in evidence following the election victory of the Liberal Party in 1906. Its term in office witnessed a slew of social reforms, including laws requiring the provision of school meals in that same year; school medical inspections in 1907 and old-age pensions in 1908. In this regard, the Liberals were clearly committed to improving the well-being of British society – and particularly the lives of children. The Liberals also formulated a bill to address the issues raised by Rowntree and Booth. In 1908, they presented it to parliament where it passed without substantial revisions, and it became the Children's Act in December of that year. Its main provisions were:

- the prevention of cruelty to children by applying a greater focus on neglect by a parent

- the requirement that anyone receiving payment for minding children under seven must inform the local government and be subject to visits

- a ban on the sale of cigarettes to children under the age of 16

- that children could no longer be executed for capital crimes or serve sentences in adult prisons. Instead, new juvenile prisons would be established

- protection of children's rights, including: the right to an education; protection of children giving evidence in court; protection against neglect through a vagrant lifestyle.

SOURCE

From Seebohm Rowntree's *Poverty: A Study of Town Life*, published in 1901. Rowntree was a social reformer whose study helped to expose the extent of poverty in Britain and added to the growing demand for greater reforms to support those below what Rowntree established as the 'poverty line'.

The life of a labourer is marked by five alternating periods of want and comparative plenty. During early childhood, unless his father is a skilled worker, he probably will be in poverty; this will last until he, or some of his brothers or sisters, begin to earn money and thus augment their father's wage sufficiently to raise the family above the poverty line. Then follows the period during which he is earning money and living under his parent's roof; for some portion of this period he will be earning more money than is required for lodging, food, and clothes. This is his chance to save money. If he has saved enough to pay for furnishing a cottage, this period of comparative prosperity may continue after marriage until he has two or three children, when poverty will again overtake him. This period of poverty will last perhaps for ten years, i.e. until the first child is fourteen years old and begins to earn wages; but if there are more than three children it may last longer. While the children are earning, and before they leave home to marry, the man enjoys another period of prosperity – possibly, however, only to sink back again into poverty when his children have married and left him, and he himself is too old to work, for his income has never permitted his saving enough for him and his wife to live upon for more than a very short time.

A labourer is thus in poverty, and therefore underfed – (a) In childhood – when his constitution is being built up. (b) In early middle life – when he should be in his prime. (c) In old age.

The Children's Act was generally regarded as a great step forward in the attempt to safeguard children. Its adoption marked a much greater responsibility for the government, which contrasted significantly with the laissez-faire, non-interventionist approach that was in place at the start of the 18th century.

The impact of the new legislation was varied. In one sense, it encouraged parents to take greater care of their children since, for example, they could now be fined £10 if they left a child under seven alone in a room with an open fire. This was undoubtedly a benefit for the very young. However, for older children some of the legislation was felt at the time to be excessively restricting – for example boys under the age of 16 could be searched by park-keepers for cigarettes if they were seen smoking in public places. While the health benefits of this legislation are unquestioned, in many regards it also removed a sense of freedom for older children by clearly setting age restrictions upon them. In this sense, the Act removed some of the trappings that made older children feel like adults and forced them to remain children until their mid-teens. By doing this, it created a clear divide between childhood and adulthood which, though promoting benefits, also restricted those who were keen to grow up.

A Level Exam-Style Question Section C

How far do you agree that the working conditions for children changed substantially in the years 1759–1928 because of deliberate government policy? (20 marks)

Tip

When answering this question you should look at the whole time frame given and judge the extent of change that took place within it – was this the result of deliberate government policy or perhaps encouraged by something else?

The initiatives of employers and philanthropists

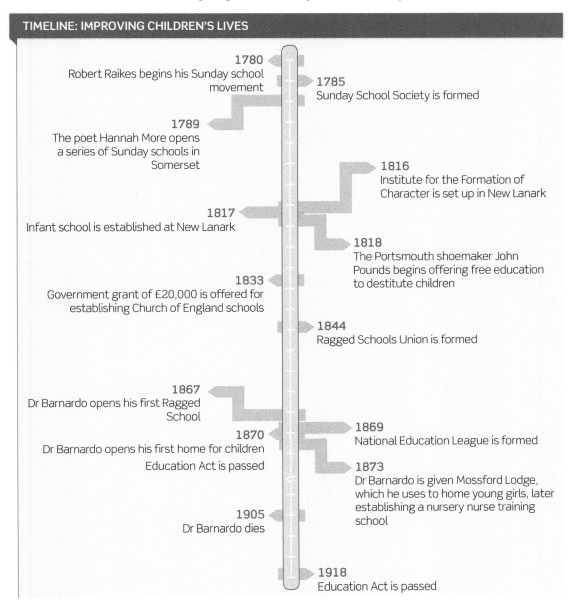

TIMELINE: IMPROVING CHILDREN'S LIVES

1780 Robert Raikes begins his Sunday school movement

1785 Sunday School Society is formed

1789 The poet Hannah More opens a series of Sunday schools in Somerset

1816 Institute for the Formation of Character is set up in New Lanark

1817 Infant school is established at New Lanark

1818 The Portsmouth shoemaker John Pounds begins offering free education to destitute children

1833 Government grant of £20,000 is offered for establishing Church of England schools

1844 Ragged Schools Union is formed

1867 Dr Barnardo opens his first Ragged School

1869 National Education League is formed

1870 Dr Barnardo opens his first home for children. Education Act is passed

1873 Dr Barnardo is given Mossford Lodge, which he uses to home young girls, later establishing a nursery nurse training school

1905 Dr Barnardo dies

1918 Education Act is passed

Traditionally, the responsibility of looking after children remained solely with the family, as governments throughout the 18th and 19th century maintained a strong commitment to non-intervention. The belief was that it was not the state's responsibility to interfere with the private lives of its citizens and to do so would undermine their own effectiveness at governing. Given the lack of political motivation to address social issues that the government did not have an interest in, early efforts at alleviating social challenges were often met by individuals – either benevolent employers or **philanthropists** who wanted to improve society. Among the earliest of these was the poet Hannah More, who set up a series of Sunday schools in Somerset in 1789 with the intention of giving children some basic schooling while they were not at work. This motivation was encouraged because of her religious conviction and general sympathy towards society's vulnerable people, of whom she recognised children to be a substantial section. Complementing her early efforts to provide educational opportunities for the country's children was the mill owner and early socialist, Robert Owen, and later, the physician Dr Thomas Barnardo, who sought to accommodate Britain's poorest children. Collectively, these individuals helped to promote the interests of children over the course of the 1800s and they contributed effectively to the emerging idea that children should not be left to fend for themselves within an adult world. Their private actions not only directly increased this belief, but also helped to influence political remedies to the growing social problems that industrialisation created.

KEY TERM

Philanthropist
A person who seeks to promote the welfare of others by either donating money or supporting action.

Robert Owen

Robert Owen was a pioneering mill owner who established a model community at his New Lanark mills in Scotland based upon **co-operative principles** and a greater sense of social responsibility. It was Owen's belief that a person's character was influenced by their environment, and that to promote better human beings it was first necessary to improve their surroundings. At New Lanark, he sought to implement his ideas and he improved living and working standards for all his employees there. After 1800, the working day was shortened to not more than 12 hours, inclusive of a one-and-a-half-hour meal break, and the minimum age at which a child could work was set at ten years old. In addition, the punishment system that was so prevalent in British mills at this time was removed. Rather than fine workers or beat children, Owen installed a 'silent monitor' above each work station, essentially a wooden block with different coloured sides to denote that worker's behaviour. A particular side would be turned to face the front according to the worker's behaviour, which would be on public display. This method sought to shame workers into improving their attitudes rather than physically punishing them. Combined with these changes, better facilities were also introduced. A shop was established that sold quality goods at little more than cost price, and the profit that was generated went back to the workers in the form of 'free' education for their children in the schools that were also created.

The first of Owen's schools was established in 1816, called the Institute for the Formation of Character, and in 1817 he established the country's first infant school on the same premises. The foundation of these institutions was Owen's belief in the importance of education beyond the traditional reading, writing and arithmetic taught in other educational establishments. He promoted the teaching of natural history, music, dancing and games – all taught through new methods that avoided the traditionally **didactic** approach taken in schools where the teacher simply dictated to the class. For Owen, the didactic approach was ineffective, and instead his schools embraced the use of a variety of techniques and resources, such as maps and pictures, to make education fun and therefore promote effective learning.

KEY TERMS

Co-operative principle
An idea centred on working together for mutual benefit.

Didactic
The deliberate intention to instruct.

Dr Barnardo

Perhaps of all the philanthropic social reformers of the 19th century, Dr Thomas Barnardo is the most well known. A Protestant Irishman who originally trained to become a medical missionary in China, his endeavours to provide both an education and, more importantly, a safe home for destitute children in Britain is world famous and the charitable organisation that bears his name continues to support children in need today.

By adopting these new methods, Owen was very much a pioneer in children's education and his schools at New Lanark became publicly regarded as a progressive enterprise that attracted significant interest from prominent figures and the broader public. The cost of this education was practically free, costing 3d a month, despite the overall expense of running the institutions exceeding £700 per annum by 1816. In this regard, it was certainly not motivated by personal gain, but rather a more benevolent desire to improve the young people in Britain at a time when commerce was otherwise exploiting them and making their difficult lives even more so.

SOURCE 4 From Robert Owen's *A New Vision of Society,* published in 1816. Owen was a social reformer who believed in the virtue of education as critical for the improvement of personal character. His schools at his New Lanark mills employed modern teaching methods and were regarded with great interest by public figures at the time.

… it must be evident to those who have been in the practice of observing children with attention, that much of good or evil is taught to or acquired by a child at a very early period of its life; that much of temper or disposition is correctly or incorrectly formed before he attains his second year; and that many durable impressions are made at the termination of the first 12 or even 6 months of his existence.

SOURCE 5 From Robert Dale Owen's *Outline of the System of Education at New Lanark,* published in 1824. Robert Dale Owen was Robert Owen's son and his description here is perhaps the fullest available about the nature of the New Lanark education programme.

The principal school-room is fitted up with desks and forms on the Lancastrian plan, having a free passage down the centre of the room. It is surrounded, except at one end where a pulpit stands, with galleries, which are convenient when this room is used, as it frequently is, either as a lecture-room or place of worship.

The other and smaller apartment on the second floor has the walls hung round with representations of the most striking zoological and mineralogical specimens, including quadrupeds, birds, fishes, reptiles, insects, shells, minerals, etc. At one end there is a gallery, adapted for the purpose of an orchestra, and at the other end are hung very large representations of the two hemispheres; each separate country, as well as the various seas, islands, etc. being differently coloured, but without any names attached to them. This room is used as a lecture- and ball-room, and it is here that the dancing and singing lessons are daily given. It is likewise occasionally used as a reading-room for some of the classes.

The lower storey is divided into three apartments, of nearly equal dimensions, 12 ft high, and supported by hollow iron pillars, serving at the same time as conductors in winter for heated air, which issues through the floor of the upper storey, and by which means the whole building may, with care, be kept at any required temperature. It is in these three apartments that the younger classes are taught reading, natural history, and geography.

Dr Thomas Barnardo (1845–1905)

Thomas Barnardo was born in Dublin to Catholic parents, although he converted to Protestantism in 1862. He was determined from a young age to become a medical missionary and travel to China and at the age of 17 he travelled to London to train as a physician. It was in London that he discovered the extent of poverty in Britain and particularly the vulnerability of children to diseases such as cholera, which was rampant upon his arrival there. Determined to help Britain's poorest children, Barnardo abandoned his China plans and instead set up a Ragged School in the East End of London where children could get a basic education. Three years later, he opened his first home for children, providing them with accommodation and also trade skills such as carpentry that might help them to secure employment. These shelters quickly grew and, before he was 30 years old, Barnardo had opened more than a dozen on the principle that no destitute child would ever be turned away. He continued to expand his network of homes and upon his death in 1905 had the responsibility for around 8,500 children.

SOURCE
6

An unattributed photograph on a postcard of Dr Thomas Barnardo produced by Stepney Causeway Studio, c1900.

Thomas Barnardo first became interested in the plight of Britain's children when he moved to London from Dublin, a time when cholera was sweeping through the East End of that city and more than 3,000 people died. It was the degree of poverty and the growing number of destitute children, many of whom were orphans having lost parents to cholera, which motivated him to take action. Funded by banker Robert Barclay and Lord Ashley, in 1867 he opened a **Ragged School**. This type of school had been developed after John Pounds, a crippled shoemaker, had begun to teach children free of charge in 1818. Using donations from wealthy sponsors such as Angela Burdett-Coutts, by 1870 350 Ragged Schools had been established across the country. At a time when government did not seek to intervene excessively in social life, these charitable actions were a prominent addition to the meagre educational provision for Britain's poorest children during the 19th century.

Ragged School
A charitable organisation that provided basic education to destitute children free of charge during the 19th century.

Having set up his Ragged School, Barnardo then organised a shelter for destitute children after being shown by one of his boys, Jim Jarvis, where many children slept at night – mostly gutters and rooftops. The first of these was opened in 1870 in Stepney Causeway and it provided both accommodation and education, generally vocational skills such as carpentry and shoemaking, for the children who were admitted. After the death of a child who was refused admittance to his shelter because of its lack of space, Barnardo vowed never to turn any destitute child away again and began establishing further shelters across the city; by 1877 he had a dozen properties. The zeal with which he attempted to address the issue of child poverty was commendable and reflected a growing sympathy for the problem more widely, particularly among evangelicals. They proved to be significant financial backers for his projects, notably in helping Barnardo set up his first home in 1870 by paying the building's rent when he ran out of money and the home had to temporarily close. In this regard, the role of religion and its general humanitarianism proved to be a definitive influence for social reform during the later 19th century, and the growing affluence of Church members facilitated quite sophisticated networks of charitable organisations. In the case of Barnardo, his shelters expanded into training schools for nursery nurses when, in 1873, he acquired Mossford Lodge in Berkshire as a wedding present from his new wife's father, and was also funded to provide separate accommodation for young girls. By the 1920s, the training that girls received at Mossford Lodge was recognised as exceptional and as such many who attended there became sought after by prominent households as nurses to their children. Even before this recognition, in 1905 when Barnardo died, 92 homes had been established and he had under his care 8,500 children, testament to his determination to support vulnerable young people in Britain.

Charitable support
1 Why do you think charity was so important to children's welfare in the 18th and 19th centuries?

2 To what extent were private efforts at addressing the problem of child poverty effective?

3 Why do you think those who sought to address the problem of child poverty placed such an emphasis upon education?

Improvements in education

The trend towards bettering the lives of children was given further reinforcement in the second half of the 19th century when governments began to legislate for improvements in education. In one sense, this reflected their established interest in workplace practices with regard to child employment, but it was also symptomatic of a broader recognition of social responsibility for Britain's youngest inhabitants. By the mid-1800s, the country had grown prosperous, and consequently attention was able to turn from the exclusively economic focus that had largely dominated the earlier part of the century, towards improving society at large. This can be seen in the provision of government grants for charitable organisations to provide children's education, but later saw a more direct involvement. Motivated primarily by the efforts of individuals such as Barnardo and charitable organisations such the Ragged School Union formed in 1844, successive governments began to legislate for children as part of a more interventionist perspective that began to evolve.

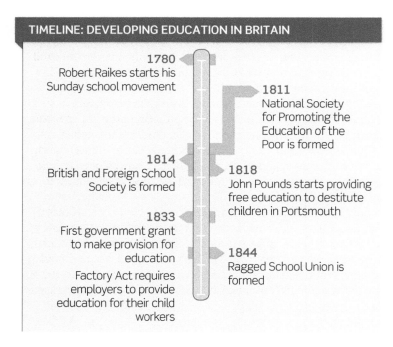

TIMELINE: DEVELOPING EDUCATION IN BRITAIN

1780
Robert Raikes starts his Sunday school movement

1811
National Society for Promoting the Education of the Poor is formed

1814
British and Foreign School Society is formed

1818
John Pounds starts providing free education to destitute children in Portsmouth

1833
First government grant to make provision for education

Factory Act requires employers to provide education for their child workers

1844
Ragged School Union is formed

The 1833 Factory Act and early factory schooling

The increasing focus upon education was also found within factory legislation primarily designed to improve the working conditions of children as early as 1833. Following the initial efforts of the 1802 Factory Act, the Factory Act passed in 1833 was considerably more wide-ranging and included a greater commitment to the education of children employed in the country's factories. This Act not only banned the employment of children under nine and restricted those over that age from working night shifts, it also required that employers provide two hours of schooling for its youngest employees – those aged 9–13 years. Proof of this schooling had to be demonstrated by the provision of a schoolmaster's certificate that stated each child had received this tuition, to be checked by the factory inspectors who had also been established under the new legislation. The provision of rudimentary education for child workers was in itself indicative of an increasingly more progressive attitude towards children as something other than cheap labour; its inclusion within what was fundamentally a piece of employment legislation suggests a growing awareness of the importance of educated workers in the competitive world created by industrialisation.

The 1833 government grant

Where formal schools did exist, they were run principally by the Church of England and therefore instructed children in that religion. One such example was the establishment of Sunday schools by the publisher Robert Raikes in 1780. The motivation behind his enterprise was his belief that vice could be better reduced through education and good moral instruction. His schools therefore sought to provide an education as well as promoting attendance at church. The spread of Raikes' schools (helped by his promotion of them in his newspaper, the *Gloucester Journal*) is testament to the growing interest in education for children. By 1831, his institutions were teaching 1.25 million children on a weekly basis – approximately 16 percent of the total child population in England and Wales. Nonconformists and Catholics objected to these schools on the basis that they forced attendance at Anglican churches and therefore the issue of children's education adopted a distinctly sectarian tone.

In 1811, supporters of the Sunday school movement set up a National Society for Promoting the Education of the Poor, which was intended to establish regular day schools in Britain's industrial towns. It was a Church of England organisation and a rival society emerged three years later called the British and Foreign Schools Society, which sought to provide the same opportunities for nonconformist children. The growth of these two distinct movements, in conjunction with factory reforms that restricted children's working hours (see pages 40–46), saw parliament vote in favour of a small grant of £20,000 in 1833 for the provision of children's education. The money was intended to be used to build and maintain small institutions of learning and is notable for being the first time the state gave assistance to schools. Part of the motivation for this grant was also the growing public interest in children's education and the awareness that by receiving a basic education, children would be better placed to become successful. More immediately, and perhaps most importantly, they would not claim poor relief and would therefore become less of a burden to both the state and its taxpayers.

Nonetheless, the government grant was meagre and was given principally to the two education societies and also to the Catholic Church, which had the organisation and network to apply these funds effectively. These institutions, however, already had funding for their educational projects, since both the Anglican and Catholic Churches had access to funds through land ownership and their congregations, while the nonconformists also had wealthy support and could also rely on their congregations. Because of this, there was some criticism that money was being granted to those who already had means rather than directing the resources to those children who did not attend church schools, primarily the poorest working class. This criticism encouraged pressure from liberal reformers for greater state involvement that could then take a more direct approach in the provision of education. In 1837, the former Whig Lord Chancellor Henry Brougham proposed an unsuccessful bill for public education and then in 1839 the government grant for the creation and maintenance of schools was made over to voluntary bodies on the condition of satisfactory inspection by government inspectors. This tentative step that the government made towards greater intervention was in a sense recognition of the need to create a more broad-based education system to reach a wider cohort of children.

Ragged Schools

Without substantial resourcing, the poorest children in Britain had to rely on alternative means for their education. Among the earliest of these were the Ragged Schools, which became very popular during the mid-1800s. These were privately organised institutions that offered the opportunity for the country's poorest children to receive a basic education. They originated in 1818 when a Portsmouth shoemaker by the name of John Pounds began offering simple education to children in his local area. The motivation for this action was his belief that existing charitable and denominational schools were not beneficial for children in inner-city areas since they often made greater demands on the children – such as attendance at church on a Sunday. He was supported in his efforts by the prominent Scottish preacher and philanthropist Thomas Guthrie, who promoted the idea of education for working-class children from his pulpit in Edinburgh and through his text *A Plea for Ragged Schools*, which was published in 1847. Guthrie himself was widely regarded in Scotland for his unusually picturesque oratory style and as such was an effective mouthpiece for promoting such an initiative. Early schools were established in vacant loft spaces or under railway arches and placed great emphasis on the traditional '3 Rs' (reading, writing and arithmetic) and also study of the Bible. In 1844, a Ragged School Union was formed by Lord Ashley, who had been instrumental in both the Mines Act and Factory Act 1847. Under his presidency, more than 350 Ragged Schools were established in Britain by 1870, educating more than 300,000 children.

The National Education League, 1869

Ragged Schools went some way towards encouraging more widespread action by both social reformers and government figures to take a more active role in the provision of education. Lord Ashley especially became a particularly vociferous advocate, pushing for reforms at every opportunity. However, it was the establishment of a more pointed political movement that ultimately made the difference. At a local level, the question

SOURCE

7 From a description of a Ragged School by Charles Dickens, published in the *Daily News*, 4 February 1846. Dickens visited a school in London and here he recalls the state of the establishment for the purposes of raising attention to the need for greater state intervention.

The close, low chamber at the back, in which the boys were crowded, was so foul and stifling as to be, at first, almost insupportable. But its moral aspect was so far worse than its physical, that this was soon forgotten. Huddled together on a bench about the room, and shown out by some flaring candles stuck against the walls, were a crowd of boys, varying from mere infants to young men; sellers of fruit, herbs, lucifer-matches, flints; sleepers under the dry arches of bridges; young thieves and beggars—with nothing natural to youth about them—with nothing frank, ingenuous, or pleasant in their faces; low-browed, vicious, cunning, wicked; abandoned of all help but this; speeding downward to destruction; and UNUTTERABLY IGNORANT.

of education for children increasingly became common and several of the larger cities in Britain had therefore become more attuned to the issue. In 1864 in Manchester and Salford, education societies had been formed with the intention of raising funds for the provision of education to their cities' children. In part, this was an economic motivation, to raise educated children who could contribute more effectively to future society and not be a burden upon the existing poor laws. This motivation was compelling. However, improving education was also a part of a broader liberal moralism that developed in the second half of the 19th century (see page 57) that began to recognise the importance of giving people the means to help themselves. This moralism became known as 'self-help' and found articulation in Samuel Smiles' book of the same name, published in 1859. The concept of self-help was not entirely new to Britain. It was an idea that had been present in the 18th century and one that developed as part of the broader industrialisation of the country, when entrepreneurial men achieved great wealth off the back of their own efforts. The returning emphasis upon self-help in the mid-19th century was initially in response to the continued high level of pauperism and a desire to place responsibility for this in the hands of the paupers themselves rather than the state. This mindset clearly had an economic motivation, but also represented a more individual way of thinking that sought to encourage greater self-sufficiency. This belief was further amplified in regard to schooling because the British state already funded education at a cost of £800,000 per annum in the 1860s. However, much of this went only to Church schools and in areas where they already existed. The argument presented by local education societies was that education should be available to all and not be as selective as it was, with significant funding going to Church-run institutions, which also overlooked new industrial areas that had very few educational establishments.

The education societies of Manchester and Salford were added to in 1867 by the Birmingham Education Society, which was established by the city's mayor, George Dixon, and Joseph Chamberlain, a future mayor himself and also leader of the Liberal Unionist Party after 1891. Like the other organisations, the Birmingham society was intended to raise funds and also promote the cause of child education. On the initiative of Dixon and Chamberlain, and 18 others who collectively subscribed £14,000, a

National Education League was established with branches across England and Wales to amplify their cause. This national body met for the first time in October 1869 and resolved to promote a bill for parliament to debate in the next session the following year. The basis of their desired bill was as follows.

- Local authorities should be compelled to provide education for all children in their district.

- Schools should be founded and maintained by public money and government grants.

- All schools that are publicly funded should be managed by local authorities rather than churches.

- These schools should be non-sectarian and admission free.

- Local authorities should have the power to enforce attendance at schools.

SOURCE

From a letter written by J. Davis, a member of the public, published in the *Spectator* on 23 October 1869. The aims of the National Education League stirred up much discussion because of their focus on education for all, free from religious influence.

Now, it is possible to defend either a secular or an unsectarian religious scheme of instruction for primary schools on grounds which would suit this class of schools exclusively. For the secular, it may be said, 'The State must insist that no child in the country shall be left ignorant of the elements of reading, writing, and arithmetic. Places must be provided at the public expense for the teaching of these rudiments, and the children now neglected and untaught must be compelled, by fines and flogging when necessary, to learn them. The State does not take upon itself the direction of education in general. It contents itself with prescribing lessons in reading, writing, and arithmetic, leaving the higher and more delicate parts of education to the voluntary care of parents and religious bodies.' For the unsectarian religious scheme, it may be contended, 'The kind of religious knowledge which it is wise and usual to impart to children is, in fact, that which is held in common by all religious bodies. Anglicans and Nonconformists alike teach their children of the love and providence of God, of the goodness and tenderness of Jesus Christ, of the duty of trying to please God, and similar universal lessons. Many earnest Christians would not care if their children of tender years learnt little beyond these rudiments of theology. But there would be no difficulty in supplying the "denominational atmosphere", and such farther instruction as might be thought desirable, at home, at church, without any want of harmony making itself felt by the children between the school teaching and the religious creed of the family.' But the case is entirely altered when the question is no longer of the bare rudiments of knowledge nor of tender years, but of the whole education of the youth. If history and the laws of life are taught on the secularist principle, you not only do not teach belief in divine purpose, you teach secularism. If you go on teaching to young men and young women the simple religion of childhood, you do in effect adopt what Mr. Lowe, I think, called a sort of Biblical Deism. Now, there is a good deal to be said for Deism, especially as a State creed, but we ought to know whether we mean to substitute it for Catholic Christianity or not.

The Elementary Education Act 1870

The argument put forward by the National Education League centred on the need to promote widespread formal education in the interest of maintaining the country's lead in manufacturing. Education, they maintained, would not only create more skilled workers, but also promote entrepreneurialism and innovation, which would continue to give Britain the edge in the increasingly competitive and industrialised world. These arguments, coming from many industrialists – Joseph Chamberlain was a screw manufacturer and George Dixon was the head of a merchant partnership – had a significant impact upon the British parliament, which was keen to maintain Britain's economic standing in the world. Collectively, these pressures encouraged the drafting of an education bill that was presented to parliament in February 1870 by William Forster and passed in the same year.

The provisions within this Act, called the Elementary Education Act, included the following.

- Elementary education should be provided for children between the ages of 5 and 13.

- Local education boards should inspect schools to ensure sufficient places are available for children in their area.

- Where inadequate provision existed in Church schools, **school boards** would be set up to establish and run secular elementary schools.

- School boards could apply for powers to make attendance compulsory.

- Schools should be publicly funded either directly by a government grant, or by a **precept** added to the local poor rate.

- Unless unable to, parents had to pay for their children's education. For those who could not afford to pay, the board would fund those children's education.

- Religious teaching in schools run by the school boards was to be non-denominational, but children could be withdrawn from these lessons if their parents required it.

- Schools were to be regularly inspected under the existing framework.

KEY TERMS

School board
An elected body of men and women who were in charge of maintaining and running an elementary school in England or Wales on behalf of the state. These boards would also set up new schools in areas where there was inadequate provision made by the Church.

Precept
A request or requisition that would be added to the local poor rate.

This Act was a substantial piece of legislation that went a long way to improve the education provision for children. Perhaps the most noticeable feature was the option for school boards to apply for powers that would enable them to make attendance on a full-time basis compulsory across England and Wales. This particular feature was significant because after 1870 parents could no longer take for granted that their children could contribute to the family income or perhaps do extensive chores around the home. In this regard, the Act effectively undermined the opportunities for children to work. In one sense this was a positive development. However, many working-class families relied on their children's contributions to pay house bills, and therefore if children were in school rather than working then often families began to struggle financially. Faced with this pressure, many children avoided going to school and continued to work despite the new law, which only compounded the challenging existence many of them experienced, of not only having to work but now also having to fend off school inspectors trying to force them into education.

Despite this resistance among some of the working class, the impact of the legislation was noticeable. Between 1870 and 1880, 4,000 schools were set up by school boards and in urban areas schooling became more rigorous, providing a range of subjects beyond the traditional '3Rs', including domestic science and gymnastics. Rural schools for their part were equally rigorous. However, many of them allowed students to leave school in order to conduct necessary agricultural labour as the need demanded. The increased formalisation of schooling signalled the start of a more robust attitude by government for managing education provision, but was not as comprehensive as the National Education League hoped.

The main drawback for the League was the failure of the Act to provide free education and to make attendance compulsory. The wording of the document gave boards the power to enforce compulsory attendance. However, there was a mixed application of this feature. By 1871, 117 boards had instituted compulsory attendance but there were also many exemptions, particularly in the rural areas. Given these limitations, the 1870 Act is perhaps regarded as the start of a new government-driven focus on education rather than as a complete solution to the issue of children's education in Britain.

ACTIVITY
KNOWLEDGE CHECK

Improving education

1 Having considered the changes that were made to education during the 19th century, plot a line graph depicting the progress made by these reforms. The x-axis should be the reforms and the y-axis the extent of progress (1 – lowest to 10 – highest).

2 Briefly justify the choices you have made and comment upon the shape of your graph. What does it suggest about the overall trend?

3 Write down your ideas as to what might have influenced the introduction of these reforms during the years before 1870.

Further legislation

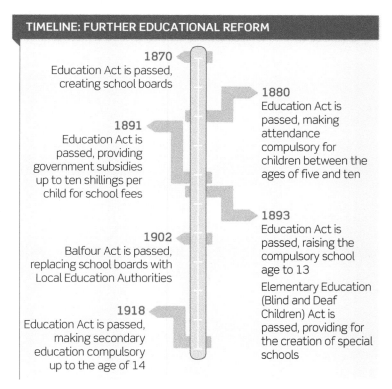

TIMELINE: FURTHER EDUCATIONAL REFORM

1870
Education Act is passed, creating school boards

1880
Education Act is passed, making attendance compulsory for children between the ages of five and ten

1891
Education Act is passed, providing government subsidies up to ten shillings per child for school fees

1893
Education Act is passed, raising the compulsory school age to 13

Elementary Education (Blind and Deaf Children) Act is passed, providing for the creation of special schools

1902
Balfour Act is passed, replacing school boards with Local Education Authorities

1918
Education Act is passed, making secondary education compulsory up to the age of 14

The passage of the Education Act 1870 signalled a more determined attitude by the British government to take an interest in the education of children, and after it came into force further legislation soon followed. The 1870 Act laid a framework that was subsequently built upon; noticeably in 1880, when compulsory education became mandatory for children between the ages of five and ten, and then in 1891 with the provision of state subsidies up to the value of ten shillings per child for school fees, making elementary education in Britain free for the first time. These reforms marked an increasing role for the state, as with each piece of legislation it added further regulations and provided more direction, taking control of education and broadening its focus. This was evident in 1893 when two new bills were passed; the first (the Education Act) extended the age of compulsory education and the second (the Elementary Education (Blind and Deaf Children) Act), provided for the creation of special schools where blind and deaf children could receive education tailored to their specific requirements. In this last regard, the state was perhaps especially progressive and was manifesting increasingly popular liberalism that emphasised the rights of all individuals and the state's responsibility to them.

The move towards greater acceptance of state responsibility in social and economic affairs began to take significant strides in the mid to late 19th century, by which time Britain had industrialised to such an extent that social problems became particularly noticeable. Towns and cities had grown substantially, and with their enlargement came greater problems associated with such urbanisation: first, sanitation and housing pressures, and then the need to improve the people themselves, particularly those who threatened the social order and respectability of the new affluent classes.

The success of industrialisation had helped to raise the standards of British society and, as the century wore on, there developed a growing demand to preserve this new-found status. It was felt that this could be achieved by greater state provision – small incursions that did not affect individual rights per se, but rather provided a means to support those deemed at risk of undermining the high standards that Victorian society had now set for the country. Education was the natural choice for such support, since it would offer the best opportunity for self-improvement in addition to installing an appropriate set of values and morals for the younger generation.

Perhaps the most significant of the post-1870 legislation that evidenced this new attitude was the 1902 'Balfour Act', which replaced the school boards and placed all schools under the supervision of Local Education Authorities (LEAs). These bodies could fund voluntary elementary schools. However, most of these were run by the Church of England and Catholic Church and because of this the legislation antagonised nonconformists. In the longer term, however, the legislation encouraged greater uniformity among all schools since they were now funded by public money and were responsible to the LEAs. Furthermore, the financial stability that such funding created saw a significant growth in secondary provision, and by 1914 more than 1,000 had been opened.

The Education Act 1918

Perhaps the most significant piece of legislation since 1870 was that created by Herbert Fisher, the president of the Board of Education, which he presented to parliament in 1918. His bill was the product of an extensive investigation of the state of British education undertaken in the years 1914–18. During this time, he visited schools across the country to inspect their quality and identify any areas of weakness. The purpose behind this investigation was a personal belief in the importance of education both for the individual and society. Equally important was the more tangible idea that British education had been hampered by the outbreak of the First World War, which saw many teachers called up for active service and children attracted to the workplace and fields. The war disrupted the education of thousands of children and if post-war Britain was to remain a dominant economic and political power in the world then it would require well-educated children to take up the mantle in the future.

EXTEND YOUR KNOWLEDGE

Herbert Fisher (1865–1940)

Herbert Fisher began his career as an historian after being educated at Oxford University, where he took a first-class degree in 1888. He was offered a fellowship at New College, Oxford, and was a tutor in modern history before becoming Vice-Chancellor of Sheffield University in 1913. He then went on to be elected MP for Sheffield Hallam in 1916. He served in David Lloyd George's government as the president of the Board of Education and was instrumental in the development of the 1918 Education Act. Fisher was also integral to the creation of the Superannuation Act in 1918, which provided teachers with a pension at the end of their working careers.

During the course of his investigations, Fisher concluded that the current system was woefully underfunded, despite the government grant having increased to over £800,000 a year by the end of the 19th century. These findings encouraged Fisher to overhaul the existing system and to find a new solution to the question of education in Britain. The remedy he settled upon was passed in the British parliament in 1918 and it provided for the following.

- The school leaving age was raised to 14.
- Local Education Authorities were empowered to provide secondary schools.
- Fees for state-run elementary schools were abolished.
- Provisions were to be made for medical inspections, nursery schools and special schools.
- Sixty percent of the costs of educational provision was to be transferred from the LEAs to central government.
- Part-time 'continuation day classes' were to be established for those children in work.

In effect, the Education Act 1918 – also known as the Fisher Act after its sponsor – was the furthest-reaching educational legislation enacted in Britain. It committed central government to this field by transferring the majority of its costs to the Local Education Authorities – an action that not only emphasised the importance of education, but also ensured that its quality would be promoted with teachers being able to access better salaries and pensions. This particular feature was very marked because it clearly shows a break from the past in that government was now more willing to accept the responsibility that it had been so reluctant to take in the previous century.

While many of the finer points of the legislation would be unachievable due to lack of financial resource in the immediate post-war period, the direction in which the Fisher Act was determined to take the British education system was a significantly more formal and uniformed one than ever before. It sought to professionalise the field and ensure a more complete and consistent opportunity for the nation's children to improve themselves.

SOURCE

From a debate in parliament on the 1918 education bill. It is from a speech by the Liberal MP for Camborne, Sir Francis Acland, on 13 March 1918.

No one who has an appreciation of what life ought to be can doubt for a moment that there should be, during the years of growth for the children of the 95 per cent roughly, of our population, who send their children to elementary schools, a far greater approximation to the conditions which have always prevailed for the children of the 5 per cent who do not send their children to that type of school. There is a general feeling that education should not be so much as it has been in the past a matter of class, or a matter of the particular amount of means which a particular class has, but that there should be something like a more general uniformity of educational opportunity throughout all classes, and that after we have all received, whatever our means may be, as good an education as the country can afford, there surely will be plenty of opportunity for people to find their own level and to segregate off into classes. I believe that in the position in which we shall find ourselves after the War industries that do not want workers with a broader outlook, a better trained character and an increased power of applying their brains, not only to the particular industry concerned but to the ordinary problems of citizenship, are not industries that we shall be able to encourage or even to keep in this country. Undoubtedly there are difficult times coming. We simply cannot afford to let our industries lack the better mental equipment which all those engaged in them will obtain if the main provisions of this Bill are carried out. We shall need to exercise national economy in every possible way. I am convinced, and I believe the House is convinced, that the truest possible national economy is wide and wise expenditure on a system of education.

A Level Exam-Style Question Section C

How far do you agree that the most significant development in children's education in the years 1759–1928 was the Elementary Education Act in 1870? (20 marks)

Tip

When answering this question, you should look at the whole time frame given and judge the extent of change that took place within it – what was children's education like before 1870 and did this change dramatically afterwards?

ACTIVITY
KNOWLEDGE CHECK

Motivation and action

1 Using your own knowledge and the information given in Source 9, answer the following questions:

   a) What are the motivations given in this source for introducing further educational reform in 1918?

   b) Do these motives suggest a significant shift in government attitudes since the last major reform in 1870?

   c) What do you think might have influenced the introduction of further reform?

   d) What reservations might you have with the information given in this source?

2 Considering the legislation passed by parliament between 1833 and 1918, do you think there was a focused and deliberate attempt to create a formal nationwide education system?

WHY DID ATTITUDES TOWARDS CHILDREN CHANGE IN THE YEARS 1759–1928?

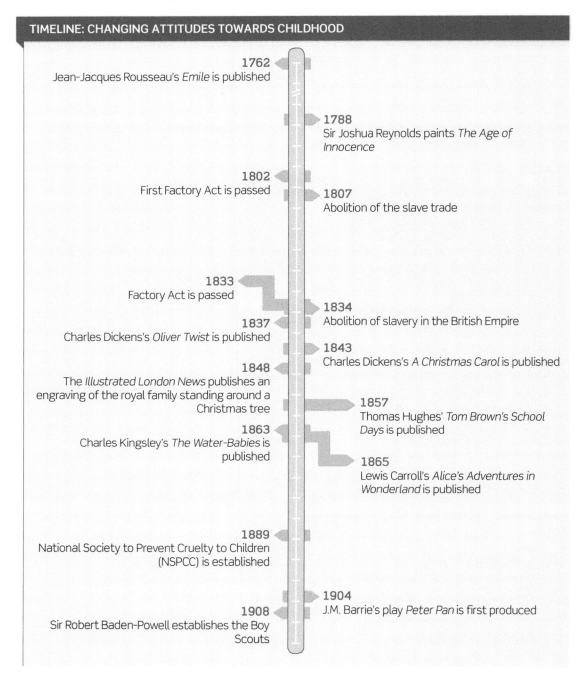

TIMELINE: CHANGING ATTITUDES TOWARDS CHILDHOOD

1762
Jean-Jacques Rousseau's *Emile* is published

1788
Sir Joshua Reynolds paints *The Age of Innocence*

1802
First Factory Act is passed

1807
Abolition of the slave trade

1833
Factory Act is passed

1834
Abolition of slavery in the British Empire

1837
Charles Dickens's *Oliver Twist* is published

1843
Charles Dickens's *A Christmas Carol* is published

1848
The *Illustrated London News* publishes an engraving of the royal family standing around a Christmas tree

1857
Thomas Hughes' *Tom Brown's School Days* is published

1863
Charles Kingsley's *The Water-Babies* is published

1865
Lewis Carroll's *Alice's Adventures in Wonderland* is published

1889
National Society to Prevent Cruelty to Children (NSPCC) is established

1904
J.M. Barrie's play *Peter Pan* is first produced

1908
Sir Robert Baden-Powell establishes the Boy Scouts

Over the course of the 18th and 19th centuries, the perception of childhood changed considerably. In the years prior to industrialisation, the attitude towards children was variable. In labouring families, children were often regarded as supplementary workers within the cottage industry – additional hands to increase the productivity of the family unit. For those born into wealthier families, there was a more romantic notion of childhood: children as innocents, untainted by the sins of the world and who became increasingly idealised as pure spirits who should be nurtured. As the Industrial Revolution took hold, this position changed, at least for the majority of working-class children, and they became integral parts of the expanding economy, performing essential and often dangerous roles that today would be unheard of. Childhood during the first half of the 19th century was especially difficult, but as the century went on so attitudes towards Britain's youngest workers matured. By the end of the century, children were very restricted in the hours of labour they could perform and were even required to attend school. In this regard, the idea of children as workers had diminished and almost been replaced with a more sympathetic attitude that placed much greater emphasis upon their well-being, recognising that children were not small adults and should not be treated as such. This transition was in part the result of the wider shift in social attitudes that demanded a greater role for the state in order to preserve social order. From this perspective, the role of children became significant for two reasons: firstly, their innocence offered the chance to instil a greater sense of morality and, secondly, their youth offered legacy for the future. In the late 19th century and early 1900s, these ideas were propagated significantly with the expansion of a deliberate children's literature that encouraged fantasy and imagination, keystones in a new construction of British childhood.

The specific factors that account for this substantial transition are varied. No single reason can be attributed, but certainly it is reasonable to suggest that in part it was industrialisation itself that started the process. As the nation grew wealthy, it developed new concepts of society and people's places within it. This was perhaps first in evidence with the great controversy of slavery, the practice of which increasingly became incompatible with industrialisation and was consequently attacked as inhuman, eventually being abolished in the British Empire in 1834. The advent of the Victorian period in particular saw the spread of a more pronounced **moralism** that significantly informed social attitudes, especially among the expanding new middle class, which came to dominate and direct the country. The traditional concept of laissez-faire individualism gave way to a policy of self-help that sought to provide those less fortunate with the means to pull themselves up and thereby add to wider society rather than be a burden upon it. Among the best examples of this principle in action was the growing determination to educate children so that they could contribute more effectively to the long-term future of Britain: Pounds' Ragged Schools and then Barnardo's vocational teaching (see page 49). These enterprises endeavoured to provide children with skills but they also created the opportunity for traditional notions of childhood to be reappraised as more attention was placed upon children's self-improvement. The concept of moralism developed as industrialisation and the national economy became more complex, binding the fortunes of both employer and employee together as one began to recognise the importance of the other. With this recognition the notion of pure individualism transformed into a more **collectivist idea** that recognised the concept of 'society' as more than just the affluent. The role of government also became more important, becoming a mechanism to support the weaker and more vulnerable elements within the country, children in particular. This moralism, therefore, applied a lens through which to view childhood and the function of children generally, and the image it projected – of youthful innocence and imagination – became the accepted reality that even now informs attitudes towards childhood. In this sense the transformation of children from workers to wonderers was the product of Victorian thinking.

Attitudes to childhood in the late 18th century

Ideas of childhood varied in the 18th century, with a broad romantic concept of innocence and purity dominating among intellectual and affluent sections of society, while a more realistic idea of children as additional wage earners existed among working families. Attitudes were inextricably tied to economic position and altered as that position changed. This is perhaps a truth that is not confined to the 18th century but could also be seen in the 19th century, where the development of class reflected equally divergent concepts of childhood, though these contrasting views would eventually be reconciled as wealth began to permeate through the whole of society and middle-class views of childhood became the accepted truth.

The idea of children as innocent beings imbued with purity was first extolled by the French philosopher Jean-Jacques Rousseau in his novel *Emile*, which was published in 1762. His theory was that corruption develops with experience and that children should ideally be left to develop naturally. This idea found significant support throughout the **Romanticism** movement of the late 18th and early 19th centuries. However, it contrasted starkly with the realities of living for poorer families. Here children were encouraged to work so as to augment the family's income and ensure that the unit was able to survive, and as such children were often regarded as an asset that could be put to work. This was especially so in the burgeoning cottage industries of Britain's rural communities, which often paid piecework rates, and children could be used to increase the productivity of the parent's work.

KEY TERMS

Moralism
An overemphasis upon morality that often governs the way in which society is judged.

Collectivist idea
Collectivism is a moral and political position that emphasises the importance of groups within society as opposed to the individual.

KEY TERM

Romanticism
An intellectual, artistic and literary movement that embraced nature and emotion over science and rationalisation. It developed in the late 18th century in part as a response to the developing Industrial Revolution.

SOURCE 10

Oil on canvas portrait of a young girl by Sir Joshua Reynolds. It is called *The Age of Innocence* and was painted in 1788. It came to symbolise the romantic notion that children were innocents in the world – a vision that would be obscured by the onset of industrialisation in the 19th century.

The campaign to abolish slavery

Despite economic imperatives, the late 18th century did see some fundamental changes in society that would indirectly challenge social attitudes towards childhood and keep the Romantic vision alive. Perhaps the most significant of these was the developing campaign against slavery and the slave trade, which grew significantly after 1787. Though orientated specifically towards the plight of African slaves, the moral and ethical arguments that were developed against the practice were equally applicable to the practice of child labour, especially in the new factory system that was being developed, where children as young as six were being forced to work 12-hour days. The growing public awareness of the slavery issue lay the foundations for future social reform as people began to adopt more humanitarian perspectives towards

particular issues. Indeed by the mid-1800s, both Lord Ashley (see page 42) and Richard Oastler, both advocates of reducing the length of the working day, made direct links between working children excessively and slavery.

Childhood in the 19th century

The drive for economic gain arguably characterised the early 19th century attitudes, but as early as 1802 legislation was already being passed to improve the conditions of young children in the workplace (see page 40). This trend continued throughout the century and with each reform, children were distanced more and more from Britain's workplaces. The motivation for this trend was a growing moralism within middle-class Victorian society that began to recognise the importance of childhood and increasingly sought to preserve their innocence in the hope of reaffirming a more orderly society. This involved the creation of an idealised image of childhood: one where children were taught obedience and manners – to respect their elders and to accept appropriate tuition so that they might offer an effective contribution to society. In this sense the reinvention of childhood was arguably a means to ensure an appropriate upbringing which not only promoted a strong set of moral values, but also allowed them to be effective citizens in the future. However, it was a slow process – following the Factory Act 1802, for example, there was no substantial legislation until 1833. The reason for such a sluggish approach was the dominance of capitalism and its demand for cheap labour. Since children were the cheapest, costing at most half as much as an adult, many business owners were reluctant to apply the same concepts of childhood that they might apply in their own homes; instead they maintained that a cheap labour supply was essential to economic expansion.

Despite reticence from economic quarters, as the country as a whole grew more affluent it became easier to consider the importance of childhood. In part this was because of the improving educational position of Britain's children following legislation from government such as the 1833 grant (see pages 50–51), which had arguably contributed to that affluence. It was also the increasingly more stable society that had developed; with clear roles being established for adults and children and with the latter, it was perceived, developing into more aspirant and motivated individuals because of the guidance received from a 'good upbringing', which had become the product of the reinvention of childhood. Furthermore, those who were able to acquire a degree of spare time, or who found their lives so overtaken by work, sought solace in the lives of their children and the opportunity they afforded of more simple things. In this regard, children, for some, became an avenue for reaching a more pure form of living. This idea reached back to the 18th century notion of innocence, which Victorian Britain sought to recapture as solace within an increasingly complicated material world.

Childhood in the early 20th century

By the end of the 19th century the formalisation of childhood through legislation and education had created an enduring image that was only enhanced by the position that Britain held within the world. As an imperial power with responsibilities across the globe, Britain developed a strong feeling that if it was to retain this position then it would be through the calibre of its younger population. Therefore, there remained a strong motivation to give children as many opportunities as they could. Perhaps the best example of this thinking was the creation of the Boy Scouts in 1908 by Robert Baden-Powell. The organisation sought to instil key virtues such as fitness and personal character, as well as an ability to face challenges in the outdoors and overcome them through both individual and team perseverance.

In addition to these imperial demands, the market economy of the previous century also promoted childhood through the vast industry that had subsequently been built around the image. Dolls, dolls houses and train sets, for example, provided good income for factories, which could now produce them in great numbers for mass consumption, reinforcing the image of childhood while also profiting from it.

The influence of Kingsley's *The Water-Babies*, Barrie's *Peter Pan* and Dickens's *A Christmas Carol*

Charles Dickens

A particular influence on the changing attitudes towards childhood was the growing body of literature that placed children central to their plots. Perhaps most famous of these in the 19th century was the figure of Oliver Twist in Charles Dickens's work of the same name published in 1837. Oliver is an orphan child and the story follows him as he leaves the workhouse and eventually finds himself in London. The tale presents a vivid picture of poor children's experiences in Britain and it arguably encouraged Victorian society to reappraise the provision for destitute children. Childhood remained a recurring theme in Dickens's writing, and his equally famous character Tiny Tim from his novella *A Christmas Carol,* published in December 1843, was equally thought-provoking. Tiny Tim is a crippled young boy whose zest for life and general gratitude for anything he receives is starkly contrasted the materialistic selfishness of Ebenezer Scrooge, the employer of Tiny Tim's father. *A Christmas Carol* presents a stark picture of society – Scrooge represents the hard-heartedness of capitalist greed and the 'less eligibility' policy endorsed in the **Poor Law Amendment Act** 1834.

KEY TERM

Poor Law Amendment Act 1834
An Act that instituted workhouses to provide a minimal level of security and benefit for Britain's poor, on the understanding that such an approach would force people to take care of themselves. Under this system, only the very needy such as the old, infirm and very young could apply for help. This approach was known as 'less eligibility'.

By drawing parallels to this legislation the novella is arguably a morality tale that seeks to educate its readers to the plight of those who are often deliberately ignored or simply unseen – especially since the passage of the new Poor Law, which saw children placed into workhouses away from public attention. The plot of the tale also takes a wider view of mid-Victorian society and depicts children as the only source of goodness in that otherwise materialistic and selfish world; the Tiny Tim character

is very much a source of hope and redemption. This view is underlined in the final pages of the story, when Scrooge is able to redeem himself by attending upon the Cratchit family and presenting them with a fine turkey for Christmas dinner, earning the gratitude of the young boy. It is here that the story ends, but the reader is left with the sense that Scrooge, and society itself, has been able to find salvation through the blessing of this child. In this sense, *A Christmas Carol* is not only a warning about the greed in society or its failings towards children, but rather a comment upon the value of children themselves. Furthermore, Dicken's depiction of Tiny Tim forced readers to confront the realities of child labour, which crippled hundreds of children each year. On a more theoretical level, the fragility of the character also underlined the vulnerability of children in the world and indirectly challenged the state to consider greater protections for them. The first print run of the novella was 5,000 and upon its publication the story was immediately popular, selling out long before Christmas Day 1843.

The impact of Dickens's creations was the humanisation of children who otherwise were not really noticed. His writing brought them to public attention and more importantly encouraged society to see them as vulnerable children rather than small adults who could be treated with disdain. In this regard, Dickens caused a reappraisal of the position of children in society and helped to usher in a more widespread acceptance of children as simply that: children.

Charles Kingsley and *The Water-Babies*

Building on the earlier works of Dickens, there emerged a growing body of literature aimed at children specifically, intended to offer instruction in morality. Since the mid-1700s, when writers began to focus on writing for young audiences, the intention was to offer instruction in religion or moral values, and they found that the most effective means was to make the lessons entertaining. These tales were deliberately creative and grew to full-length novels. Writers continued to produce didactic stories for children in the 19th century, and among the most significant was Charles Kingsley's *The Water-Babies*, published in 1863. Kingsley was a Church of England minister whose book was intended as both as support for Charles Darwin's book on evolution, *On the Origin of Species*, and also as a commentary on the issue of child labour in Britain. The plot is a fantastical story about a young chimney sweep who falls into a river and becomes a 'water-baby'. In this form he undertakes good deeds and is reborn once more in child form at the end of the novel. It was a creative idea designed to appeal to children specifically, although it also found favour with adult readers. Its central purpose was in the same tradition as the didactic novels of the 18th century and it intended to convey clear moral messages to those who read it.

Additionally, the story is more than a simple comment upon child labour, as it also serves as a morality tale. The central character of Tom the chimney sweep is presented as a reckless young boy who seems to have no moral virtue or sense of purpose beyond his own indulgence. It is from this position that his misfortune to fall into the river and be taken by the 'water-babies' stems. While under the water he gets involved in many adventures, but the main plot involves him having to rescue his hated master,

Mr Grimes, who also drowned in the river. Tom is supported by spiritual guides in his quest – fairies by the name of 'Mrs Doasyouwouldbedoneby' and 'Mrs Bedonebyasyoudid'; here the Christian virtues of forgiveness are hard to ignore. In writing the book, Kingsley was commenting upon the continuing need for such Christian moral sentiments in a society that was increasingly motivated by material gain and which had therefore encouraged exploitation to achieve it. Reinforcing this sentiment is the overarching theme of personal responsibility and the benefits of repentance. Tom initially fell into the river after being chased out the house of a young girl called Ellie and he is able to restore himself to human form by helping his hated master find atonement for his own misdeeds towards his young apprentices.

In terms of the significance of this book, in one sense it reasserted the effectiveness of the didactic novel; presenting complex moral values in simple, albeit eccentric, ways that children in particular could absorb. Indeed, it is perhaps the eccentricity of the book that is its greatest value to children; it was not a preaching book and did not present its moralism in a manner that discouraged their interest. At a time when children were not formally compelled to attend school, this avenue for instruction was of immense value because it became accessible for all children – even those who did not attend school.

SOURCE
11 From the moral in Charles Kingsley's *The Water-Babies*, published in 1863.

One thing, at least, we may learn, and that is this—when we see efts in the pond, never to throw stones at them, or catch them with crooked pins, or put them into vivariums with sticklebacks, that the sticklebacks may prick them in their poor little stomachs, and make them jump out of the glass into somebody's work-box, and so come to a bad end. For these efts are nothing else but the water-babies who are stupid and dirty, and will not learn their lessons and keep themselves clean; and, therefore (as comparative anatomists will tell you fifty years hence, though they are not learned enough to tell you now), their skulls grow flat, their jaws grow out, and their brains grow small, and their tails grow long, and they lose all their ribs…, and their skins grow dirty and spotted, and they never get into the clear rivers, much less into the great wide sea, but hang about in dirty ponds, and live in the mud, and eat worms, as they deserve to do.

But that is no reason why you should ill-use them: but only why you should pity them, and be kind to them, and hope that someday they will wake up, and be ashamed of their nasty, dirty, lazy, stupid life, and try to amend, and become something better once more. For, perhaps, if they do so, then after 379,423 years, nine months, thirteen days, two hours, and twenty-one minutes (for aught that appears to the contrary), if they work very hard and wash very hard all that time, their brains may grow bigger, and their jaws grow smaller, and their ribs come back, and their tails wither off, and they will turn into water-babies again, and perhaps after that into land-babies; and after that perhaps into grown men…

… Meanwhile, do you learn your lessons, and thank God that you have plenty of cold water to wash in; and wash in it too, like a true Englishman. And then, if my story is not true, something better is; and if I am not quite right, still you will be, as long as you stick to hard work and cold water.

But remember always, as I told you at first, that this is all a fairy tale, and only fun and pretence: and, therefore, you are not to believe a word of it, even if it is true.

ACTIVITY
KNOWLEDGE CHECK

Changing attitudes towards children

1 Using the material you have read and your own knowledge, write a paragraph explaining how economic developments helped to encourage the changing attitudes towards childhood.

2 In what way did the modernisation of the economy help to change attitudes towards children in the workplace?

3 How influential do you think the growing focus of children in emerging literature was in changing personal attitudes?

J.M. Barrie and *Peter Pan*

The enduring influence of *The Water-Babies* was the importance of imaginative literature that appealed to children. This literature allowed for covert moral instruction, but also served as a means to construct a new idea of childhood, which Victorian society was beginning to promote in the second half of the 19th century. This particular interest had slowly grown over the course of the 1800s as concern developed over the treatment of children. This concern was manifested in the form of various Factory and Education Acts, along with private charitable activities, which took place throughout the period, gradually redefining children as distinct from the small adults that they had been considered before. Having recast children as children, literature therefore became a way of promoting this new idea – a way of giving back a concept of childhood that had been lost to many people during the high days of the Industrial Revolution, when profitability had been the main focus.

The motivation for this transformation was a growing sense of moral propriety that developed as the nation prospered. Through more affluent eyes, the plight of children was eventually recognised and addressed, and having taken the majority of children from the workplace by the end of the century, there was a great effort to create a new sense of childhood, one that reignited the Romantic notions of the late 18th century and promoted hopes and dreams for the young. In this last regard, literature was an ideal platform for constructing a new child identity and it was seen in an early form with Kingsley's *The Water-Babies*, but it appeared most clearly upon the stage in 1904, when J.M. Barrie's play *Peter Pan, Or the boy who wouldn't grow up*, was first performed.

Upon its first performance *Peter Pan* became instantly popular and it ran in London until 1913. Based upon the success of the play, Barrie published a novelisation of the story as *Peter and Wendy* in 1911. The story of the boy who would never grow up struck a chord with early Edwardian society because it represented a certain freedom of mind that many individuals, adults and children alike, found attractive.

This story is a tale about the children of a middle-class family being drawn into a world of fantastical adventure by a boy named Peter Pan who cannot grow up and is able to fly. The story is based in a place called 'Neverland' and sees the characters doing battle with pirates. The play's plot has subsequently become a template for classic children's adventure storytelling because it offers a wonderful world of make-believe where children do not have to grow up and therefore live in a perpetual state of wonderment.

It is this particular quality that perhaps singles out *Peter Pan* as an important contribution to the new image of childhood that was established by the end of the Victorian period. The central character of Peter Pan constantly wrestles with the prospect of growing up and this is a continual torment for him, particularly when challenged on the issue by Wendy. The idea that childhood was so valuable that to give it up would be a significant loss is perhaps the starkest example of how much the concept of childhood had transformed. Early in the 19th century children were simply additional sources of labour, but one hundred years later they were more than this – they now fulfilled a more

important role in society and this was something that should not be given up lightly. Barrie did not specify exactly what this role was. However, it would be reasonable to suggest that an active childhood served to create a bright young mind that could contribute more fully to the modern world – thinkers and wonderers whose unstifled creativity might improve the fortunes of society. Outside of this economic context, it is also reasonable to suggest that a childhood full of exploration and imagination also offered a healthy way to meet the demands of the modern world; a mind unfazed by problems and pressures.

It is reasonable to suggest that *Peter Pan* is perhaps the first literary construction to clearly establish the purity of a newly created idea of childhood; one in which imagination and innocence is able to run free and children can simply enjoy their emersion in it. In effect, it is the first fully formed manifestation of the Victorian idealisation of childhood.

SOURCE 12 The frontispiece of J.M. Barrie's *Peter and Wendy*, first published in 1911. The illustration is by F.D. Bedford.

J.M. Barrie (1860–1937)
James Matthew Barrie was a Scottish writer and playwright who took his MA in Literature at the University of Edinburgh in 1882. Since he was a young boy, he had settled upon a career as an author, despite the misgivings of his family who encouraged him to pursue a more stable career as a civil servant. While at university, he wrote reviews of plays for the *Edinburgh Evening Courant*, and after graduating he wrote several short pieces for the *St James Gazette*, although his interest lay in drama. His first few plays received mixed reviews and it was only in 1901–02 that he began to achieve any noteworthy success. In 1904 he wrote *Peter Pan*, and following its success he continued to enjoy positive reviews until his last play in 1936. Upon the success of *Peter Pan*, he rewrote the play as a novel entitled *Peter and Wendy* in 1911 and in 1929 gave the copyright to his *Pan* works to Great Ormond Street Hospital.

The influence of Prince Albert

As important as the development of children's literature was to the changing attitudes towards childhood, it was perhaps stimulated by the support of Queen Victoria's husband, Prince Albert of Saxe-Coburg-Gotha – the **prince consort** after 1857. Prince Albert was particularly concerned with social welfare and took a great interest in the experiences of children in Britain. After the death of Lord Melbourne, the queen's adviser and prime minister between 1835 and 1841, Albert was able to take a greater interest in these affairs, and in 1842 invited Lord Ashley to discuss the issue of child labour with him at Buckingham Palace. He had also sent Lord Ashley a letter of support for his Mines Act of the same year. Unlike Lord Melbourne, who had encouraged Victoria to not think about social affairs, Albert promoted the cause as well as he could, and this had a substantial bearing upon the changing attitudes of government. The relationship that Albert enjoyed with the queen was a very close one and, as his wife, Victoria took a great deal of interest in what he said. Though parliament retained ultimate authority over the passage of laws and the administration of the country because of Britain's use of a **constitutional monarchy**, the interest of the queen certainly registered with politicians, and as such it is reasonable to suggest that through this indirect manner, Albert was able to exert some influence over the issue of social welfare, and particularly the experiences of the young.

Prince consort
The title given to the husband of a reigning queen who is not himself a king.

Constitutional monarchy
A system of government whereby the monarch exists as the head of state but operates within a clearly defined set of rules, usually a constitution.

Such was Prince Albert's interest in social welfare that he served as president of the Condition of the Labouring Classes – a group interested in improving the experience of Britain's working people. In 1848, with revolution abroad, he made a speech in which he made clear his sympathy with those less fortunate in British society. By publicly declaring his support, he not only gave personal weight to the cause of poverty, but also acted as a figurehead under which others could align. In effect, he became a prominent figure to spiritually lead the fight for improvements in Britain's social condition, of which children's experiences became a central target.

SOURCE

13 From a speech made by Prince Albert in his role as President of the Condition of the Labouring Classes in 1848.

[We must have] sympathy and interest for that class of our community who have most of the toil and fewest of the enjoyments of this world… [it is the] duty of those who, under the blessings of Divine Providence enjoy station, wealth, and education… to assist those less fortunate than themselves.

In addition to the issue of child labour and the experience of the labouring classes generally, Prince Albert was greatly interested in education reform and believed that schooling was integral to a better life. He had arranged the schooling of his own children and was intent on supporting wider educational reform, making many speeches on the importance of education. In 1847 he was elected as Chancellor of Cambridge University, and in this position he pursued reform and sought to have new subjects accepted in the university. His interest was substantial and he took a very active role in promoting greater accessibility to the institution as well.

In terms of promoting children's experiences and changing attitudes, Albert was of important public significance. His position gave him access to the queen, and Victoria's influence over government, though limited, was still weighty. As such, the opportunities of effecting change became more positive with the support of the prince consort. Additionally, as such a public figure who after 1851 had become more popular in Britain, Albert was able to mobilise public support for change in an indirect way that quietly encouraged the gradual change in attitudes towards children to which the 19th century bore witness.

Perhaps more significantly than talks with politicians and the influence he had over the queen, Albert also helped to facilitate a wider appreciation of family life and the value of harmony within it. As both a husband and father, the prince was devoted to his family and he revelled in the company of his nine children. Victoria and Albert went to great lengths to ensure their children remained happy and fulfilled – for example Albert helped to popularise the now accepted tradition of having a Christmas tree indoors when, in 1848, an engraving of the royal family together around such a tree was published by the *Illustrated London News*. Albert brought this German tradition to his family's celebrations and together they would decorate the tree with baubles and other trinkets. In many regards, this particular image – a family around the Christmas tree – represented a model example of harmony within the family unit and this ideal gradually became more prominent within wider society, as the example set by Albert and Victoria became a measure of respectability in Britain.

THINKING HISTORICALLY   Change (8a, b & c) (I)

Imposing realities

I hear that Victorian society is starting to promote the interests of children.

Yes, but I don't think much of the education programmes they are offering.

Answer the following:

1 Explain why the conversation in the cartoon above would not have happened.

The shape of history is imposed by people looking back. People who lived through the 'history' did not always perceive the patterns that later historians identify. For example, some people living through the Industrial Revolution may have understood that great change was taking place, but they would not have been able to understand the massive economic, social and political consequences of industrialisation.

2 Consider the beginning of reforms to child labour.

a) Who would have made the decision as to when this took place?

b) Could anybody have challenged this decision?

c) Explain why someone living in the 19th century would have been unable to make a judgement about the beginning of a new era.

3 Who living at the present time might regard the beginning of child labour reforms as an important event?

4 What does this cartoon tell us about the structure of history as we understand it?

A Level Exam-Style Question Section C

How far do you agree that attitudes towards children changed substantially in the years 1759–1928? (20 marks)

Tip

When answering this question you should look at the whole timeframe given and judge the extent of change that took place within it – what was the attitude towards children like at the start of the period and how different was it by the end? You could also consider who held these attitudes – is there any difference between the working class and the middle class, for example?

ACTIVITY
KNOWLEDGE CHECK

Influencing change

1 What influenced the changing attitude towards children over the period 1759-1928?

2 Of these influences, which do you feel is the most important?

3 Do you feel there were sufficient other changes that would have promoted a new perspective towards childhood?

ACTIVITY
SUMMARY

Improving lives

Using your own knowledge and the material you have read complete the following tasks:

1 Identify and write down the events that you feel are most significant to the improvement of children's lives during the years 1759-1928.

2 Which of these events do you think is most important and why?

3 In your opinion why might it be said that improving children's lives took longer than it should have done?

WIDER READING

Cunningham, H. *The Invention of Childhood*, BBC Books (2006)

Heywood, C. *A History of Childhood: Children and Childhood in the West from Medieval to Modern Times*, Polity Press (2001)

Humphries, J. *Childhood and Child Labour in the British Industrial Revolution*, Cambridge University Press (2011)

Kirby, P. *Child Labour in Britain, 1750–1870*, Palgrave Macmillan (2003)

Murphy, D., Staton, R., Walsh-Atkins, P. and Whiskerd, N. *Britain 1783–1918*, Collins Educational (2003)

Wilkes, S. *The Children History Forgot*, Robert Hale Ltd (2011)

3.3

Josiah Wedgwood: china and canals, 1759–87

KEY QUESTIONS

- In what ways did Wedgwood's innovations in production and design influence taste and style for ceramics in elite society?
- How important was the construction of the Trent and Mersey canal and the linking of the canal network for the development of Wedgwood's business?
- What was the motivation for Wedgwood's involvement in the campaign to abolish the slave trade?

INTRODUCTION

Josiah Wedgwood was an icon of the early Industrial Revolution, the period that saw the rise of a new class of entrepreneur involved in the manufacture of goods. Yet, as the historian Brian Murphy notes, unlike cotton spinning, which saw the mechanisation of a process of production that was able to exploit a mass market for cheap cotton cloth, Wedgwood chose instead to create products that catered for more exclusive consumers, who were concerned with style, quality and taste. At his Etruria factory near Stoke-on-Trent he sought to create a model of efficiency that combined large-scale production with the aesthetics of good design. The whole building was a testament to the scale of Wedgwood's ambition to be regarded not only as a great manufacturer, but an arbiter of fashion. Wedgwood would make his mark not just as an industrial innovator and a producer of iconic ceramics but also as a marketing pioneer who conquered continents with his stoneware and porcelain.

SOURCE

1 From the second edition of Wedgwood and Bentley's catalogue in 1769. At the end of the catalogue Wedgwood sets out his ideas on design, production and the importance of maintaining quality.

The desire of selling much in a little time, without respect to the taste or quality of the goods, leads manufacturers and merchants to ruin the reputation of the articles which they manufacture and deal... whilst those who buy for the sake of a fallacious saving prefer mediocrity to excellence.

Beautiful forms and compositions are not to be made by chance, and they never were made nor can be made in any kind at a small expense; but the proprietors of this manufactory have the satisfaction of knowing by a careful comparison, that the prices of their ornaments are much lower, and of all of them as low, as those of any other ornamental works in Europe of equal quality.

1759 – Wedgwood's Etruria factory is established

1762 – Wedgwood presents Queen Charlotte with a breakfast set of cups as exemplification of his products

1766 – Construction of the Trent and Mersey canal begins

1777 – Trent and Mersey canal is completed

| 1755 | 1760 | 1765 | 1770 | 1775 | 1780 |

1761 – Bridgewater Canal opens

1765 – Queen Charlotte commissions a dinner service from Wedgwood

1770 – Catherine the Great commissions a dinner service from Wedgwood

Source 1 can be seen as Wedgwood's manifesto that he intended to focus on excellence of design and quality of production, but to do it as efficiently as possible so as to control price. He saw himself as a combination of designer and manufacturer who was able to successfully market his vision of what was considered tasteful and elegant. It was Wedgwood the genius in marketing, as much as Wedgwood the technical innovator, who was to make his name in the British pottery industry and become a leading figure in 18th-century commercial society. His was a story of combining what he would have seen as art and industry to create items of ornament and function that would be found in the homes of the respectable classes, as well as the homes of the political and social elite.

Josiah Wedgwood was born in Burslem, Staffordshire, in 1730, the youngest of 11 children. He was from a dynasty of potters who could trace their ancestry in the Burslem area back to the early 17th century where they had enjoyed some notable prosperity. However, the strand of the family to which Josiah belonged had not been as successful and, when his father died in 1739, debts took away Josiah's inheritance and the family struggled to keep the business going. In 1744, he was apprenticed for five years to his older brother, Thomas, and began work at his late father's works the Churchyard Pottery in Burslem. Wedgwood learnt much about the techniques of the skilled potter and became adept at **turning pots**. However, a bout of smallpox left him with a weakened knee and meant that he was not able the work the treadle on the potter's wheel. Though the apprenticeship gave him an understanding of the process of making pottery, he was critical of the quality of the work produced by his brother and the lack of attention paid to design and form.

In 1752, Wedgwood left his brother's employment and went into partnership with John Harrison, the son of a banker from Stoke-on-Trent. This arrangement lasted only two years and after a disagreement the partnership was dissolved. In the same year, 1754, Wedgwood entered into a five-year partnership with the renowned potter Thomas Whieldon, of Fenton Low in Staffordshire. Here Wedgwood was finally free to experiment and develop his ideas on design and taste.

KEY TERM

Turning a pot
Where clay was worked into a pot by placing on a turntable or wheel, which was turned by a treadle mechanism by the potter.

EXTEND YOUR KNOWLEDGE

Thomas Whieldon (1719–95)
Thomas Whieldon was a successful potter who produced high-quality ceramics. The quality of his work was recognised outside Staffordshire and he found a ready market for his tortoiseshell designs, which were multicoloured and produced an unusual clouded effect. In addition, his black ware, known as the Jackfield type (after the Jackfield area near Coalport where the material was first used) was a very hard earthenware which was finished in a strong black glaze that produced a very glossy finish. He also produced grey-white salt-glaze stoneware, although he is perhaps best known for his tortoiseshell pottery. He is famous as the master of a number apprentices who would go on to have successful careers in the pottery industry, such as Aaron Wood, who was very skilled at moulded pottery and is said to have invented early creamware, and Josiah Spode, the inventor of bone china.

1787 – Wedgwood joins the Society for Effecting the Abolition of the Slave Trade

Wedgwood produces his slave medallion

1807 – Britain abolishes the slave trade

| 1785 | 1790 | 1795 | 1800 | 1805 | 1810 |

1795 – Death of Josiah Wedgwood

IN WHAT WAYS DID WEDGWOOD'S INNOVATIONS IN PRODUCTION AND DESIGN INFLUENCE TASTE AND STYLE FOR CERAMICS IN ELITE SOCIETY?

Location of the industry

In Wedgwood's 1765 monograph *Staffordshire Pottery and its History*, he asserts that in 1710 there had only been 52 pot-works in the area: 43 in Burslem, seven in Hanley and two in Stoke-on-Trent itself. By the mid-18th century they were so numerous that the area became known as the Potteries. The pottery trade had developed in north Staffordshire for a number of reasons. The area was rich in red clays for making earthenware and these could be accessed from the open seams of the locality's coal mines. Below these seams were fire clays that had a refractory property: it retained its strength at high temperatures so that it could be used to make firebricks for lining the **kilns**, **saggars** to hold the pots in the kilns while they were fired, and **glazed** sewage pipes. The Middle Coal Measures in the region contained much Sencroft and Peacock coal, which were long-flame coals ideal for firing a kiln. When many of the local potteries moved from earthenware to stoneware, the nearby village of Mow Cop provided silica sand for the process, while salt came from just over the border in Cheshire.

Partnership with Thomas Whieldon

Wedgwood's partnership with Whieldon was to provide the first opportunity for him to demonstrate how innovations in production and design could be used to capture a market, and he was to show how one had to combine the skills of craftsman with those of the businessman. The Fenton Low works were larger than most in the region and exemplified the best work in Staffordshire, producing marbled ware such as tortoiseshell plates and tea sets. Whieldon had been innovative in the way he produced his ceramics, in his use of glazes and focus on the quality, but by the 1750s his work was losing ground to competitors and it was clear to Wedgwood that the business needed to further industrialise and innovate to improve its consistency. There was a need for new products and most importantly new markets beyond those that traditionally purchased Staffordshire pots.

Wedgwood observed that the variation of finish meant that there were differences between batches that made it difficult to produce large sets of pottery. He was also despairing of the fact that the highest-selling item, the white stoneware, had seen its price so reduced because of the increase in competition that there was little incentive to improve either its design or invest in improvements to its production. It was, therefore, his view that the pottery had to invest in new styles and experiment with different glazes to create goods that would find a new market.

Wedgwood's experimental work

The ceramics produced by Wedgwood were heavily influenced by the classical world. The late 18th century saw a return to **neoclassical** design in architecture, which also affected decoration. Leading architects such as Robert Adam promoted a style of design called **rococo**, which was echoed in the work of Wedgwood. These two forces defined the period.

On the one hand, we see the wider focus on the arts of Greece and Rome, while on the other we encounter the reinterpretation by individuals such as Wedgwood, Spode, and Adam, who brought them to a new market. The creamware of the Wedgwood factory was heavily indebted to Etruscan pottery in terms of shape and embossed patterning, while later decorative items such as black basaltware and jasperware used classical forms, but often with contemporary decorative themes.

Green glaze

The dominant form of decoration in the Staffordshire potteries was salt-glaze, a translucent brown finish created by combining silica with common salt. There had been some experimentation to offer different colours and an off-white shade had been made using flint chippings mixed with the salt base, though the shade varied greatly. For Wedgwood, salt glaze typified the lack of innovation in the potteries and the need to search for new and novel forms of decoration. In March 1759 came Wedgwood's first breakthrough in attempting to improve colour and constancy. His notebook makes reference to the development of a green glaze from vitrified flint glass, red lead and white enamel,

KEY TERMS

Kiln
At this time a kiln was a bottle-shaped structure known as a bottle kiln, which was used to heat pottery to a high temperature, causing a chemical change in the clay to create a hard and durable material.

Saggar
A container made out of fire clay in which pots were stacked for firing, enabling large numbers of pots to be loaded into the kiln.

Glaze
A coating added to a pot for decoration, protection or to prevent it from being porous. Once the glaze has been added, the item is put into a kiln where heat is applied to it. Once the item has been fired (heated), a chemical reaction takes place and the coating turns into a type of glass.

Neoclassical
Design based on forms of architecture and decoration encountered in ancient Rome and Greece. It consisted of buildings that have a balanced form in terms of their symmetry and a use of columns.

Rococo
A style that added decoration to the simple classical form, and can be elaborate in the way it is arranged, with the use of organic forms that sit in juxtaposition to the formality of the straight lines of the classical form.

along with calcined copper. The combination gave a consistent rich dark green colour to the pottery. The discovery of the green glaze was followed by a yellow glaze in 1760, which in his notebook is listed as experiment 100. The combination of yellow and green glazes was used in Wedgwood's early coloured pottery, most notably the pineapple teapot with its green leaves and yellow pineapple dome, and his cauliflower ware. The design of the leaves is often attributed to Whieldon, but refined and developed by Wedgwood and potter and designer William Greatbatch.

SOURCE
2 An example of a cauliflower ware teapot from 1765, held in the Wedgwood museum. It shows the dark green and cream glazes developed by Wedgwood as well as the attention to design and the excellence of the workmanship that he was able to bring to the production process.

Creamware

From the 1720s there had been experimentation in producing white or cream glazes. Early attempts combined lead ore into the glazing paste, which then was fired at a low temperature but in the same kilns as the salt-glazed wares. The results were uneven and there were wide variations in colour. Enoch Booth of Tunstall improved the method by introducing **twice-firing** to the potteries of Staffordshire, which made the coverage more consistant. Wedgwood first encountered creamware at Whieldon's Fenton pottery and began experiments to try to create a consistent, even colour. Though the pottery sold well, batches could vary from a light primrose or straw colour to the deepest saffron. Consistency was key to long-term commercial success, as purchasers would become disenchanted with the product if they could not replace broken pieces with items of the same shade or were restricted in the size of their purchase if services were confined to what could be had from a single firing.

Wedgwood conducted around 400 experiments, combining differing proportions of lead ore, flint and kiln temperature until he was able to produce an even, translucent glaze. Even so, he still faced problems over the desired shade as was expressed in his correspondence regarding the problems of marketing his creamware.

KEY TERM

Twice-firing
Where pottery is fired once to what is described as a biscuit state, then dipped in a suspended solution of lead ore, ground flint and pipe-clay dusted with colouring reagents and fired again. The result is an even glaze, if not one that is always a consistent shade.

SOURCE
3

Letter from Wedgwood to his London office regarding the colour of his creamware. While he had been able to produce a uniform colour, there were issues over which shades would prove to be most popular and the difficulty in varying production.

With respect to the colour of my ware, I endeavour to make it as pale as possible to continue it cream-colour, and find my customers in general, though not every individual of them, think the alteration I have made in that respect a great improvement. But it is impossible that any one colour, even though it were to come down from heaven, should please every taste, and I cannot regularly make two cream colours, a deep and a light shade, without having two works for the purpose. Nor have I any clay to make with certainty a very light colour for tea-ware.

As can be seen from Source 3, the art of the potter was not confined to the technique of production, but also needed to focus on the art of marketing. Creamware would be Wedgwood's most popular product and brought him to the attention of an important elite who defined taste. However, this was not done through quality of production alone. There were perhaps more than a hundred potteries selling versions of creamware by 1774, but it was Wedgwood's that was able to define the market and set the standard through a highly effective marketing strategy.

Wedgwood on his own

The partnership with Whieldon lapsed in 1760 and Wedgwood decided to go into business on his own. He moved back to Burslem and took a lease on the Ivy House Works. Here he began to develop his ceramics, focusing on combining colour and design. In the latter matter he was aided by William Greatbatch who was an excellent modeller and craftsman that he had come to know through his work at the Fenton pottery. Skilled labour was to remain at the heart of the Wedgwood business, and, though he would refine the process of production, Wedgwood's reputation would ultimately come to rest on the abilities of his workforce.

The Ivy House pottery was of a quality and style that became popular outside Staffordshire, bringing Wedgwood's work to the attention of a wider audience. However, this did not always mean that he was able to demand the highest price. Also, during this time he often found himself continuing to supply older-style salt-glazed goods, which remained in great demand. An order from a Dutch retailer, dated 1763, requested items of traditional enamel, salt-glazed and redware to be supplied, which should be pretty but not expensive.

Workforce

Throughout Wedgwood's time in business, the organisation and discipline of his workforce was to be a perpetual problem. While the potteries of Staffordshire could supply him with skilled labour – as well as providing access to large amounts of raw materials such as clay – the operatives were not used to regular hours and indulged in practices that could disrupt the process of production. Wedgwood made his works a place of rules and regulated work, where traditions such as **Saint Monday** were discouraged, and discipline was enforced through fines and threats of dismissal. In 1764, Wedgwood obtained a lease on the Brickhouse Works in Burslem, which became known as the Bell Works due to the use of bells to call the operatives to work and regulate the day. These methods became part of the factory environment and were characteristic of what was happening in other industries where large workforces needed to be organised to improve the output of the enterprise.

SOURCE
4

From an interview, transcribed by John Ward, with two potters who grew up with Josiah Wedgwood in Burslem. John Tellwright tells of a society in his youth where master potters were close to their men and drink affected the operation of the business.

Just as soon as they had placed the ware in the ovens, off they'd go and make straight for ye alehouse on Swan Bank. And there they'd drink n' drink till the ware would be ready to taken out, or so they thought, relying on guesswork and the state of intoxication they found themselves in. The master potters always took their labourers with them to the alehouse, and when they were all half drunk, many a row and fight would break out, each man taking his turn in the arena, arguing over whose turn it was to pay. And when they eventually returned to their oven with sore heads, all their pots would be spoiled.

Wedgwood would not tolerate the behaviour outlined in Source 4, particularly if it had the potential to cause such damage to his business. His time was taken up with improving the efficiency of production, which required ever greater specialisation. Tasks were divided between skilled workmen and as the **division of labour** increased so did the skill and knowledge in particular specialist areas. Wedgwood wanted to abandon the 'careless methods' that were characteristic of the traditional potters for a more scientific approach. Kilns had to be monitored and temperatures checked regularly; in later life he was made a Fellow of the Royal Society because of his development of a device for accurately measuring high temperatures encountered when firing pottery. Wedgwood also maintained his contact with his labourers and was prepared to negotiate directly with them. In 1776, he was confronted by a large crowd of labourers and craftsmen outside his residence at **Etruria**, demanding an increase in wage rates. Unperturbed, he approached them and debated the issues raised, though he finally lost his temper and threatened to dismiss them and find a new workforce, at which point he was able to persuade them to return to work. As the factory continued to grow, it became increasingly difficult to maintain direct contact with the employees, yet the paternalist approach continued well into the 1790s.

Etruria Works and innovations in production

To capitalise upon the growing success of his pottery manufacturing, Wedgwood wanted to construct a larger plant and to take advantage of new techniques in production, such as the machines to shape and decorate pots. In 1767 he bought the Ridge estate not far from his old factory for £3,000. Here he built a large house, Etruria Hall, for himself and his large family of eight children. He also had constructed a large factory, the Etruria Works, and a workers' village. The factory opened in 1769 and was a purpose-built structure for the large-scale production of pottery, which together with Etruria Hall, cost in the region of £10,000 to complete. From the start, Wedgwood attempted to separate out tasks and divide production between what he termed 'useful ware', consisting of creamware, and 'ornamental ware' such as vases and plaques. In continuing his scheme for regulating the work culture of his employees, Wedgwood introduced a primitive clocking-in system to maintain work discipline and discourage employees from turning up when it pleased them. In time, Wedgwood would retrain the workforce to specialise as mould-makers, seal-makers, moulders, lathe-turners, spout-makers, engravers, dippers, firemen for the kiln and many other trades, as well as increasing the number of overlookers and foremen to manage the process of production. There would no longer be general potters, just operatives with specialist skills. With this systematic division of labour, Wedgwood was able to remodel the process of production, increasing efficiency of production, constancy of quality, as well as reducing waste. Wedgwood would also become known for his increased use of machinery in the manufacture of pottery, for example lathes were employed to add decoration. At the Etruria Works, a water wheel was also set up to power grinding pans for flint to be added to the stoneware and later it was used in the development of porcelain. Wedgwood would later go on to purchase a steam engine from his friend the manufacturer Matthew Boulton to pump water to fill the mill pool to power the water wheel in times of drought.

The more artistic and interpretative work was put into a separate part of the factory where the artists were taught their trade through an apprentice system that would produce generations of renowned designers and painters. Prominent painters and sculptors, such as John Flaxman were brought in to support this process and improve Wedgwood's designs. By 1787, the works would employ 278 men, women and children and be the largest factory in the Potteries.

ACTIVITY
KNOWLEDGE CHECK

Improving the product
1 With a partner make a mind map. In the centre write 'Wedgwood's improvements' then draw links to the headings 'Labour', 'Design' and 'Experimentation'. Now add some brief notes to these points on what Wedgwood did to improve his products.

2 Look at your notes and discuss with your partner the following question: Why did Wedgwood need to make such improvements if he wanted to market his pottery beyond the Midlands?

3 Write a paragraph on why it was necessary for Wedgwood to try to exert control over his workforce.

The role of Queen Charlotte

Wedgwood's confidence in the quality of his creamware was demonstrated in 1762 when he made a present of a breakfast set of cups and bowls to Queen Charlotte, wife of King George III – though it is not clear if at this time he had sufficiently perfected his glazing technique to make a large run viable. The gift was also a shrewd marketing move as it brought his work to the attention of those who defined fashion and so might promote his goods among high society. His generosity paid off three years later in 1765, when the queen placed an order for an entire service. The provincial industrialist was summoned to attend on the queen at Buckingham House, for which audience it is recorded that he dressed in his finest brown dress wig, red silk waistcoat and blue velvet jacket, while around his waist hung a recently purchased sword. Such passing detail is important, as he did not come as a tradesman offering his goods for sale, but as a gentleman who represented the manufacturing class and looked to assert his position within the social hierarchy. The commission for the production of queensware indicated royal approval of the pottery, but it is not recorded what the queen's personal feelings were. The closest we can get to ascertaining her assessment of Wedgwood's work is from the diary of Mrs Papendiek, Assistant Keeper to the Wardrobe of Queen Charlotte (a position of considerable rank at court). She records that their tea and coffee was taken from Chinese export porcelain, but they dined on a stoneware dinner service, which among their position could not be bettered.

SOURCE

A creamware plate from 1769. The sophistication of the design can be seen, with its complex scalloped edge and embossed mouldings in the centre in the form of a Tudor rose, as well as the hand-painted additional decoration.

The commission from the queen was the key moment in establishing Wedgwood's reputation and he was quick to capitalise on it, styling himself as Potter to Her Majesty in 1766, in advertisements promoting his pottery. This branding also extended to his creamware, which morphed into queensware to emphasise its quality and style. New patrons soon followed, such as the Duchess of Argyll, who had a set decorated to her own design. In 1770 came perhaps his most famous commission, from Empress Catherine II (Catherine the Great) of Russia. Again Wedgwood had not been slow to promote himself. In 1768 he had contacted the empress though the Russian ambassador and provided specimens of his work for her consideration. The order when it came was for a vast dinner service to be supplied with hand-painted designs and decorated with a frog motif. The scale of the project caused some concern as there were questions as to the willingness of the empress's court to meet the costs of the service should there be a cooling in British–Russian relations. Yet Wedgwood was firm in his conviction that it would provide a way to further promote the reputation of his Burslem pottery. In the end, Wedgwood was paid £3,500 for the completed service, which cost him in the region of £3,000 to manufacture and decorate.

The production of queensware involved Wedgwood in developing and refining decoration. As can be seen in Source 5, creamware was not without adornment, and this required the employment of skilled artists. In 1770, he established a workshop in Cheyne Row in London under the direction of his new partner, Thomas Bentley, to provide hand-painted decoration for his pottery. The importance of the London location was that it was convenient for his elite clientele, who could discuss with the artists the decoration that they required. Wedgwood employed many talented painters to produce his famous landscapes that appeared on the dinner service supplied to Catherine the Great. As well as painted designs, Wedgwood offered a range of transfer prints which were printed by Sadler and Green in Liverpool. This arrangement was not always satisfactory and correspondence between Wedgwood and his printers suggests some irritation with their workmanship. In 1784, the arrangement came to an end and Wedgwood decided to start transfer printing at his Etruria Works in Staffordshire.

A Level Exam-Style Question Section B

How far were Wedgwood's innovative designs responsible for the success of Josiah Wedgwood's business? (20 marks)

Tip
Reflect on how far Wedgwood's designs were key to his success, balanced against, for example, his ability to target specific wealthy patrons.

EXTEND YOUR KNOWLEDGE

Thomas Bentley (1731–80)

Thomas Bentley was the son of a gentleman of some property from Derbyshire. He was well educated, though due to his theological beliefs, which were those of a Protestant dissenter from the established Church, he was not permitted to attend the universities at Oxford or Cambridge. Bentley became a merchant in Liverpool and became widely read in philosophy, science and religion. He first met Wedgwood in 1762 and a firm friendship developed. They shared views on religion, politics and an interest in science. Bentley was part of a group of similar-minded individuals such as Birmingham industrialist Matthew Boulton, scientist and one of the drafters of the US constitution Benjamin Franklin, and preacher and chemist Joseph Priestley. Bentley became a partner in Wedgwood's marketing arm, where he oversaw the placing of orders and the delivery of finished goods.

Patronage and the invention of marketing

Historian Neil McKendrick has argued that chief of Wedgwood's contributions to commerce was that he almost single-handedly invented modern marketing. While other historians, such as T.S. Ashton and G.M. Trevelyan, have offered narratives that emphasise Wedgwood's ability to innovate and improve production through greater division of labour, it is far from clear how these attributes on their own would have assured his success in a market that was filled with competitors; for example Meissen in Germany and Spode in Staffordshire were selling high-quality china. Wedgwood used patronage to define what the fashion should be. However, he was no sycophant; for example, he made no secret that his politics were radical, which was often in contrast to many of his customers' political opinions. What he contrived to do was to set the standards for taste, which he could then exploit. He resisted competition on price, as in 1773 when he held out against a falling market for ceramics to maintain his reputation for exclusivity. As he argued in a letter to his partner Bentley in 1772, the middle class, though more numerous than the upper classes, would want to buy his work at a reduced price and they were not leaders of fashion, but followers of it. If one could be the fashion then the middle class would be prepared to purchase at a premium price. To aid in this, Wedgwood set up his London salesroom carefully to display his entire range of wares. Prospective purchasers could walk in off the street and marvel at the latest offering from the Wedgwood works.

The salesroom became a place of social gathering that saw the titled elite rub shoulders with the upwardly mobile of 18th-century society.

SOURCE

6

From a letter by Miss Hulton of Brookline, Massachusetts, to Mrs Adam Lightbody of Liverpool in 1772. This request for Wedgwood pottery points to the way in which those from the respectable middle class approached the purchase of fashionable items. It also indicates that Wedgwood's reputation had spread as far as the New World.

There is another commission which I am desired to beg the favour of you. That is a small crate of Staffordshire ware, if it be bought at Liverpool. I sent a crate of the Yellow Ware (some form of creamware) from thence which cost about £3 to my Brother and they are now demolished. My Sister liked them much and desires to have another crate, if it could trouble you to buy [th]em, but she says if there's any new fashion of invention of Mr Wedgwood of this kind to ware, that is approved, should prefer it to the Yellow Ware over again.

ACTIVITY
KNOWLEDGE CHECK

Making a name for himself

1 Look at Sources 1 and 4. Make a list of the challenges that Wedgwood faced in marketing his pottery.

2 Looking at the list you have made, consider how the commission from Queen Charlotte helped to deal with those challenges.

3 Which was the most important factor in Wedgwood's success: design, excellence or marketing?

The role of Sarah Wedgwood and the need for capital

Josiah's wife, Sarah (1734–1815), usually called Sally, was his third cousin, being the daughter of Richard Wedgwood, a wealthy merchant from Burslem, whose fortune permitted him to live the life of a country squire. Though Sarah was from a wealthier background than Josiah, Wedgwood's biographer, Brian Dolan, argues that it was not a marriage of money but a love match, with the two sharing similar interests. Sarah, like Josiah, was a member of the **Unitarian Church** and held strong views on theology, society and particularly the institution of slavery, of which she was a fervent opponent, like her husband. She was a woman of noted tastes in terms of design and style, which were seen in the way she furnished the Wedgwood home, and she participated in the discussions when Wedgwood entertained his political friends. Sarah was also learned, reading widely, so much so that in the early years of their marriage she was able to help her husband with his accounts. Historian A.M. Shardrake notes from a survey of Sarah's correspondence that she wrote fluently and easily, unlike her husband, who had a rather halting style. Sarah also took an interest in Josiah's work, being described by him as his 'chief helpmate' with his experiments to perfect white. They even developed their own secret code to protect their recipes for commercial success.

KEY TERM

Unitarian Church
A branch of Protestantism that disagrees with the tenets of the established Church. It particularly endorses the idea that God embraces all people equally and therefore spiritual meaning can be found in all faiths.

The road to matrimony was not smooth, however, as there was opposition to the match from Sarah's father, who was not convinced that Josiah would be able to keep his daughter in the style she might expect. It took considerable negotiation to reach agreement – Wedgwood had to give assurances over his projected income. He also offered to enter into a business agreement with Sarah's uncle, who also ran a pottery. Finally, in January 1764, they were married. She was 30 and he 34, which for the period was relatively late. The acquisition of a wife was not just a question of sentiment, but also one of commerce. In the long term Sarah stood to inherit half her father's estate, which at today's prices was worth about £1.4 million. She also came with a £4,000 dowry that was placed under Josiah's control. Dolan notes that Richard Wedgwood also started to funnel funds into Josiah's business as well as providing the dowry settlement. Though it might have been considered a love match, the union had important financial implications for the development of Wedgwood's pottery. Yet, despite the acquisition of this financial windfall, by 1769 Wedgwood still found himself indebted to the tune of £4,000 as he invested heavily in expanding his business.

The marriage appears to have been a happy one, with Sarah bearing Josiah eight children in 14 years, four boys and four girls, though one son, Richard, died in infancy. The eldest, Susannah, married Robert Darwin, the son of Josiah's close friend Erasmus Darwin, and was the mother of the famous naturalist Charles Darwin.

Porcelain: the impact of trade with the East

Porcelain first made its way from China to Europe on the ships of Portuguese traders in the 1550s. Around the 1640s, Dutch merchants began to import it into the northern European market and its popularity increased rapidly. The blue and white pottery had been made in China for centuries and was different to anything that could be produced in Europe. The surfaces were hard, with a translucent effect when held up to the light; it often appeared to be less a piece of pottery than a form of glass. Demand for the product became so great that Chinese potteries began to manufacture items specifically for the western market. By 1730, the British East India Company was importing over 517,000 pieces a year, and the pottery became a popular way of representing one's wealth and taste.

The demand for Chinese porcelain provided the entrepreneurial Wedgwood with further opportunity to expand his business. In China particularly, there had developed a very strong trade in porcelain teaware, which became increasingly fashionable among the aristocracy in Britain, partly because of the whiteness and purity of its glaze, but also for the sense of exoticism and clear evidence of wealth that such pieces exhibited. The demand for these goods increased as aspirational families sought to emulate those in higher society and as such there was a considerable porcelain trade developing between Britain and China by the late 18th century.

The significance of this trade to Wedgwood lay in the potential for imitation. The costs of transporting Chinese porcelain to Britain were extensive; directly in terms of actual financial outlay, but also because of the potential for damage to these fragile goods – being shipped thousands of miles significantly raised the possibility of breakage. Given these drawbacks, Wedgwood, who was known for his entrepreneurial spirit and willingness to experiment, began to produce his own variation on the chinaware using hard-paste porcelain from 1782.

Making porcelain

The process to produce this exotic commodity would elude the potters on the continent until the early 18th century, until Johann Friedrich Böttger discovered the secret around 1705. In 1710 the firm of Meissen was set up in Saxony to produce hard-paste porcelain to Böttger's formula. The output of the factory was targeted at a select market and did little to dent the importation of Chinese porcelain. What Böttger had found was that porcelain was an amalgam of kaolin (soft white clay) and a type of feldspathic rock called petuntse. The kaolin binds the ceramic together while the petuntse fuses into a type of natural glass that gives smoothness and brilliance to the item when fired at 1,400 °C. In 1745, William Cookworthy, a Quaker chemist from Plymouth in Devon, discovered deposits of kaolin in Cornwall – the material would later be known as china clay. In 1768, Cookworthy set up a factory to produce porcelain in Plymouth and gained a patent not only for the process, but also a monopoly over all the kaolin in Cornwall. Cookworthy later sold his patent and his sole rights over the process to Richard Champion, who moved the factory to Bristol in 1770.

EXTEND YOUR KNOWLEDGE

Types of porcelain
There are basically three types of porcelain.

- Hard-paste porcelain, which is of fine quality, uses materials similar to those used in China and was manufactured by Meissen in Germany and the Bristol potteries.

- Soft-paste porcelain, which has a softer finish and can be worked with a file, tends to be fired at a lower temperature to hard-paste porcelain, at around 1,200 °C. It is not always smooth or translucent and tends to be somewhat porous. Soft-paste porcelain was produced by factories such as Chelsea, which was on the same street as Wedgwood's workshop for the decoration of creamware in London.

- Bone china, which comprises the same material as porcelain, but with the addition of bone ash, gives a finish similar to hard-paste porcelain, but is fired at a lower temperature. It was first produced in England at the Bow factory in 1750, and was rapidly taken up by other factories such as Chelsea in London and Spode in Staffordshire.

Wedgwood's experiments

According to historian Brian Dolan, there had been a number of bankruptcies among those attempting to make porcelain – the process appeared to be too complex to be easily transferred to existing plants. However, Wedgwood was mindful that he needed to add to his range of ceramics and began experiments with the production of porcelain. In 1766, inventor and physician Erasmus Darwin had written to advise him of a French method for the production of porcelain, while a year later because of financial difficulties, the Bow factory offered him the patent for soft-paste porcelain. Wedgwood declined it, saying he did not wish to produce an inferior product to the original imported china.

With the restriction on the use of kaolin from Cornwall, Wedgwood imported a large amount Cherokee clay from the Americas in 1768. This was similar to china clay and suitable for the making of porcelain. The problem was that the cost of bringing it across the Atlantic was high and it was questionable as to how far it was economically viable. Following the lapse of Cookworthy's porcelain patent, Champion lobbied for an extension to his period of sole rights over the process and a continued monopoly of the use of china clays. Wedgwood and his fellow manufacturers lobbied parliament to oppose this, not least in Wedgwood's view because Champion was attempting to benefit from something he had not developed himself. The result was a victory for the potteries of

Staffordshire, as although Champion was granted an extension to the patent, he lost the monopoly of the Cornish clays. Manufacturers soon began to import these clays and use them to whiten their ceramics as well as to try to use them in the production of porcelain.

SOURCE

From an entry in the handwritten notebook of Thomas Bentley, Wedgwood's business partner, dated November 1768. It contains notes of an experiment Wedgwood and Bentley were conducting.

Nov. 27 1768

Experiments. Hints and Memorandums

Experiment 1. Have cleaned and polished several of the brown teapots that had an ugly whitish scurf upon them, with skimmed milk. It gives them a good polish and leaves them of an uniform agreeable colour. I suppose this is the wash used to glaze pipes but there may be some particular manner of applying it. Q?

Experiment 2. One of these pots Gilt does not look amiss but the heat of the stove raises small scurf in the hollow parts. I suppose from the milk. This may be prevented by gilding the pots first and applying the wash afterwards.

Q?. Whether a little fine ground whiting or pounded clay should not be added to the milk, when it is applied to white biscuit.

Experiment 3. We have gilt two Etruscan vases, the gold comes to a better colour upon these than any other articles and has a fine rich effect, but might not the colour be still finer if it was laid in with a yellow size. I think the red size affects the colour of the gold upon all the ware. Would not then black vases have a good effect mounted, mottled and sprigged with silver as well as gold?

Experiment 4. Have ordered some black – to be washed over to try the effect of mechanical smallness produced that way.

To sprinkle biscuit ware with gold powder or Aura Mosaicum and glaze it over, especially dark coloured cement for joining alabaster, marble, porphyry – and other stones – Dolpie.

Experiment 5.

Bees Wax ... 2

Resin ... 1

Of the matter to be joined ground fine 1. ½

This recipe is taken from Hunchell and altered a little. I suspect for the worry See page ... 402...

Melt the two first ingredients together, stew the powder into the melted mixture and stir it continually, pour the mass upon the water and knead it well in.

A Level Exam-Style Question Section A

Study Source 7 before you answer this question.

Assess the value of the source for revealing how Wedgwood went about developing his products and also the success of his pottery during the mid to late 18th century.

Explain your answer, using the source, the information about its origin and your own knowledge about the historical context. (20 marks)

Tip
When answering this question you should consider why Bentley would be recording their experimentation and also why they are experimenting in the first place.

Ornamental ware

The market for what Wedgwood termed 'useful ware' had proved to be highly profitable; in 1769 the company sold £7,000 worth of these items, mainly creamware. However, they were only half the story. Wedgwood had already made a name for himself, producing complex items such as his green-and-yellow-glazed teasets, but in the 1770s he went on to develop a range of 'ornamental ware' that was to define his reputation as an innovator, designer and key promoter of the classical style.

EXTEND YOUR KNOWLEDGE

Problems with payment
The link between sales and profits is not always clear when talking about Wedgwood. By 1768 he was running out of capital as he had had to invest heavily in his new works and, though there was demand for his goods, bad debts depleted his earnings. He employed William Cox to go round London collecting outstanding debts and promoting his new works by going door to door. The tactic paid off – the money owed began to be received as well as new orders for the new ornamental ware.

Financial year	Goods sold	Expense of manufacture and selling	Goods in hand at end of year	Profit
Aug 1769–Aug 1770	£2,404	£1,921	£3,164	£2,561
Aug 1770–Aug 1771	£3,955	£2,372	£4,411	£2,830
Aug 1771–Aug 1772	£4,838	£2,924	£8,187	£5,691
Aug 1772–Aug 1773	£4,244	£2,303	£9,069	£2,823
Aug 1773–Aug 1774	£6,168	£2,937	£10,144	£4,307
Aug 1774–Dec 1774	£2,065	£946	£10,261	£1,235
Jan 1775–Dec 1775	£6,418	£3,804	£11,190	£3,545

Figure 3.1 Profit and turnover of Wedgwood's ornamental ware, 1769–75. The data illustrate both the profitability of Wedgwood's business and the demand for ornamental ware, as well as the fluctuation in profitability and production over this six-year period. The problem with the interpretation of these data is that the profits do not reflect the amounts sold in a particular year but the returns from sale in that year, and so can be payments for goods supplied some time before. Likewise there is no link to the cost of having to keep goods in hand.

Jasperware

Jasperware first appeared around 1776 and was described in Wedgwood's catalogue as 'white porcelain biscuit with raised figures'. The intention was to produce a type of pottery that could be used to create cameos and plaques as well as decorative vases. From these experiments came jasperware, which used china clay and ground flint to produce a hard translucent material. To market his new product Wedgwood brought in designers such as John Flaxman to develop shapes based on classical examples of the Greek and Roman world, as well as friezes to be applied to the surface. Jasperware items were moulded then assembled, the bodies having being formed from coloured clay then the decoration added. It is interesting to note that it is around this time that Wedgwood began to introduce women and girls into the workforce, who tended to be employed in the parts of the factory dealing with the application of decoration. The designs captured the taste for the neoclassical, which would be found in both the drawing rooms of the titled as well as the parlours of the middle class. Its form was also used in the production of personal items such as brooches and watch cases.

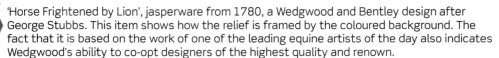

SOURCE

8 'Horse Frightened by Lion', jasperware from 1780, a Wedgwood and Bentley design after George Stubbs. This item shows how the relief is framed by the coloured background. The fact that it is based on the work of one of the leading equine artists of the day also indicates Wedgwood's ability to co-opt designers of the highest quality and renown.

ACTIVITY
KNOWLEDGE CHECK

Ornamental ware

1 With a partner discuss the reasons why Wedgwood might have wanted to develop his ornamental ware rather than just producing 'useful ware'. Think about issues of market and reputation and how those might be enhanced by the production of such goods.

2 Look at Figure 3.1 and draw two simple graphs, one showing sales and one showing profits. Do they show a steady increase in both or sharp fluctuations? Why might we need to be careful in assessing this data when trying to see if ornamental ware was a profitable avenue of production?

3 Draw a mind map with a centre label of '1769–80'. Now list the innovations in products and production and challenges that Wedgwood faced in this period.

HOW IMPORTANT WAS THE CONSTRUCTION OF THE TRENT AND MERSEY CANAL AND THE LINKING OF THE CANAL NETWORK FOR THE DEVELOPMENT OF WEDGWOOD'S BUSINESS?

KEY TERMS

Turnpike road
One where a fee (toll) was charged to use it, which was often used to straighten a particular route and improve the road surface. Turnpike roads were managed by trusts established by individual Acts of Parliament.

Vested interest
A deliberate interest in a particular event or situation because the person or group has a direct interest in the potential outcome.

The economist and early social statistician Arthur Young remarked in the early 1760s on the poor state of the roads and the difficulty this posed for the traveller in north Staffordshire. There were few **turnpike roads** in the area and those that existed did not always extend into the Potteries. However, roads were not the only form of transport available in the region; extensive use was also made of the river network. The Trent had been made navigable up to Stoke-on-Trent and provided a means for the transport of raw materials such as coal and finished goods. Nevertheless, rivers had their drawbacks: drought or heavy rain could render them impassable and carriage on some inland waterways was monopolised by certain **vested interests**, which raised costs. Coastal shipping was also used to bring flint and clays from other parts of the country to supply the expanding pottery industry, but this still required packhorses on land to transport goods from factory gate to the nearest port. It was asserted in a petition for a turnpike road linking the Potteries to London, given to parliament in 1762, that around £5,000 a year was paid in duties to the government to ship goods internally from the ports of Liverpool and Hull into Staffordshire. The cost of transporting goods and the difficulty in carrying them to market led to Wedgwood's involvement in promoting improvements to the system.

Turnpike roads

The need to improve the transport infrastructure of the region was to make Wedgwood into a key figure in local politics. Though he would never hold national office, by the early 1770s he would be the key mover and shaker in promoting the interests of the Staffordshire potteries. He first became involved in agitation for an extension of the existing turnpike road network to Stoke-on-Trent. In 1765, he wrote to his brother John (see Source 9) to outline the difficulties faced in trying to get such a project approved. All such proposals needed a private Act of Parliament, which would entail the mobilisation of support throughout the county. However, such improvements often ran contrary to certain vested interests, which could prove destructive to the project.

SOURCE

9

From a letter by Wedgwood to his brother John in 1765. It outlines the pressures and problems faced in trying to get approval for the project and the difficulty in convincing all involved of agreeing to a route that was beneficial to the potteries at Burslem.

We have another Turnpike broke out amongst us here betwixt Leek & Newcastle, & they have let Armies mounted me upon my hobby-horse again, & a prancing rouge [rogue] he is at present, but hope he will not take the route of London again. He carried me yesterday to Leek, from whence I am just returned much satisfied with our reception there. Tomorrow I wait upon Sir Nigel to beg his concurrence & on Monday must attend a meeting to settle the petition, etc., at Mony Ash at your friend Isaac Whieldon's. We pray to have the Utoxeter & Burslem Turnpikes joined, & to have the Road made Turnpike from Buxton & Bakewell to Leek, & from Leek to Newcastle. Whether or not our good friends at Newcastle will give us battle on this occasion we do not know.

As can be seen from Source 9, Wedgwood was very active in seeking broad support for the proposed road across the county. In a time when the right to vote was limited, it is interesting to reflect on how public meetings were used to gain support for activities that today would be a function of government. The petition for the road was unfortunately not successful, as publicans objected to proposed changes in the route that would bypass their premises and cause them to lose passing trade.

Canals

Waterways had provided a means for the transportation of goods since at least the early Middle Ages, if not before. Inland ports such as Gloucester acted as trading hubs for goods being shipped into the Midlands. However, their utility could be limited; a fall in the level of a river could hinder passage, while flooding might render it impassable. River **navigations** also had to be maintained by regular dredging to keep channels open, which incurred significant costs. Most problematic of all, however, was that river navigations were not always where they were most needed. Despite these problems, water transportation remained a significant feature of Britain's growth, and as such these difficulties were an important step on the path to the later development of canals. These manmade channels would, for a time, offer a significant contribution to the development of British manufacturing by providing a more bespoke opportunity to transport goods.

In 1757, St Helens was joined to the river Mersey by the Sankey Brook Navigation, which had been intended as a combination of river navigation and **artificial waterway**, but in the end became a canal. Its prime purpose was to carry coal from St Helens to the port of Liverpool. A few years later, in 1761, the 3rd Duke of Bridgewater, with the aid of his chief engineer James Brindley, constructed a canal from his coal mines at Worsley to nearby Manchester. The canal made transporting bulky low-value goods more efficient and also cheaper to bring to market, which made the duke considerably wealthier.

The Duke of Bridgewater and the need for patronage

The lack of success in the promotion of turnpike roads led Wedgwood to look at the possibility of the construction of a canal linking the Trent to the Mersey so as to carry the increasing export trade in Staffordshire pottery. Historian Michael McCahill observes in his work on patronage in the early Industrial Revolution that industrialists tended to lack direct representation in parliament and so were forced to lobby in support of their interests. These included issues over the extension of patents as well as the need for private Acts of Parliament for projects such as the creation of turnpike trusts and canal building. Even as late as the 1780s, there was no representative of Black Country ironmasters, West Riding woollen producers or Lancashire cotton mill owners in the House of Commons. Among the leading advocates on behalf of industry were Josiah Wedgwood and Matthew Boulton, who together became the most active of political lobbyists for the manufacturers in the Midlands.

Francis Egerton, the 3rd Duke of Bridgewater, was known to Wedgwood as he had built a windmill in Burslem to grind flints to supply a pottery belonging to Wedgwood's uncle, John Wedgwood. The duke was interested in commerce and had been responsible for greatly increasing his own fortune. In 1761, Bridgewater and his engineer James Brindley had overseen the construction of what is considered the country's first canal, between the coal mines on Bridgewater's estate at Worseley and

KEY TERMS

Navigation
A series of manmade channels that runs alongside an unimproved existing river and which shares its drainage basin.

Artificial waterway
A manmade channel for a body of water that is still subject to tidal influence.

Manchester, a distance of eight miles (in 1776 it was extended as far as Liverpool). The effect was to make a rich man into an exceedingly wealthy one. Historian William Chaloner estimated that in 1791 the canal earned £19,455 from the transport of coal, with a further £30,000 from the carriage of other goods, such as rock salt (figures have not been adjusted into present-day prices). It was on the basis of this enterprise that Wedgwood approached him to see if he would support a plan to link the Potteries to the Mersey. Such support was crucial; the aristocracy regularly participated in the preparation of private bills and as major landowners their support was key in gaining approval for the construction of such projects. Wedgwood was gratified by the reception his proposal received from the duke and it was suggested that the duke's brother-in-law, Lord Gower, would be prepared to support a proposed bill in parliament. In 1766, a bill to connect the Mersey and Trent rivers was finally passed and that same year work began on the ambitious project, which had been estimated would cost £77,939.

The progress of the bill had not been easy and the patronage of the duke was key to its success. There had been much opposition from waggoners and packhorse interests as well those involved in coastal trade who were able to bring their grievances to parliament. Bridgewater had, however, managed to assemble a formidable lobby in favour of the scheme, including Lord Grey, Thomas Anson the MP for Lichfield – who was the cousin of the Earl of Macclesfield – and Thomas Gilbert MP for Newcastle-under-Lyme, who was a close friend of Bridgewater's cousin Lord Gower. Such networks of kinship and patronage underpinned the structures of 18th century British society. Political power, historian Thomas Heyck has argued, remained for the most part in the hands of the landed elite, who nevertheless developed relationships with the emergent industrial capitalist class, such as the Wedgwoods and Boultons. It has been suggested that this produced a deferential society where patronage was the key currency for advancement. In that sense the 18th century was the opposite of the 19th, where ideas of merit and achievement were considered to be the essential virtues on which society should be based. Though Bridgewater was central to the success of the plan to build the Trent and Mersey canal, it is not always clear how deferential the relationship between the duke and Wedgwood was. While it was necessary to maintain good relations, disagreements did occur. Wedgwood was forceful in his arguments with the duke to respect the backers of the project, particularly the industrialists in the Staffordshire towns that would be disadvantaged by any

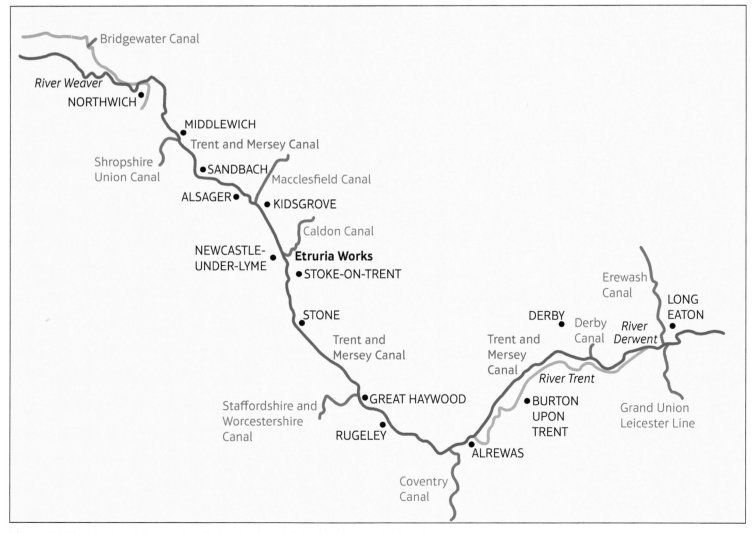

Figure 3.2 The Trent and Mersey Canal, showing how it linked to the canal network.

amendments to the scheme. While Bridgwater remained the leading advocate for the canal project in parliament and used his influence to placate landed interests that expressed concerns regarding the impact of the canal, such as Sir Richard Brooke who feared the boatmen would poach his game and wildfowl, it was Wedgwood who would lead the industrial interests.

Political leadership

Much responsibility was placed on Wedgwood to guide the construction of the canal to completion. He was elected honorary treasurer and subscribed £1,000 of his own money towards the cost of the scheme and pledged another £10,000 as security. The canal was not Wedgwood's pet project, but one of a joint stock company that had investments from many other industrialists in the area. While the aristocracy might be involved in promoting the canal, the financing was based on popular support. It was this latter point that gave Wedgwood most concern, as disputes developed over the proposed route of what then was called the Grand Trunk Canal (though it has since become known as the Trent and Mersey Canal). The investors became concerned that the duke wanted to almost bypass Staffordshire and instead link his canal with the salt towns of Cheshire. This caused a great deal of tension and led Wedgwood to put his case most forcefully to Lord Gower to respect the need to make sure the canal served its backers. There was also local opposition from the River Weaver Navigation Company, which saw the project as competing with its trade in Cheshire salt. However, Wedgwood proved successful in furthering his cause and in gaining backing from other regional industrialists such as Matthew Boulton in Birmingham and the Birmingham Chamber of Commerce. Such solidarity among manufacturers also illustrates the reciprocity of the relationship with the aristocracy. If politically the nobility were prepared to promote projects advantageous to industrialists, it was the financial backing from this class that paid for their completion. In the view of the historians Michael McCahill and J. Money, there was a net gain for both parties to such arrangements.

SOURCE 10

A letter from Josiah Wedgwood to Thomas Wedgwood in 1765, regarding the problems faced in gaining support for the canal scheme. It illustrates the effort Wedgwood put into gaining support for his cause and also the groups that might be won over to his side and those who would oppose him.

Mr. Taylor is just entered into partnership with one Mr. Lloyd in the Banking business (in Birmingham), and Mr. Lloyd, it seems, is one of the proprietors in the Burton [river] Navigation which will be injured by our intended Canal, as it is proposed to carry it beyond Burton to Wilden in order to keep clear of their locks and shallows. We made it appear pretty evident to the Gentlemen of Birmingham that £10,000 per anum would be immediately saved to them in [carriage] to and from the River Trent, so soon as the Canal was brought to their Town* which would it is apprehended be in less than three years after it is begun upon.... This scheme of a navigation is undoubtedly the best thing that could possibly be planned for this country & I hope there is a great probability of its being carried into execution.

*The Trent and Mersey canal did not go to Birmingham but rather would be joined to a canal linked to the town.

Completion of the canal

The cutting of the first sod at Brownhills near Stoke-on-Trent took place in July 1766. However, it would not be until 1777 that the canal was completed, including an arm that joined up to Wedgwood's Etruria Works. It had initially been intended to build the link in a curve to balance out the landscape and the factory, but Brindley would not contemplate the extra expense and time and insisted on a more direct connection to the main canal. Nevertheless, contemporary illustrations show the canal framing the factory in a way that is more reminiscent of a stately home than a place of industry.

The canal proved to be profitable for the investors, with regular dividends. More importantly for Wedgwood and the other manufacturers, it provided a means to supply them with raw materials and a way to safely export the products of the Potteries. This was particularly important, as unlike the Duke of Bridgewater, Wedgwood was more concerned with shipping expensive finished goods than the bulk transport of raw materials. Being able to send his creamware and jasperware by canal rather than packhorse reduced breakages and increased the potential volume of goods that could be transported.

SOURCE 11

An illustration produced in the early 19th century of Wedgwood's Etruria factory. This image depicts how the factory would have appeared in 1777, when the canal was first opened in order to link the factory to the Trent and Mersey Canal.

A Level Exam-Style Question Section B

To what extent did the building of the Trent and Mersey Canal show Wedgwood to be an important regional champion of Midland manufacturing rather than just another businessman looking to satisfy his own narrow ends? (20 marks)

Tip

Think about the benefits for Wedgwood and the other manufacturers from the construction of the canal. Try contrasting this with the difficulties faced in obtaining support for the canal and the role Wedgwood played in pushing the project to a successful conclusion.

ACTIVITY
KNOWLEDGE CHECK

Patronage and canals

1 Make a list of reasons why Wedgwood and the other pottery manufacturers would want to improve the transport network in Staffordshire. With a partner try placing them in order of importance.

2 Why were there objections to the improvement of the transport system and what were the reasons for the objections? Write a sentence about each one.

3 What did Wedgwood gain from the patronage of the Duke of Bridgewater? Write a short paragraph of not more than 100 words. Compare your answer with that of a partner and then discuss any differences of interpretation.

EXTRACT

From *The Canal System of England* by Hubert Gordon Thompson (1904). Thompson was a surgeon at Birmingham General Hospital after 1905, having graduated from Liverpool College in 1903. His work here on the canals of England originated from a prize-winning essay that he submitted while completing his studies.

Before the completion of these great schemes the natural increase of commerce in the middle of the 18th century was greatly hindered by the heavy expense and the lack of adequate means of conveying produce to the ports. Thus, about the year 1750, the cost of goods by road between Manchester and Liverpool was 40/- per ton, but by the Mersey and Irwell the water rate was only 12/- per ton, and after the opening of the Bridgewater Canal the cost was reduced to 6/- per ton, and a better service was given than that provided by either of the fore-mentioned routes. Again, the cost of transport of coal which up to this time was carried by packhorse from Worsley to Manchester, and which had been from 6/- to 8/- per ton, was reduced to 2/6 per ton on the canal.

EXTRACT

From the Canal & River Trust website. Canal historian Mike Clarke describes the problems with the canals and their profitability.

When the first canals were built, people were unsure about the future return on their investment. The result was that just over one quarter of the UK's waterways were built as narrow canals, with locks just seven feet wide, in the belief that it would make them less expensive.

These narrow canals were certainly marginally cheaper, but their small size made them less able to cope with the increasing traffic that developed, particularly in the second half of the nineteenth century. During this period, most new trade was increasingly carried by railways, and a few canal companies built railways along their waterways to offer an improved service.

For some canal companies, their income was insufficient to pay even for improvement of their waterway, and the less successful were taken over by railway companies. However, successful canals held on to their traffic during the nineteenth century, and some increased the tonnage of goods they carried. It was the First World War which really marked the beginning of the end for carriage of goods by canal.

EXTRACT

From *The Archaeology of the Roman Economy* by Kevin Greene (1986). Greene discusses the motivation behind the development of a canal system in Britain in the 19th century as part of his broader focus upon Roman canal systems.

Britain's spate of canal building in the eighteenth and nineteenth centuries, although soon overshadowed by the railways, was motivated by the needs of growing industries for fuel and raw materials, but the canals also facilitated the distribution of industrial products.

THINKING HISTORICALLY   Change (8a, b & c) (II)

Judgements about change

If two professionals were asked to track a patient's health over time, one might approach this task by measuring heart rate, weight and cholesterol, while the other professional might assess the patient's mental well-being, relationships and ability to achieve their goals. Both are valid approaches, but result in different reports. What is true in this medical case is true in historical cases. Measuring change in something requires: (a) a concept of what that something is (e.g. 'What is "health"?' 'What is an "economy"?'); (b) judgements about how this thing should be measured; and (c) judgements about what relevant 'markers of change' are (how we distinguish a change from a temporary and insignificant fluctuation).

Historians have differed in their accounts of economic change and development in England in the 18th and 19th centuries and debated the reasons for this change.

Look at Extracts 1–3 about the growth of the canal system and answer the following questions.

1 Do all three accounts agree that canals were fundamental to the development of British manufacturing?

2 Do all three accounts agree in the chronology of change (do they see it happening in the same time periods and at the same pace)?

3 Do all three accounts agree in characterising decline as (a) rapid, (b) dramatic and (c) impacting the economy as a whole?

4 Do the historians all think of the economy in the same way (for example, do they all focus on manufacturing and trade markets)?

5 Generalising from these examples, to what extent do historians' judgements about change depend upon what historians decide to look at and how they decide to measure change?

WHAT WAS THE MOTIVATION FOR WEDGWOOD'S INVOLVEMENT IN THE CAMPAIGN TO ABOLISH THE SLAVE TRADE?

In politics, Wedgwood was a seen by contemporaries as a radical dissenter. His religion was not that of the established Church, the Church of England, but instead he was a follower of Protestant nonconformist theology. It was this, along with his relatively humble background, which placed him outside the social elite whom he spent most of his time cultivating as customers for his ceramic ware. Wedgwood took social responsibility seriously and believed that individuals had a duty to use their resources to support just causes for the betterment of humanity. In 1760, at a time when he faced considerable challenges to developing his business, he nevertheless gave £10 to build a free school for the community in Burslem. In 1792, he donated £250 to the people of Poland to fight against the Russian invasion of that year. However, money was not his only contribution; he was also prepared to give his time and position in support of causes he felt were important.

The issue of the slave trade

The existence of the slave trade with the West Indies and the Americas was a key factor in the process of industrialisation of Britain. The labour of African slaves on plantations producing cotton and sugar fed the demand in Europe for both of these commodities, in addition to generating substantial profits for British traders. Moral questions regarding the practice were interwoven with economic interests, which drew in many early industrial manufacturers and merchants. Samuel Greg, an early pioneer of the industrialisation of cotton spinning and a man considered humane in the treatment of his workforce (see Chapter 4), benefited greatly from cotton produced on plantations in the southern states of America. However, for others involved in trade and industry slavery was thought of as a moral stain on what was considered civilised society, and Wedgwood firmly belonged to this group.

It is not clear when Wedgwood became active in the movement to abolish the slave trade, but key figures in his life were vocal opponents of the institution. His partner Bentley was one of the few Liverpool merchants who was willing to express his opposition to the trade, given its central role in the commerce of the port. Wedgwood's friend Erasmus Darwin was equally as vocal in his rejection of the slave trade. In 1787, a group of 12 activists met in London to form the Society for Effecting the Abolition of the Slave Trade, which was dedicated to the ending of the slave trade throughout the British Empire. Thomas Clarkson, one of the co-founders of the society (the other founding member was Granville Sharp), was a close friend of Wedgwood and was able not only to encourage him to support the society financially, but also to lobby on its behalf so as to gain influence.

Wedgwood's first action was to write to his friends to try to persuade them of the moral argument for the abolition of the slave trade. Though he was sincere in his arguments, not all were convinced by his case and felt that economic necessity was greater than any moral issue regarding the enslavement of

EXTEND YOUR KNOWLEDGE

Thomas Clarkson (1760–1846)

Unlike the majority of the founding members of the Society for Effecting the Abolition of the Slave Trade, who were Quakers, Clarkson was the son of an Anglican clergyman. When at the University of Cambridge in 1785, he had written a Latin essay on the evils of the slave trade. Much of Clarkson's work for the society was focused on gathering research on the nature of the trade and using it in his writings. It was Clarkson who first made contact with William Wilberforce, who became the organisation's mouthpiece in parliament and was the key mover behind the 1807 Act that prohibited British ships from carrying slaves.

other peoples. Even where there was revulsion at the cruelty of the slave trade, some were less than enthusiastic in championing the cause for abolition.

In 1789, William Wilberforce, MP for Kingston-upon-Hull, introduced proposals for the abolition of the slave trade in the House of Commons (but not at that time for the end to slavery in the colonies). Though his proposal gained some support from fellow MPs, it was ultimately rejected in 1791. Undeterred, Wilberforce continued to work hard with the campaign outside parliament to lobby MPs and, in 1796, managed to win backing in the Commons for the reading of his bill to end the slave trade in British shipping. However, the measure was held up in the House of Lords, which used delaying tactics to impede its progress. The agitation against the slave trade was also increasingly viewed with suspicion by some. Historian T.H. Dickinson has argued that it was seen to be associated with radical ideas that appeared to echo those of the French Revolution, where the National Convention had abolished slavery in 1794. As the threat of revolution subsided in the early 1800s, the bill finally won a third reading and was passed into an Act in 1807.

Historians remain divided as to how far the agitation by public opinion led to the ending of the slave trade. In 1788, 102 petitions were presented from across the kingdom demanding an end to the slave trade. The agitation increased in 1792 when 502 petitions were sent to parliament from places such as Manchester, where 20,000 people signed. However, Trinidadian historian Eric Williams has suggested that slavery was becoming less economically viable, as it was seen as increasingly unprofitable, and it was material self-interest rather than morality that won the day. Williams' evidence has been questioned by historian Seymour Drescher, who has pointed to the continued profitability of the plantation economy – in 1807, he argues, trades could still make a ten percent profit on the sale of slaves – and that abolition damaged British economic interests, this being the central theme of the pro-slavery propagandists (see Source 12). For Drescher, therefore, it was the moral rejection of slavery that was more important in ending the trade. More recently, historian James Walvin, in his *A Short History of Slavery*, has suggested that economic factors should not be ignored, but they were not the paramount reason; rather they were a factor alongside the moral case and changing social attitudes that the anti-slavery movement had done much to promote.

The importance of the slave medallion

SOURCE 12

From an exchange of letters between Wedgwood and Ann Seward of Litchfield, a poet who held progressive ideas on female education. The letter from Wedgwood outlines his moral argument, while that of Seward, though supportive, indicates economic interests as an underlying concern.

Dear Miss Seward

I need no assurance of your sentiments of humanity and mercy to our brethren of every tribe and colour, for a mind like yours cannot be limited by any trivial circumstances in its benevolent wishes, and exertions too upon all proper occasions. But many objections, and of great seeming weight, have been made by some, and acquiesced in by others, with the best intentions, to the effectual extension of the hand of mercy to our poor African brethren.

It has happened, by my being one of the Society in London, and upon the Committee, for abolishing the slave trade, that the facts and arguments on both sides have pretty generally come to my knowledge, I mean those who are for abolishing, and those who wish only for a regulation of this traffic, for I do not know of any who say there is no necessity for either....

Dear Mr Wedgwood

I am honoured and obliged by your endeavours to enlighten me on a subject so important to human virtue and human happiness...

I have had long acquaintance with a Mr. Newton of this place, who made a large fortune in the East, where slavery pervades every opulent establishment. He constantly assured me, that the purchase, employment, and strict discipline of the negroes were absolutely necessary to maintain our empire, and our commerce, in the Indies. As constantly did he affirm, that they were of a nature so sordid and insensible, as to render necessary a considerable degree of severity, and to make much lenity alike injurious to the indulger and the indulged; that the accounts of the cruelties practised upon the slaves by their masters were false, or at least infinitely exaggerated.

Beneath the force of that melancholy conviction, I avoided reading anything upon the subject; flattering myself, that if the abolition of a traffic so lamentable could be safely effected by our legislators, they, as Englishmen and Christians, would listen to merciful remonstrance, and feel themselves impelled to abolish it. Your letter, and the tracts which accompanied it, have changed my ideas on the subject. They have given me indignant convictions, decided principles, and better hopes that the flood-gates of this overwhelming cruelty may be let down without injuring our national interests.

If letters as a form of propaganda advocating the abolition of the slave trade were limited in their impact, Wedgwood's other contribution was far more effective in raising the profile of the campaign. He offered to produce a cameo medallion promoting the campaign. Such medallions had been a staple of Wedgwood's production for a decade. He had produced images of leading figures of the day, such as the astronomer Sir William Herschel, scientist and theologian Doctor Joseph Priestley and the explorer Captain James Cook, and there had also been series produced of famous writers including Shakespeare and Voltaire, as well as contemporary actors such as David Garrick and Sarah Siddons. These had sold very well and were often produced in glass cases to be exhibited on sideboards. They had also been used to promote political causes; portraits of George Washington and Benjamin Franklin were produced during the struggle for American independence. The image for the anti-slave trade medallion was that of an African slave in chains surrounded by the words 'Am I not a man and a brother?' (see Source 13). It is not clear who finalised the design of the cameo, though it is suggested that it was the work of Wedgwood's best modeller William Hackwood, though others have suggested Henry Webber was responsible or even John Flaxman. The cameo was produced in jasperware with a black figure on a white background, though it was soon copied and appeared on tapestries, tokens and china.

SOURCE 13

The anti-slave trade medallion produced by Josiah Wedgwood in 1787. The design focused on the idea of a brotherhood of humanity and was a graphic critique of the institution of slavery, with the slave depicted asking 'Am I not a man and a brother?'

A Level Exam-Style Question Section A

Study Source 12 before you answer this question.

Assess the value of the source for revealing Wedgwood's motives for getting involved with the campaign for the abolition of the slave trade and the role he performed in it.

Explain your answer, using the source, the information about its origin and your own knowledge about the historical context. (20 marks)

Tip

When answering this question you should carefully consider the nature of the source. In this case, they are letters, so you should consider the potential reasoning behind such correspondence – in addition to simple communication, why else might people write letters?

Impact of the slave medallion

The medallion proved to be a great success. Thousands of the cameos were produced and distributed; the abolition activist Thomas Clarkson accounted for 500 alone, giving them out to supporters to help promote the cause. Wedgwood sent some to his friend Benjamin Franklin in America to give to supporters there. It was Franklin's opinion that the medallion would have equal impact to a well-argued pamphlet. The popularity of the image became a general fashion, making it a way to raise political awareness. It even led to an early form of fair-trade marketing, with suppliers offering items in containers that promised sugar not produced by slave labour. In marketing the anti-slave trade image, Wedgwood might be considered as a pioneer of the political marketing that has become commonplace in the modern world such as the red ribbon for Aids awareness or the wristbands associated with many campaigns.

The slave trade was finally abolished in Britain in 1807 after a tireless campaign by men such as Clarkson and Wedgwood. The extent to which this decision was the direct result of their efforts is hard to say definitively. However, the growth in public support that they were able to create, together with the awareness that the slave medallion generated, certainly encouraged parliament to consider more carefully their attitude towards the practice.

Conclusion

Josiah Wedgwood's role in the early stages of the Industrial Revolution was one of innovator and regional political organiser. His use of marketing to promote his pottery and political ideas would not be out of place in the contemporary world. What Wedgwood was able to do was transform a commodity that only had local utility in providing something to eat off or drink from into a brand that defined status and fashion. With first the use of green glaze and then later cream glaze, products were produced that changed public tastes. Wedgwood, the man of science, who carefully recorded the outcome of each experiment in developing his glazes, was also Wedgwood the designer, who looked for inspiration in the classical world to produce ceramics that had a quality and style unique to his pottery. The success of his approach sported many imitators, but they lacked the royal and aristocratic patronage Wedgwood enjoyed. He also did much to promote his products and so he remained the leader of taste and fashion rather than a follower of it. Unlike other industrialists, such as those involved in the cotton trade, Wedgwood's strategy was to define and cultivate an elite market with the hope it would invest in brand loyalty, rather than cultivating mass markets for cheap goods.

While the output of the Etruria Works might have been lower than that of Samuel Greg's cotton-spinning mill in nearby Lancashire, like other industrialists of the 18th century Wedgwood was interested in improving the methods of production. He took what had been a process heavily dependent on skilled (and sober) craftsmen, oversaw production and modernised it through the separating out of tasks where repetition increased the skills of the operatives and improved the speed at which items were produced. The division of labour and specialisation were key elements in Wedgwood's method of manufacture. He was also quick to employ new technologies such as a lathe for adding decoration to pots, and the development of new methods to monitor the temperature of his kilns so as to be able to produce more uniform pottery. Finally, there was his ability to produce new and innovative designs through the use of different clays and adding minerals to them. Key among these was the development of jasperware, with its coloured body and white embossed decoration that was moulded and added before firing.

Finally, the ability of Wedgwood to gain and mobilise patronage for the promotion of particular ends made him an important political actor. The improvement of the transport network in Staffordshire was not just a question of having capital to finance it, but also requiring backing from the aristocracy to gain the required legislation to permit it to be built. It was Wedgwood's acquaintance with the Duke of Bridgewater as well as his skills as an organiser among the manufacturers that saw the Trent and Mersey Canal built. The completion of this waterway linked the Potteries with the ports of Hull and Liverpool, and later it also connected north Staffordshire to London and the industrial Midlands. The new waterway provided a way to transport coal and clay to Stoke-on-Trent and gave Wedgwood a way to move his finished items in a more safe and secure way than on the back of a packhorse. Aside from his role as a leader of industry, Wedgwood the humanitarian was prepared to put his resources at the disposal of causes that he felt to be important. The abolition of the slave trade became one of the key issues in his later years. His contribution was to create a product that combined a slogan and an image that made the case for abolition more eloquently than a pamphlet. The words 'Am I not a man and a brother?' defined the moral case for the ending slavery in England and its acceptance into fashionable society added to its potential to raise the profile of the issue and gain the attention of those who might be persuaded to act in parliament to end this trade.

ACTIVITY
KNOWLEDGE CHECK

The slave trade and business

1 What were Wedgwood's objections to the slave trade?

2 How important would you say Wedgwood was to the cause of abolition?

3 Was Wedgwood's involvement motivated by humanitarian concerns or was abolition a useful campaign to promote both his products and personal image? Justify your response to this question in 200 words.

THINKING HISTORICALLY Cause and consequence (7c)

The value of historical explanations

Historical explanations derive from the historian who is investigating the past. Differences in explanations are usually about what the historians think is significant. Historians bring their own attitudes and perspectives to historical questions and see history in the light of these. It is therefore perfectly acceptable to have very different explanations of the same historical phenomenon. The way we judge historical accounts is by looking at how well argued they are and how well evidence had been deployed to support the argument.

Here are three approaches to success.

Approach A	Approach B	Approach C
Success is personal. It is dependent upon the internal motivation of the individual.	Success is entirely dependent upon circumstances and requires the right conditions before any progress can be made.	Success is a personal goal that can be achieved even without optimum conditions because the individual can always adjust their goal.

Work in groups of between three and five.

1 In your groups, devise a brief explanation for the success of Josiah Wedgwood of between 200 and 300 words that matches one of Approaches A, B or C above. Present your explanation to another group, who will decide on two things:

a) Which of the approaches is each explanation trying to demonstrate?

b) Considering the structure and the quality of the argument and use of evidence, which is the best of the three explanations?

2 If you choose a 'best' explanation, should you discount the other two? Explain your answer.

ACTIVITY
SUMMARY

1 Create a mind map that reflects on Wedgwood's many talents. In the centre of the sheet of paper write 'Wedgwood's Achievements'. From the central bubble, add three other bubbles with the titles 'Science and Production', 'Patronage and Politics' and 'Markets and Marketing'. Go through the chapter and add your findings to this mind map.

One of the challenges we often face in history is to understand how differing aspects of the past interact. Looking at your mind map, consider the strengths and weaknesses of the following statements:

a) Wedgwood's reputation rests on marketing his ceramics rather than real innovations in design and production.

b) Patronage of the aristocracy was more important than his ability as a designer and a pioneer of how to market his products.

c) Without his innovations in production and design, there would have been no product to market or patronage to seek. Wedgwood's reputation as a man of science and industry is what defines his legacy.

2 What might have been the outcome had Wedgwood decided to market his products to the middle class and labourers instead of seeking elite patronage and setting high prices? Speculate on what would change. You might want to discuss this with a partner or have a group discussion.

 WIDER READING

Dolan, B. *Josiah Wedgwood: Entrepreneur of the Enlightenment*, Harper Perennial (2004)

Kelly, A. *The Story of Wedgwood*, Faber and Faber (1975)

Long, D. 'The power of an image: Wedgwood's slave cameo', *Oakland University Journal* (2004)

McCahill, M. 'Peers, patronage and the Industrial Revolution 1760–1800', *Journal of British Studies*, Vol. 16 No. 1 (1976)

McCraw, T.K. *Creating Modern Capitalism; How Entrepreneurs, Companies and Countries Triumphed in Three Industrial Revolutions*, Harvard University Press (1998)

McKendrick, N. 'An eighteenth-century entrepreneur in salesmanship and marketing techniques', *Economic History Review*, Vol. 12 No. 3 (1960)

McKendrick, N. 'Josiah Wedgwood and factory discipline', *The Historical Journal*, Vol. 4 No. 1 (1961)

Mankowitz, W. *Wedgwood*, Spring Books (1966)

Stoke-on-Trent and the Potteries: www.thepotteries.org/history.htm

Wedgwood Museum: www.wedgwoodmuseum.org.uk

3.4

Samuel Greg: cotton and cottages, 1784–1816

KEY QUESTIONS

- What influenced the growth of Quarry Bank Mill in the years 1784–1816?
- How successfully did Samuel Greg deal with the labour problem at Quarry Bank Mill?
- How significant was Quarry Bank Mill in the development of the cotton industry in Lancashire?

INTRODUCTION

Eminent historian Eric Hobsbawm has argued that it was the growth of the cotton industry in the late 18th century that was the key revolutionary element in the story of British industrialisation. From the 1750s there had been a general expansion in the production of manufactured goods in Britain. Yet for many industries, such as in the metal trades, manufacture remained centred on traditional workshop production that used skilled handcraft. As output grew, so did the number of workers, meaning that productivity did not improve. Cotton was different, however, because its production saw the increased use of machinery, which made it cheaper and more efficient to manufacture. The focus upon the development of this commodity was indicative of a trend that would have a profound and long-term effect on all aspects of society. The use of powered machinery and the development of the factory system meant that a worker in the cotton industry produced more in 1816 than they could have done 60 years earlier. Samuel Greg was one of the leading figures in the cotton industry in Lancashire, which would become the hub of a new global trade. His mill at Quarry Bank, which had begun production in the 1780s, was among the largest and most advanced of its day, and sat at the centre of his growing textile empire.

Samuel Greg was born in Belfast in 1758, one of 13 children of Thomas Greg and his wife Elizabeth Hyde. Thomas was a successful merchant and shipowner and Elizabeth was the daughter of a Lancashire landowner who had interests in the Belfast linen trade. Both families were from a Protestant dissenting background, and were attached to the Unitarian Church. Thomas had a range of business interests from Russia and the West Indies to North America, however, at times he overextended his resources and found himself in severe financial difficulties. It was during one of these periods of financial strain that Elizabeth's childless brother, Robert Hyde, offered to adopt and educate the eight-year-old Samuel. The move to England – Ardwick Hall in Manchester specifically – would make Samuel's fortune and set him on the road to becoming an important industrialist.

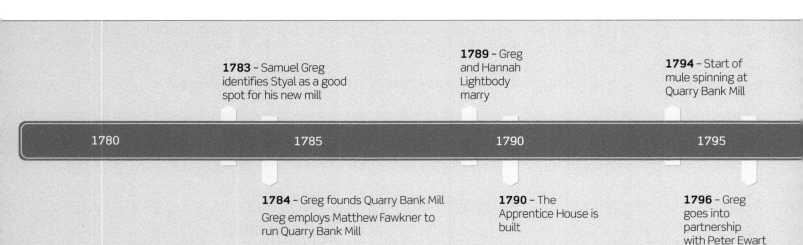

1783 - Samuel Greg identifies Styal as a good spot for his new mill

1789 - Greg and Hannah Lightbody marry

1794 - Start of mule spinning at Quarry Bank Mill

| 1780 | 1785 | 1790 | 1795 |

1784 - Greg founds Quarry Bank Mill
Greg employs Matthew Fawkner to run Quarry Bank Mill

1790 - The Apprentice House is built

1796 - Greg goes into partnership with Peter Ewart

Hyde and Company – learning the trade

Robert Hyde and his brother Nathaniel had done much to expand their father's textile business in Manchester. By 1762, they had capital of £20,000 and their trade consisted of importing linen yarn from Hyde's Belfast firm and 'putting this out' to Lancashire cottagers to be woven into **fustian** cloth. The '**putting out**' system linked merchants to domestic production and presented certain advantages in the early industrial period. The merchants controlled the trade in yarn and cloth, supplying the weaver with yarn and providing a market for the finished goods, but actual production was undertaken by weavers operating from their domestic premises. The system, known as 'cottage industry' (see page 11), was flexible, easily able to adjust production to demand and did not require any large capital investment.

It was into this business that the young Samuel Greg was inducted after being taken in by his uncle's family. Having initially been educated at a school in Harrow (not the famous Harrow School), he was sent to the continent to take orders for his uncle's firm, and it was here that he learnt the essential skills of a textile merchant. In 1780, at the age of 22, he completed his apprenticeship and was made a junior partner in Hyde and Company. Two years later, Robert Hyde died and Greg inherited an estate worth £10,000. Robert's brother Nathaniel, the senior partner in Hyde's, was at the same time forced to retire due to his alcoholism and Samuel found himself in charge of a firm with assets estimated at £26,691, a considerable figure for the time. Greg, with a new business partner, John Middleton, was quick to look at ways in which to take advantage of the increasing demand for cotton cloth. It soon became clear that there was a need to increase the supply of good quality yarn to their weavers. To ensure the continuity of both quality and supply, they decided to build their own mill in the village of Styal, ten miles outside Manchester.

KEY TERMS

Fustian
A heavy cloth made from a combination of linen and cotton threads that were woven together using the stronger linen thread for the warp and the weaker cotton for the weft. The material was heavy and durable but it would be the more delicate pure cotton cloths with their wider range of applications that would become the focus for the growing textile industry.

Putting out
A system where merchants who traded in cloth would send out orders to producers for goods, then collect the finished items. Later the cloth merchants would become the key suppliers of raw cotton as well as credit to the producer.

SOURCE 1

An oil painting attributed to the artist Strickland Lowry c1765 of Thomas Greg with his family. It includes Samuel Greg, fourth from the right dressed in the blue jacket and breaches.

1797 – Greg family move into Quarry Bank House, built for them close to the mill

1806 – Greg's programme to erect purpose-built cottages in Styal village begins

1810 – First steam engine installed at Quarry Bank Mill

1800   1805   1810   1815

1801 – Construction of the weir to increase the power of the mill
New wooden overshot wheel installed at Quarry Bank and the River Bollin dammed to help increase water power to it

1807 – New 8ft iron wheel installed to help generate more power for the mill

WHAT INFLUENCED THE GROWTH OF QUARRY BANK MILL IN THE YEARS 1784–1816?

Choosing the site at Styal

Proximity to Manchester and Liverpool

The selection of Styal for the erection of the cotton mill was very deliberate for several reasons, not least its proximity to Manchester and Liverpool, which made good commercial sense since these were increasingly important towns in the development of manufacturing particularly and British industry more broadly. The location of Styal within a 30-mile radius of these towns gave the prospective mill an excellent opportunity for exportation, since Liverpool was the site of Britain's largest docks and a primary point for international trade. Access to this port was possible because of a nearby canal, which had been built by the Duke of Bridgewater in 1761. By siting the mill at Styal, the potential for developing effective trade links was very possible. This, to an entrepreneurial businessman such as Greg, was a critical consideration if his mill was to be successful. Furthermore, Manchester was a centre of commerce with its growing population: in 1773 only 22,481 people lived there but by 1788 there were 42,821 residents.

In addition to the convenience of exportation, Styal also had the advantage of being next to the fast-flowing River Bollin, which would consequently be able to meet his need for a reliable power supply. This particular requirement was fundamental for Greg's business, since he wanted to base his manufacturing around Richard Arkwright's new water frame – a machine that dramatically sped up the creation of cotton thread – and these new machines were powered by water. Using the force of the river, a water wheel would be rotated, which in turn generated power to operate the machinery in the mill; without the river, those machines would not function and therefore such a feature, alongside the availability of a labour force, was critical in the selection of a new site. That Styal had good access to the river made it a very attractive possibility for Greg when he was undertaking his search during the early 1780s.

Costs

Another advantage Styal offered over other areas was that there was a quarry nearby. To build the mill, the necessary building materials would need to be easily obtainable and, of equal importance, not at an excessive cost. The local quarry would be able to supply the necessary materials and, being so close, the cost of transportation would not be prohibitive. This financial advantage was enhanced by the relatively cheap price of the site itself, since it was boggy and therefore unfarmable. Greg paid £50 for the land and buildings, and then 2 shillings and 8 pence rent per year on the site afterwards. This was a very reasonable figure compared with the higher costs of land in Manchester – the result of a growing population.

The mill cost £3,000 to build and equip, which was in line with other similar ventures such as Jedediah Strutt's mill at Belper, in Derbyshire, which cost £5,000 to build in 1793. For Greg, the risk of investing in fixed assets was balanced by the size of his inheritance and the value of the turnover of his main Manchester business. Though he had spent a not inconsiderable sum on Quarry Bank Mill, for such a wealthy merchant it was not that large an investment in comparison to his interests elsewhere.

The development of spinning

> **KEY TERM**
>
> **Bourbon West Indies**
> The Caribbean islands under French rule such as Haiti and Martinique

The mill employed about 150 operatives in 1795, spinning relatively coarse yarn. Greg appeared to have little concern as to where his cotton came from, using any that could be got. Most came from the **Bourbon West Indies** and was best for thicker threads, though he also obtained raw cotton from Brazil. This was imported into the docks at Liverpool and then put onto barges, which were then taken up the canal to the site of Quarry Bank Mill. In fact, it was the water links with Liverpool that made the site at Styal attractive to Greg when he was originally looking for a place to locate his mill. The Rathbones of Liverpool, who would become leading traders in raw cotton, had started to import American cotton in the mid-1780s, which could be used to spin finer yarns, but it would not be until 1808 that the United States would become the major supplier for Quarry Bank Mill. In early years of operation, Samuel Greg invested little additional capital into the venture, which would suggest that Quarry Bank Mill was peripheral to his other commercial interests. It would not be until 1793, with the outbreak of war with France, that a major shift in emphasis and a rapid expansion of the spinning side of the business would take place.

SOURCE 2 Quarry Bank Mill in 1897. At the right of the building you can see the tower for the bell that was used to summon the workers for their shifts.

© The Francis Frith Collection

ACTIVITY
KNOWLEDGE CHECK

Cotton spinning

1 Create a timeline of the key innovations in the cotton industry.

2 What reasons might there have been for Greg to move out of domestic production in spinning and weaving? Make a list for and against that option.

3 From your own perspective, write a brief explanation of not more than 200 words either supporting or challenging Greg's decision.

The impact of the French wars, 1793–1815

In 1789, the absolutist monarchy in France was overthrown in the French Revolution. Over the 26 years that followed, the consequences of these events would plunge Europe into a series of wars in which Britain would be heavily involved. Though Britain did not initially seek confrontation with France, it joined in the War of the First Coalition against the revolution. Britain would become one of the main financial backers of the countries opposed to French dominance of the continent, and by 1808 it was sending its army to fight in the Spanish Peninsular War against the French armies. The French wars presented both opportunity and risk for the textile trades. With the war came disruption of markets and fluctuations in demand as large parts of the mainland European market became closed to British exports, especially after 1806 due to Napoleon's **continental system**. In response to Britain's naval blockade of the French coast, Napoleon imposed a ban on British goods entering the continent. The ban was far from effective and led to much criticism of Napoleon's rule, but it did affect markets for British goods.

KEY TERM

Continental system
Napoleon's embargo on all trade with Britain as a result of the Royal Navy's blockade of the French coast.

While there was a decline in cloth exports to Europe, new international markets in South America and India were quickly exploited, especially as there was relatively little competition from the continent. Demand for yarn also increased rapidly and with rising wartime prices mill owners saw profits increase.

In the 1790s, Greg's interests, like those of other textile merchants, turned towards the Atlantic trade with the Americas. He had a wide range of contacts in Philadelphia, and his brother-in-law, James Lyle, who had been involved in the trade for many years, became his partner. Greg expanded his production at this time, presumably in the hope of exporting it to the US, with 59 percent of his stock being shipped across the Atlantic. In this sense, the war with France forced Greg and other merchants to look to new markets and, given the majority of cotton products were going to the US, it can be suggested that the closure of European doors in fact opened far more lucrative American ones. Between 1804–06, for example, the market accounted for £8.2 million worth of Britain's textile trade.

The profitability of yarn

Yarn exports to South America also increased markedly throughout the French wars as demand for cotton cloth continued to rise. This growth increasingly compensated for the difficulty of trade in Europe and also the closed markets of the US after 1807, following the passage of the Embargo Act in that country (repealed in 1809). In 1804, for example, Greg's profits in his spinning business were running at about 18 percent of turnover, and historian Mary Rose has suggested that it had been this growth in profits at Quarry Bank Mill that were behind Greg's decision to transfer the bulk of his operations away from trading and into spinning. It was also a business that was easier to manage than the Atlantic trade, as he supplied other merchants directly who then took on the risk of exporting the yarn or finished woven goods. The switch in focus, however, increased the need for capital investment at Quarry Bank Mill. If Greg was to take advantage of these developing markets, he needed to expand the mill's capacity. Fortunately, he had access to considerable funds that had been accumulated over time. Unlike other manufacturers, he was able to improve his factory and make it more competitive without increasing business debt. The emphasis on the spinning trade did not free the undertaking from risk in other areas, essentially due to Greg's poor judgement. In 1814, at the end of the Napoleonic Wars, Greg incurred massive losses of £31,864 from his dealings in Spain. The situation was not disastrous as profits continued to be healthy in spinning, which helped to offset the losses made in other areas that in lesser enterprises would have led to bankruptcy.

Samuel Greg

Having entered the manufacturing business in the late 18th century, Greg would prove to be instrumental in the development of Britain's economic position in the world. His business acumen and opportunism, together with substantial wealth bequeathed to him from his family, gave him an advantage in the fast-changing economy that presented numerous opportunities for those prepared to take a chance. In particular, Greg would be fundamental to the growth of Lancashire as a pillar of Britain's cotton manufacturing, as his mill at Quarry Bank was both one of the largest mills in the country and one of the most successful – benefiting from Greg's willingness to buy in many of the new technological innovations such as the water frame, which helped to promote efficient large-scale production processes. By taking the lead in such practices and succeeding, Greg's example encouraged others to develop along similar lines, and consequently his influence helped to professionalise the industry.

In addition to encouraging the Lancashire cotton industry to adopt more modern techniques such as steam power, Greg was also a pioneer in the promotion of improved conditions for those who worked in his mills. This facet of his public contribution is perhaps more enduring than that of his commercial enterprise, since the improvement of workers themselves arguably encouraged a much longer-term benefit for the region itself, and also the profitability of the cotton industry, since workers were not only better looked after, but as a result of ventures such as the apprentice house they became more loyal and therefore reliable employees. The basis of this gradual loyalty was the philanthropy that Greg practised during his lifetime. While philanthropy was not unknown among the mill owners of Lancashire, the picture that is most often presented in popular literature is that of the factory masters as hard-faced men out to make a profit. Although in many parts of the country, and indeed Lancashire, there was certainly many such individuals, historian Michael Sanderson points to Samuel Greg as a more progressive figure; he was undoubtedly motivated by profits, but he was also one of the most prominent advocates of education for workers in the region. One of the reasons we know so much about Quarry Bank Mill was that it attracted the attention of contemporary commentators on industrial matters such as Andrew Ure, who held it up as an exemplar of what might be achieved. Greg also influenced other manufacturers such as Henry Ashworth at the New Eagley Mill in Bolton, who set up a day school in 1818.

As an entrepreneur, Samuel Greg was always looking for a new opportunity to secure his business fortunes. He also tried to diversify his interests, which in 1782 amounted to £36,000, by engaging in large-scale investment in land. He purchased property in Reddish, near Stockport, in 1804, and continued to expand the estate until 1815. While the returns on land were not as high as profits in textiles, it was considered a safe repository for spare capital that would be protected from the fluctuations in the cotton trade. Besides his holdings in Britain, Greg also had sizeable investments in the West Indies and New York State, where he had inherited land from his father and uncle. In 1813, only about 63 percent of his wealth was based in the cotton industry, while around 26 percent was held in land. By spreading this risk, Greg demonstrated a keen awareness of the flexibility of markets, reasoning that by diversifying his portfolio he not only made his investments more secure, reducing the risk, but this also offered new avenues to generate more income. Greg enjoyed a great deal of success with his investments and by 1814 his assets were worth in excess of £230,711. As a businessman, he was very astute and his businesses enjoyed financial security.

Matthew Fawkner

Greg, like many involved in commerce, had little knowledge of how to operate a mill; in many ways he continued to see himself as a merchant rather than a manufacturer – he continued to describe himself as such up until the 1800s. To help him with his new venture, he advertised in the Manchester press for a technically competent partner to oversee the building and equipping of the new mill. The mill at Styal was built under the direction of John Massey, his chosen partner and a man who had knowledge of the spinning business. Unfortunately, he died suddenly in 1784, just before the mill was due to open. Greg was in a quandary about what to do. He had neither the time nor the expertise to oversee the mill and time was too short to look for another partner. His solution was to place his faith in the works manager, Matthew Fawkner, who had been appointed by Massey to run the mill, an arrangement that would continue for the next 12 years. Unlike Greg, who was often absent from the mill, Fawkner was a constant presence at Styal and under his direction Quarry Bank grew to become one of the most successful mills in the country – single-handedly accounting for 0.6 percent of world supply by the mid-19th century.

Central to this success was the work ethic that Greg and Fawkner encouraged at the mill and also the adoption of Richard Arkwright's water frame, which sped up the process of manufacture by introducing a mechanical advantage, allowing for both greater efficiency and production in greater volume – albeit at a greater initial cost of £3,000. As the manager responsible for overseeing the working day at the mill, Fawkner was evidently trusted by Greg, who remained in Manchester at least until 1796, at which time he was persuaded to move closer to the mill by his wife.

Peter Ewart

What might seem surprising is that throughout his life Samuel Greg developed little knowledge of the process of spinning. He was not an engineer or manager, but remained first and foremost a merchant who understood commerce. The lack of technical ability, in many ways, held back his undertaking at Quarry Bank Mill. To address these shortcomings, in 1796 Greg took on a new partner, Peter Ewart. Ewart was a highly competent engineer who had served his apprenticeship among the best practical mechanics of the day at the engineering firm Boulton and Watt in Birmingham. He met Greg when he was in the north-west of the country marketing steam engines to cotton manufacturers to power their factories. Greg was keen to have Ewart's expertise at his disposal and offered him a highly lucrative partnership. For a capital investment of just £400, Ewart was to receive a quarter of the profits from spinning and a sixth from marketing.

Boulton and Watt

Matthew Boulton was originally a leading producer of small decorative metal items at his Soho works in Birmingham. The scale of the factory at Soho was vast by contemporary standards, with power provided by a water wheel. In the late 1760s, Boulton became the sponsor of James Watt's endeavours to improve Newcomen's atmospheric steam engine to fill his mill pool at Soho in the summer months. One would eventually be used to power his factory at Soho. Watt changed Newcomen's boiler design to utilise the power of expanding steam rather than atmospheric pressure. Atmospheric engines had been used to pump water from coal mines where its heavy fuel consumption was not a problem. Watt's more efficient design opened up the possibility of utilising steam beyond the coal fields, and eventually supplanted water power. The partnership between Boulton and Watt would provide designs for steam engines to their customers, which would then be built under the supervision of Boulton and Watt's own engineers.

KEY TERMS

Muslin

A fine cotton cloth, originally handwoven, which came from India. It was light, thin and translucent and became popular in the late 18th century among fashionable women. One famous portrait of the French queen Marie Antoinette depicts her wearing a flowing white muslin dress.

Calico

A printed cotton fabric from India. In the late 18th century, bright calico fabrics became very popular. The introduction of the mule and the development of a dyeing and printing industry permitted the cloth to be home-produced rather than imported.

Among the first changes at the mill was the introduction of Crompton's spinning mule. Samuel Crompton had developed his machine in 1779 as a hybrid between the spinning jenny and Arkwright's water frame, hence the name mule. The mule was capable of spinning strong, thin yarn that was suitable for use as both warp and weft thread. Mule yarn could be used to produce a much wider range of cotton fabric, including fine **muslin** cloths and printed **calicos**. The main drawback was that it needed the right type of raw cotton to work efficiently, whereas the water frame, which created coarser spun yarn, could use any type available. With the use of better-quality cotton at Quarry Bank Mill – with most of the raw cotton now coming from the southern states of the US – it was decided to use mule spinning to produce a product that had a greater potential market. The water frame was soon eclipsed by the mule, which would become the mainstay of the spinning trade for the next century.

SOURCE

From *History of the Cotton Manufacture in Britain* by Edward Baines (1835). Baines was the son of Edward Baines (Snr), the owner of the *Leeds Mercury* and Liberal MP. Although both he and his father supported political reforms, such as extending the vote in 1832, they were against factory reforms such as that challenging child labour. His book was a defence of the factory system.

The water-frame spun twist for warps, but it could not be advantageously used for the finer qualities, as thread of great tenuity [thinness] has not strength to bear the pull of the rollers when winding itself on the bobbins. This defect in the spinning machinery was remedied by the invention of another machine, called the Mule, from its combining the principles of Arkwright's water-frame and Hargreaves's jenny. Like the former, it has a system of rollers, to reduce the roving; and, like the latter, it has spindles without bobbins to give the twist, and the thread is stretched and spun at the same time by the spindles, after the rollers have ceased to give out the rove. The distinguishing feature of the mule is, that the spindles, instead of being stationary, as in both the other machines, are placed on a moveable carriage, which is wheeled out to the distance of fifty-four or fifty-six inches from the roller-beam, in order to stretch and twist the thread, and wheeled it again to wind it on the spindles.

As production increased, Ewart began a series of improvements to the mill. In 1801 a stone weir and dam were created to control the flow of water and two new water wheels were installed. The year 1807 saw the installation of another water wheel and the building of a tunnel to take off the headwater of the river, which increased the available power to 40 horsepower (hp). Finally, in 1810 a 10 hp Boulton and Watt steam engine was added to provide supplementary power for the factory. The adoption of steam not only permitted an increase of productive capacity, but it meant that work was not interrupted by low water levels in the summer months. In nine years, a sum of £8,622 had been invested in the mill. Ewart's adoption of steam would, in many ways, prove to be the most significant innovation at Quarry Bank Mill. Steam power meant that mills no longer needed to be sited in remote areas to take advantage of the available water power. Though, as Peter Mathias notes in his book, *The First Industrial Nation*, demand was so great for cotton that, despite the mass expansion of steam-powered factories, new water mills were still being built until the 1830s. The installation of a steam engine at Quarry Bank Mill was to increase the available power to the mill, permitting it to further expand its productive capacity. For example, in 1805 the mill produced 213,616 lbs of yarn, while ten years later in 1815 that number had risen to 342,578 lbs.

SOURCE 4

An illustration of Crompton's mule. Note the carriage that moved back and forwards while the cotton was spun into thread. Though it might have been Arkwright's water frame that helped the expansion of the cotton trade, it was the mule that would lead the way in the production of a wide range of cotton fabrics.

The development of steam power provided an opportunity for Greg to expand the business further, given the rising demand for mule-spun yarn due to the French wars. However, instead of adding capacity to Quarry Bank, he decided to start a new venture in Manchester. Why he chose this option is far from clear, but it could have been related to the relatively high costs of running an additional steam engine at Quarry Bank, as well as having a readymade workforce on his doorstep in Manchester. Greg started his mule-spinning factory in 1807 at Peter Street in Manchester, which by 1811 had capacity for 12,400 spindles, which was more than at Quarry Bank. Despite the lack of investment in increasing the amount of power available, output continued to rise at Quarry Bank Mill, which saw an increase of over 50 percent in the ten years between 1805 and 1815. With the end of the Napoleonic Wars in 1815, the market for yarn declined sharply and, in an industry that now found itself with far too much productive capacity, Greg decided to sell the factory in Peter Street.

The importance of Peter Ewart to the productivity of Quarry Bank Mill and Greg's success there lies in the partnership the two men enjoyed. Though Greg was able to appreciate the potential for profit in spinning, it is unclear if he would have been able to take advantage of the situation without the technical skills of Ewart, both in terms of mechanical innovation and as an effective organiser of the productive process. In this sense it would be quite reasonable to suggest that Ewart provided tangible and necessary support for the realisation of Greg's ideas.

Hannah Greg

In 1789, Samuel Greg married Hannah Lightbody, the daughter of Adam Lightbody, another Unitarian merchant. The Lightbodys and the Gregs moved in the same social circles in Manchester comprising nonconformists with interests in various forms of commerce. Protestant **dissenters** such as Hannah's great-grandparents had been excluded from the professions and prevented from taking university degrees, which had led to many becoming involved in business. Dissenters would play an important role in the process of industrialisation, from the Quaker Abraham Darby in the iron industry to the Unitarian M'Connels and Gregs in cotton. Marriage within these groups created family connections that helped build networks that aided their commercial interests.

A Level Exam-Style Question Section B

How far did the French wars change the nature of Samuel Greg's business in the years 1793–1815? (20 marks)

Tip

Think about how little he invested before the wars with France and consider where his profits came from between 1796 and 1815. You might also contrast his fortunes in the spinning trade with his ventures in exporting cloth to the United States.

KEY TERM

Dissenter
A member of a Protestant sect that was not part of the established Church of England. These sects included Unitarians, Methodists, Baptists and Quakers. They had faced a certain amount of persecution and been excluded from the established universities of Oxford and Cambridge as they were not members of the Church of England. They played an important role in promoting various independent colleges and new universities, such as the University of Manchester, founded in 1824.

Hannah was a devout in her religious beliefs, principled in her views of society and well educated. She had attended a boarding school at Ormskirk, but after her father's death in 1778, she went to London to study at the new dissenting academy Hackney New College. She was an enthusiastic scholar who believed that education was a key not only to social progress, but also to society's general well-being. It was at this time that she became convinced that social reform was needed to address the problems of poverty and to make politics less corrupt. In part, this was due to her contact with radical reformers such as Dr Richard Price, who was a dissenting minister and polemical writer for social reform.

Price held progressive ideas about the education of men and women and was a vocal supporter of the American and French Revolutions. He was friends with eminent figures of the Enlightenment such as Joseph Priestley and Benjamin Franklin. Hannah was also influenced by one of Dr Price's associates Mary Wollstonecraft, who would become one of the leading advocates of female emancipation.

SOURCE 5

From Hannah Greg's contributions to *The Monitor*, a collection of aphorisms published in 1804. Here she writes about her views on the social responsibilities of the wealthy.

To see the poor adequately rewarded, to prevent exertion from exceeding strength or extinguishing spirit, to suppress the deficiencies occasioned by sickness, to procure for the mothers of families the ease necessary for rearing healthy children – to afford hours of pleasure and relaxation to the young, and years of cheerful inactivity to the old. It is, in short, to make man contented with his lot, that the rich should use their fortune and should consider themselves as stewards.

SOURCE 6

Miniature portraits depicting Samuel and Hannah Greg c1790. Miniatures were often presented as gifts within lockets so that they could be worn by the owner.

The marriage to Samuel Greg was not without affection, but convention restricted Hannah's ability to express her views publicly, particularly if they were at variance with those of her husband. She also had responsibility for managing a large family of 13 children, which restricted her time to write or to help the poor in her community. She was a lifelong supporter of education as a means for self-development and believed it to be the best means to improve both the individual and society as a whole. This led to her becoming infuriated with her husband's subordination of education to just learning how to run his business, as can be seen from Source 7.

SOURCE
7

From a letter from Hannah Greg to her daughter Elizabeth Greg in 1816. She comments on Samuel Greg's desire to have his son, John, involved in the family business.

I rather hoped your father had forgotten or relinquished the idea of sending John to Liverpool this vacation, but yesterday, on his asking leave to have Mr Dalton's instruction this summer, your father told him he must learn the business.

Despite their differences, there is evidence that she managed to create a reputation for operating an open house that welcomed the visits from literary figures both British and continental. We have from a number of memoirs a vivid portrait of the type of society that Hannah Greg wished to promote.

SOURCE
8

From the autobiography of Eliza Fletcher, published in 1784. Fletcher was an English writer and literary patron, notably of Hannah More, who supported parliamentary reform and liberal politics. Later in her life, she became friends with Elizabeth Gaskell, who would write about the lives of the working classes.

We stayed a week with [the Gregs] and admired the cultivation of mind and refinement of manners which Mrs Greg preserved in the midst of a money-making and somewhat unpolished community of merchants and manufacturers. Mr Greg was most gentlemanly and hospitable, and surrounded by eleven clever and well-conducted children. I thought them the happiest family group I had ever seen.

ACTIVITY
KNOWLEDGE CHECK

Greg and his entrepreneurialism

1 Make a list of the businesses in which Samuel Greg had an interest.

2 Make a mind map and list the ways in which Peter Ewart was essential to the success of Quarry Bank Mill.

3 Looking at your evidence from activities 1 and 2, what arguments might be offered to support the statement that 'Samuel Greg was less an innovative industrialist than a traditional cloth merchant who happened to own a mill.'

HOW SUCCESSFULLY DID SAMUEL GREG DEAL WITH THE LABOUR PROBLEM AT QUARRY BANK MILL?

Early textile mills tended to be located in relatively sparsely populated parts of the country so as to take advantage of the available water power, which was the case with Quarry Bank Mill. As a consequence, it was difficult to obtain suitable labour to work in the new mill. It is not clear where the original workforce for Samuel Greg's new venture came from. However, it is believed that many of the skilled operatives were recruited from Eyam, in Derbyshire, some 30 miles away. Eyam had been an early centre for industrial cotton spinning and Greg had financial interests in the area. However, maintaining a workforce continued to be a struggle in the early years of the operation at Quarry Bank Mill since the local population, who were generally employed on the 'putting out' system, were less enthusiastic about the more formalised working practices of the factory system. They were not used to factory discipline and were considered unreliable, preferring to tend their cottage allotments on fine days rather than work in the mill. The lack of discipline of the early mill worker was a common problem for 18th-century factory owners. Workers in the domestic industries were used to working at their own pace and in a way that suited their way of life. Greg, therefore, had to look at ways to recruit a reliable labour force to keep Quarry Bank Mill running.

Connections with the Poor Law system

The Poor Law before 1834

Under the existing Poor Law in Britain during the late 18th century, responsibility for relief was left to the local parish authorities and was funded by local poor rates, which were an additional tax levied to generate the necessary money for this support. Such support – usually in the form of allowances or residence in a **poorhouse** – was not systematic and its quality varied from parish to parish, creating an ad hoc and rather chaotic system, which did not efficiently address the issue of poverty. It also placed a great burden on the local taxpayers and increasingly this became a point of pressure into the mid-19th century.

Greg and the Poor Law

To help overcome the shortage of labour, Greg began to take pauper apprentices from the local Wimslow poorhouse. This arrangement was agreed between Greg and the local parish guardians, who entered into a contract with Greg to supply him with child labour on the understanding that he would provide work, lodgings and food for the children for an agreed fixed term – usually until the age of 18. In return, Greg got his cheap and ready supply of labour along with several guineas per child, since he was relieving the Poor Law by accepting the 'burden' that the children created upon it. Initially the numbers were small and the apprentices lodged with the local cottagers.

In 1790, Greg decided to expand the provision and spent £300 building an apprentice house to accommodate 90 children. Child labour would play an important part in the development of Quarry Bank Mill and represented half the labour at the mill until the early 1840s. Child labour was cheap since they were provided with education, lodgings and food in lieu of actual wages. They were also quick and nimble, ready to carry out complex tasks and able to get under the moving machinery to remove jams and clean out cotton debris, which covered the floor of the mill. Historian Mary Rose has suggested that, despite some runaways, children offered a generally more pliant workforce that could be better controlled than adult mill workers, who might be more resistant to the discipline of the factory.

A Level Exam-Style Question Section A

Study Source 9 before you answer this question.

Assess the value of the source for revealing the level of support for Greg's decision to use pauper children in his mill and the success of his actions.

Explain your answer, using the source, the information about its origin and your own knowledge about the historical context. (20 marks)

Tip
When answering this question you should consider what benefits the apprentice system offered in terms of the context of the time and particularly the attitudes towards poor relief.

SOURCE

From Joseph Townsend's *A Dissertation on the Poor Laws*, written in 1786. Townsend was the rector of Pewsey, a prominent religious figure, as well as a physician who criticised the existing Poor Laws because in his eyes they encouraged indolence. His dissertation was widely read and influenced the developing debate about poor relief, which was later addressed with the Poor Law Amendment Act 1834.

To a man of common sensibility nothing can be more distressing, than to hear the complaints of wretchedness, which he hath no power to redress, and to be daily conversant with misery, which he can neither fly from, nor relieve. This at present is the situation of the clergy, who, in virtue of their office, are obliged to visit the habitations of the poor. Here they see helpless infancy and decrepit age, the widow and the orphan, some requiring food, and others physic; all in such numbers, that no private fortune can supply their wants. Such scenes are more distressing, when, as it sometimes happens, the suffering objects have been distinguished for industry, honesty, and sobriety. The laws indeed have made provision for their relief, and the contributions are more than liberal which are collected for their support; but then, the laws being inadequate to the purposes for which they were designed, and the money collected being universally misapplied, the provision, which was originally made for industry in distress, does little more than give encouragement to idleness and vice. The laws themselves appear beautiful on paper, and will be the admiration of succeeding ages, when, in the revolution of empires, the whole fabric of our government shall be dissolved, and our nation, as a separate kingdom, shall exist no more. These laws, so beautiful in theory, promote the evils they mean to remedy, and aggravate the distress they were intended to relieve. Till the reign of Q. Elizabeth they were unknown in England; and to the present moment, they have never been adopted by any other kingdom upon earth. It has been most unfortunate for us, that two of the greatest blessings have been productive of the greatest evils. The Revolution gave birth to that enormous load of debt, under which this nation groans; and to the Reformation we are indebted for the laws which multiply the poor.

The apprentices supplied from parish workhouses were mostly orphans. The parish apprentice system dated back to the time of the Tudors and had been designed to provide destitute children with a trade to support them through life. However, by the 18th century the system was under strain; in the expanding cities, such as London, Manchester and Liverpool, workhouses were struggling to meet their commitments and were only too glad to offload this heavy drain on the local rates. The readiness to provide labour for the growing textile mills is attested to by the letter in Source 10 from the vicar of Biddulph.

SOURCE

10 From a letter from the vicar of Biddulph, in Staffordshire, to Samuel Greg, dated 1817. The relationship between the vicar and Greg developed after Greg expressed a wish to employ children from the parish. The vicar was keen to rid his parish of poor children, who were regarded as a burden on the poor rate.

The thought has occurred to me that some of the younger branches of the poor of this parish might be useful to you as apprentices in your factory at Quarry Bank. If you are in want of any of the above, we could readily furnish you with ten or more at from 9 to 12 years of age of both sexes. My wife desires to join in best wishes for Mrs Greg and family.

These parish apprentices were bound to their master for around seven years, meaning that they could not leave and were liable to be punished if they were found slacking off work. Often they would have to work extra hours to pay the fines imposed for infringements of the mill rules.

Greg was by no means the first to use child labour of this sort. In the 1770s, Richard Arkwright had employed pauper children in his Derbyshire mill, and at one point they accounted for over half his workforce. The first batch of new apprentices supplied to the Quarry Bank Mill apprentice house in 1790 came from the Newcastle-under-Lyme workhouse, the same place Arkwright had obtained his workforce. Later on, Liverpool workhouses would become an important source of pauper children.

As well as approaching parish guardians himself, Samuel Greg had agents who went about the local parishes in search of apprentices. Knowing the pressure that was being placed on the system by a growing population of paupers, Greg was prepared to drive a hard bargain. He would charge the parish £2 for every child that he took, rising to £4 for the poorest parishes who were most desperate to rid themselves of this burden. It was also expected that the apprentices were supplied with smocks and other clothing by the parish and before they were accepted they had to pass a medical examination. The apprentices accounted for about 50 percent of the workforce at Quarry Bank Mill in 1800, though this had fallen to about 36 percent by 1816.

EXTEND YOUR KNOWLEDGE

Apprentice system
This system gave young people the opportunity to learn a trade by matching them up to a skilled tradesperson who could teach them. In return for developing skills, the apprentices would work for little or no payment and undertake any task required of them, usually performing menial and laborious jobs integral to the trade they were learning.

Accommodating and managing the workforce

The apprentice house was in part financed by Hannah Greg's dowry and was completed in 1790. According to Andrew Ure in his 1835 book *The Philosophy of Manufacture*, there was space for 90 children, with about 60 girls and 30 boys occupying separate floors in the house. What we know of the conditions in the apprentice house at Quarry Bank Mill is in part provided by observers such as Ure, as well as contemporary documents. They indicate that the environment was clean and basic physical needs were met. The accounts of a number of runaways provide a fascinating picture of day-to-day life at the mill. Joseph Sefton, who ran away in 1806, told the court at Chester that he had been thirteen-and-a-half when he was indentured as an apprentice. Part of his testimony to the court is given in Source 11.

SOURCE 11

The typical experiences of apprentices at Quarry Bank Mill from two runaways, Joseph Sefton and Thomas Priestly, who left in 1806 to visit their families. The evidence was given at a court in Chester since running away was considered a crime.

The rooms were very clean the floors washed frequently... aired daily and whitewashed once a year... On Sunday we had for dinner boiled pork and potatoes. We also had peas, beans, turnips and cabbages in their season.

Monday we had dinner milk and bread and sometimes thick porridge. We always had as much as we could eat

Tuesday, we had milk and potatoes

Wednesday, sometimes bacon and potatoes and sometimes milk and bread

Thursday, if we had bacon on Wednesday then we had bread and milk

Friday, we used to have lob scouse [a type of stew]

Saturday we used to dine on thick porridge

We had only water to drink, when ill we were allowed tea.

EXTRACT 1

From the online article 'Legal Child Abuse' by Wendy McElroy (2001).

Greg saw himself as a humanitarian and, by contrast with workhouse officials, he probably was. In *The Philosophy of Manufactures* (1835), Andrew Ure wrote: 'At... the great firm of Greg and Son... stands a handsome house, two stories high, built for the accommodation of the female apprentices. They are well fed, clothed and educated. The apprentices have milk-porridge for breakfast, potatoes and bacon for dinner, and meat on Sundays.'

But no amount of decent treatment can obscure the fact that the children were stripped of the one thing they possessed—their labour and the right to contract. Nothing can convert the violation of their rights as labourers into an act of benevolence by Greg or by government officials.

EXTRACT 2

From *Child Workers and Industrial Health in Britain 1780–1850* by Peter Kirby (2013).

The isolated rural setting of many early water-powered textile mills sometimes provided opportunities for the schemes of utopian industrialists such as Robert Owen and Samuel Greg. Such early industrial visionaries often attracted praise for removing poor children from the moral and spiritual degradation of urban life. Many early textile mills were looked upon as charitable enterprises.

 THINKING HISTORICALLY Evidence (6c)

Comparing and evaluating historians' arguments

Extracts 1 and 2 give two accounts of mill owners using child labour.

1 Compare the two accounts above and identify factual statements or claims that they both agree upon. Make a list of these points.

2 Look carefully at how the authors use language. Do they both use equally cautious language in making their claims or is one more confident and assertive than the other? Is one (or both) of the historians over-claiming?

3 Look at Source 11. Do both authors appear to have made equally effective use of the trial evidence?

4 Are both of the accounts equally credible or are there reasons to prefer one account more than another?

At Quarry Bank Mill, the apprentices received a basic education provided by Samuel Greg and supported by his wife Hannah. After work, the children attended classes from eight to nine o'clock in the evening. They were taught to read and write with the use of slates and sand boxes to practise their letters, and girls were also taught sewing. In evidence given to a parliamentary select committee on the condition of apprentices in 1816, it was revealed that the girls were responsible for making both their own clothes and the boys' shirts. Though the instruction was minimal by modern standards, it was provided at a time when few from the working class could read and write. William Greg, one of Samuel's sons, even asserted to a select committee, which had been convened in 1833 to investigate factory conditions, that the education of the mill operatives at Quarry Bank Mill was far in advance of that received by the children of the local agricultural labourers. The mill also offered opportunities for some of the male apprentices to advance their situation. Historian T.S. Ashton notes that a number were able to rise to more senior positions at the mill. One example was Robert Venables, who started as an apprentice in 1816, but by 1839 had been put in charge of one of the weaving rooms.

SOURCE 12

From evidence given by William Greg to the Select Committee on Manufacturers in 1833. This committee was convened to investigate working conditions in Britain's factories and would lead to the passage of the Factory Act 1833.

Question: Have you or any of your family been in the habit of paying attention to the physical and moral condition of those apprentices out of the mill hours?

Greg: We have engaged a man and a woman, who take care of them in every way; we have a schoolmaster and schoolmistress; and in addition to that, my sisters have been in the habit of superintending the education of the girls, and my brother or myself, when on the spot, that of the boys. At present we have very few boys, and are increasing the number of girls.

Question: What is the kind of education they receive?

Greg: Reading, writing and arithmetic, and the girls sewing, and the necessary domestic occupations.

EXTEND YOUR KNOWLEDGE

Child labour

The question of child labour was much debated in the early part of the 19th century and reflects the development of an idea that childhood was different to the adult world. In the 18th century, childhood as we would understand it was absent, except among a wealthy few. Children were expected to play their part in the family economy. This has resulted in much debate among historians as to how to view the widespread use of children in the Industrial Revolution. Reformers in the 19th century were quick to see the moral danger posed by children being forced to enter the adult world too early as well as the harmful effects of long hours working in a factory, as found in the works of writers such as Charles Dickens. On the other hand, mills such as Greg's and Peel's offered a basic education and the possibility to advance one's position in life.

The apprentices were permitted time off on Sundays. On these days, Hannah Greg would visit the apprentice house with her whole family to participate in an act of worship. The presence of the family both narrowed the social distance between the employer and employed, and emphasised their position at the centre of the Quarry Bank Mill community. Though Greg might have been more humane than many, discipline was strict. Corporal punishment was administered on occasions, though fines were also used to keep the apprentices in line. For breaking a lamp glass, the fine was 4 shillings; for breaking a windowpane it was 1 shilling and 4 pence, and for 'standing on the lodge steps and going out' it was 5 shillings. However, good work could be rewarded too, with apprentices finding a sixpence left on their machine by Greg himself or one of his overseers. In the long term, the apprentice system proved successful, with around 70 percent of apprentices remaining at the mill when they reached adulthood.

Housing the workers

From the time of the completion of the mill in 1784, it was realised that it would be necessary to provide some sort of accommodation for the workforce. The motivation for this was first and foremost to retain the workforce he had developed through his apprentice house. Greg was also keen to ensure his employees were healthy since this would encourage more effective working practices and reduce the loss of work days due to ill-health. Supporting this commercial interest, Greg was also motivated by a sense of social reformism and sought to improve the conditions of those less fortunate simply from the position of moral duty.

Greg began by converting a number of agricultural buildings such as barns to provide dwellings for the first group of mill operatives. In 1789, he used some of Hannah's dowry to invest in the mill and built another 16 worker cottages. By the standards of the day, these were substantial buildings, costing between £50 and £100 each. As part of Greg's intention to improve the lives of his workforce long term, the homes he built at Styal each had access to their own allotments so that workers might develop a greater sense of self-sufficiency, and every house had its own **privy** unlike the slum dwellers of Manchester or Birmingham, who had to share one between five or six households.

The design of the cottages was far superior to that of the worker housing found in nearby Manchester and they were constructed to attract workers to the mill. In the 30 years after their construction, the village of Styal grew gradually as more housing was added to cater for the growing workforce. Rents tended to be low by urban standards as Greg based them on average agricultural wages rather than for those of a mill worker, who tended to earn more. Workers paid between 1 shilling and 2 shillings and 6 pence a week rent, which was deducted directly from their wages. Cellars were rented separately, often to widows who no longer had any dependent children.

In addition to the homes he created, Greg also founded a village shop, which was well stocked with all the necessities, including churned butter, fresh bread and tea. It operated on a 'truck system',

KEY TERM

Privy
A common term for a toilet, which at this time consisted of a separate shed construction in a yard over an earthen box cess pit that had to be emptied periodically by night soil men.

SOURCE

13 An illustration from the novel *The Life and Adventures of Michael Armstrong* by Frances Trollope, 1840. Trollope was an active campaigner against the use of child labour in British factories. The scene shows apprentices helping to operate a mule spinning machine. Note the number of threads being spun and the child crawling from under the mule having cleaned out the cotton waste. Also notice the white flecks in the hair of the apprentices, a reference to the cotton debris in the air that covered the workers' heads and coated their lungs.

which did not use cash but rather involved the shopkeeper maintaining a written record of all purchases made; the bills were then paid by deductions taken directly from the salaries of those workers who had run the bills up. The use of this system was both practical and also financially beneficial to Greg. From the point of practicality, it enabled workers to acquire the goods they needed without having to worry about being able to afford them at a given time, while for Greg it ensured that they bought directly from him rather than perhaps shopping elsewhere. It also helped to create more of a community feel to the village, consequently adding to the overall sense of well-being that Greg sought to generate.

The building of the workers' village points to the fact that Greg had to do all he could to maintain his workforce. He relied on their skills to maintain the profitability of his factory and, even though he was more philanthropic than many manufacturers, the investment in housing made sound business sense.

In the mill

The apprentices worked long shifts, up to 12 hours a day, often starting early in the morning and finishing in the evening. At Quarry Bank Mill, breakfast break was at 8.30, followed by lunch at 12.30 and finally more milk and bread at 5 p.m. However, unlike other mills in Lancashire, there was no night working. The first job an apprentice would learn would be to 'piece up', which was to repair the broken yarn as they removed the full **bobbins** from the machines.

KEY TERM

Bobbin
Cone-shaped form that the cotton yarn was wound onto.

SOURCE

14 From the testimony at a Chester court of Joseph Sefton, a runaway apprentice from Quarry Bank Mill. He ran away from the mill in 1806 to visit his family (running away was deemed a crime). Here he describes his work as an apprentice.

[At the age of thirteen] I was first employed to drop bobbins (that is, taking a full bobbin off the spindle and putting an empty one on). I then saved straps and put these round the binders. I used to oil the machinery every morning…

Working conditions in early cotton mills were poor. The atmosphere was humid so as to prevent the threads from snapping, so it was often hard to breathe, causing eyes to stream; the air was thick with small, white fibres that collected in the workers' hair and coated their lungs. As well as the humidity and the dust, the apprentices had to deal with the constant noise of the mill. The apprentices were given clogs to wear, but they would often remove them when they were working as they impeded movement and caused sparks that might ignite the cotton waste that covered the floor. As noted above, children were not only responsible for the operation of the spinning machines, but also had to maintain them, which often required them to be at work before the shift started.

In the cotton mill, operatives had to be careful of unfolded cuffs or loose shirt sleeves that might get caught in the machines. The medical officer's records at Quarry Bank Mill chronicle many incidents of apprentices suffering injuries to their eyes and legs as well as their hands while working in the spinning rooms. For example, Thomas Priestley, an apprentice in 1806, had the forefinger of his left hand ripped off when it became entangled in one of the machines. In addition, exposure to cotton fibres, 12-hour shifts and noisy machinery led to long-term health problems such as respiratory difficulties and deafness. For the apprentices, the exposure to such dangers would continue until the passing of the Factory Acts later in the century that would end child labour in the cotton mills. However, adult workers endured these conditions well into the 20th century.

A Level Exam-Style Question Section B

To what extent was the problem of reliable labour solved by the adoption of the apprentice system at Quarry Bank Mill? (20 marks)

Tip
When answering this question you should consider the broader nature of the apprentice system and how it influenced productivity at the mill. Considering the expense involved and the attitudes of many of the apprentices who continued to run away, was the overall impact more positive than not?

ACTIVITY
KNOWLEDGE CHECK

The problems of labour

1 In pairs consider what problems Samuel Greg had in attracting a suitable workforce to his mill at Quarry Bank Mill. Agree a list with your partner.

2 Why might child apprentices have been a preferable solution to trying to attract adult workers from nearby Manchester? Make a list with a partner.

3 Looking at both lists, how might you respond to the statement that 'Without child apprentices Samuel Greg's mill would have failed'?

EXTRACT 3

From 'British mercantilist policies and the American colonies' by John McCusker in *The Cambridge Economic History of the United States* by Stanley Engerman and Robert Gallman (eds) (2008).

Mercantilism's infatuation with expanding overseas trade was reinforced by an important corollary. The promotion of one's own merchants diminished the power of foreign merchants...

EXTRACT 4

From *Mercantilism* by Laura LaHaye (2008).

Mercantilism is economic nationalism for the purpose of building a wealthy and powerful state. Adam Smith coined the term 'mercantile system' to describe the system of political economy that sought to enrich the country by restraining imports and encouraging exports.

EXTRACT 5

From 'Mercantilism: a lesson for our times?' by Murray Rothbard (1963).

Far from being true friends of laborers, the mercantilists were frankly interested in exploiting their labor to the utmost; full employment was urged as a means of maximizing such exploitation. Thus, the mercantilist William Petyt wrote frankly of labor as 'capital material... raw and undigested... committed into the hands of supreme authority, in whose prudence and disposition it is to improve, manage, and fashion it to more or less advantage.'...

THINKING HISTORICALLY   Cause and consequence (6c)

Connections

Extracts 3–5 show some typical aspects of mercantilism.

Work in groups or individually and answer the following questions.

1 Read Extract 3. How might this be seen as similar to Greg's determination to be more successful than his rivals?

2 Read Extract 4.

   a) What did Greg believe about the importance of exportation?

   b) How is this similar to LaHaye's ideas about mercantilism?

3 Read Extract 5. How did Greg's actions reflect this description?

4 Make a list of other similarities between mercantilism and the activities of Samuel Greg. How did mill owners' understanding of mercantilism affect their actions during the 19th century?

5 Why it is important for historians to see these links across time and be able to explain how causal factors can influence situations much later in time?

HOW SIGNIFICANT WAS QUARRY BANK MILL IN THE DEVELOPMENT OF THE COTTON INDUSTRY IN LANCASHIRE?

From workshop to factory

By the 1740s important changes had begun to take place in Britain's industries. John Kay's flying shuttle of 1733 not only speeded up the weaving of cloth, it also meant that wider strips of material could be woven. A relatively simple device, it was originally introduced for use in weaving woollen fabric before being used for cotton cloth. The increased productivity of the weaver created a growing demand for yarn. In an attempt to raise the productivity of spinners, a number of devices were developed in the 1760s, the most successful of these early machines being James Hargreaves' **spinning jenny** of 1764. Hargreaves was a weaver from Blackburn, Lancashire, who took out a patent on a hand-powered machine that could spin multiple even threads. Although there were small numbers of factories using spinning jennys by the 1770s, the domestic form of production continued to be the norm.

EXTEND YOUR KNOWLEDGE

Spinning machines
Hargreaves was not the first to try to develop a spinning machine. In 1733, a Mr Wyatt from Lichfield had invented a machine for spinning cotton and on the basis of it two factories were built, one in Northampton and one in Birmingham. However, the venture failed and there is no record of what the machines were like or how they worked. It would not be until the 1760s that there would be further development of spinning machines. The lack of success experienced by Wyatt highlights that innovation in production was not guaranteed to turn a profit – the market had to be ready for them.

The jenny had a limited impact on the way the textile industry was organised as it produced a weak, fine thread only suitable to be used as **weft**. But Richard Arkwright's water frame, patented in 1769, would have a more profound effect. While weaving remained an artisanal trade, the spinning of yarn became an industrial one. The water frame produced a yarn of sufficient strength to be used as **warp** threads. This led to an increase in pure cotton fabric, replacing the cotton and linen mix that had been common. In this way, it could be said that it marked the true start of the British cotton age.

The water frame needed a power source greater than could be provided by a single human operative. Arkwright had originally considered using horses to drive his machine but this was soon abandoned in favour of water. This changed the economics of spinning as it became necessary to invest capital in fixed assets in the form of mill and machinery to produce yarn. It also saw the dispersal of the industry to take advantage of the available water power. Arkwright went into production with the water frame in the early 1770s in the small village of Cromford in Derbyshire (see Chapter 1). The mill that he built was large by the standards of the day and made full use of the abundance of water to drive its machinery. With this venture, the factory age had arrived, although it would take decades before all aspects of the domestic textile industry would vanish completely.

EXTEND YOUR KNOWLEDGE

Innovations in production: the water frame
This was a mechanical, multi-spindled, frame that was powered by water and designed to spin cotton into thread. Without the development of the water frame, the cotton textile trade would have been confined to the production of goods with relatively limited markets. Arkwright continued to develop the water frame until the late 1770s, adding extra spindles to the original design. However, Arkwright was more an entrepreneur than an innovator – most of the original design work for the water frame was done by John Kay, a clockmaker from Warrington. The water frame would later be superseded by Crompton's mule, which could spin a finer thread.

The impact of Quarry Bank Mill

It is not always easy to get a clear picture of the impact of Quarry Bank Mill on the development of the cotton industry in Lancashire. Although by the early 19th century much of the cotton trade became concentrated in that county, there remained a great deal of diversity among manufacturers in terms of scale of production, quality of goods and business management. While the factory system replaced the domestic industry, first in spinning and later in weaving, not all manufacturers followed the same path. Some remained purely spinners of yarn, while others focused on weaving alone. One way in which Greg stood out was in the way that he was able to obtain sufficient capital to expand the business without increased indebtedness. The key to this lay in the maintenance of large sums, kept in reserve from other investments and accumulated profits, which often were greater than the mill's fixed and working capital. This was particularly important as yarn prices began to fall in real terms and there was a need to invest in new machines so as to maintain profits. Other enterprises were not so fortunate and so were not able to take advantage of the rising market as effectively as Ewart and Greg did. By 1801 cotton would account for 17 percent of value added to the British economy

Year	Value
1780	£355,060
1787	£1,101,457
1790	£1,662,369
1800	£5,406,501

Figure 4.1 The value of cotton yarn exported by Britain, 1780–1800.

As can be seen from Figure 4.1, the value of the cotton trade grew rapidly, particularly at the time of the French wars. However, despite the increase in demand, bankruptcies among spinners peaked in 1805 at around 3.5 percent. In Peter Solar's survey of bankruptcies in the cotton spinning trade between 1780 and 1840, he suggests that over-reliance by small firms on the export market resulted in too great an exposure to fluctuations in the international trade without the compensation of an expanding home market. It was also at a time when firms were changing from using Arkwright's water frame to Crompton's mule, which placed a strain on firms looking for additional investment capital. By contrast, Greg and the other large producers were able to ride out these difficulties and had sufficient recourse to meet their obligations even in times of stress.

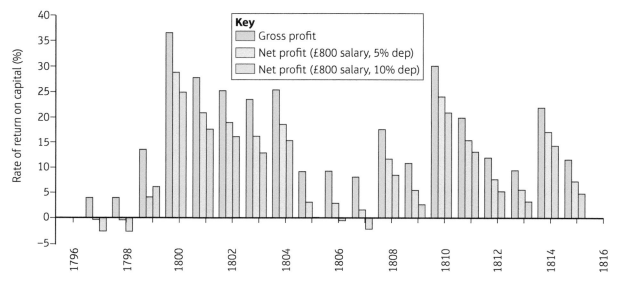

Figure 4.2 Greg's profits for Quarry Bank Mill between 1797 and 1815. It shows gross profit as well as calculations of net profit taking account of capital depreciation – at estimates of both 5 percent and 10 percent, and also Greg's salary of £800. It points to how the market in cotton fluctuated widely over this period, as did the profits to be made. From 'Was technological change in the early Industrial Revolution Schumpeterian? Evidence of cotton textile profitability' by C. Knick-Harley (2012).

Developing the workforce

The growth of Quarry Bank Mill was an essential feature in the development of Lancashire as a centre for cotton production because it helped to focus attention on that growing industry and increasingly offered a source of reliable employment for those who wanted it. By 1816, for example, Quarry Bank Mill employed 252 operatives, which was large for Lancashire, where before the 1840s the average workforce per mill was less than 200. For Greg, therefore, the need for labour was more acute than for smaller firms that might have been able to subsist on whatever workforce was locally available. Nonetheless, many of the smaller firms took on pauper apprentices in what historian

Karina Honeyman has argued was a tactic solely to take advantage of the cheap labour provided by children. In these cases, many of the mill hands were dismissed when they reached adulthood and could demand higher wages. Such actions stood in sharp contrast to Greg's regime at Quarry Bank Mill that was far more interested in retention of the workforce than maintaining margins by keeping the wage bill as low as possible. The provision of housing and the development of the village of Styal drew the attention of the chroniclers of the early industrial revolution and explains why Greg was to receive such positive press from the likes of Andrew Ure in his 1835 work, *The Philosophy of British Manufacturers*.

SOURCE
15

Andrew Ure's book *The Philosophy of British Manufacturers* was written in 1835 as a result of his travels around industrial Britain. It was condemned by factory reformers because it claimed that child workers in factories and mills were treated well. Ure himself attacked factory reformers, claiming that they exaggerated the health problems of factory workers.

The proprietors have engaged a man and women, who take care of them in every way; also a schoolmaster and a schoolmistress, and a medical practitioner. The Messrs Greg are in the habit of looking after the education of the boys, and their sisters superintended that of the girls, who are taught reading writing, arithmetic, sewing, and other domestic avocations. The health of these apprentices is unequalled by that of any other class of work-people in any occupation. The medical certificate laid before the Factory Commissioners proves that the deaths are only one in 150, being no more than one third of the average in Lancashire. Their ages vary from ten to twenty one years. When they grow up they almost always marry some of the men belonging to the factory. [They] often continue to work, and receive better wages than the other operatives (at other mills) as they are obliged to take houses for themselves. Only one or two instances have occurred in the course of forty years, since the system was begun by Mr Greg, sen. of any of them coming on the parish. The apprentices have milk-porridge for breakfast, potatoes and bacon for dinner, and butcher-meat on Sundays. They have bacon every day. About 550 of this description have passed through that mill in the course of forty years. Mr W. R. Greg says, that the general state of education among their mill hands is remarkably superior to that of the agricultural people. He has attended sometimes a sort of little club established near one of their country mills, to which some of the farmers' people came, and he found an astonishing difference between their intelligence and that of the mill workers. He has observed, that the children are a great deal more fatigued and less willing to go to school after a holiday, than after the business of an ordinary day. They all attend school with regularity.

By providing housing for his workforce, Greg arguably pioneered a new way of ensuring a reliable supply of labour and, in achieving this, his mill was able to be successful without the continual worry of a labour shortage. In this regard, the consolidation of a sustainable workforce also helped to solidify the new trend for a factory system rather than the traditional putting-out system that had previously been employed. By promoting this particular measure, Greg was one of the most influential figures in the development of cotton manufacturing in Lancashire, helping the county to become the largest centre for production in Britain in the 19th century.

Powering the industry

Greg's mill was innovative in the way in which it employed power. The early mill used a standard wheel, but under the direction of Peter Ewart the capacity of the mill increased rapidly. In 1810, steam power was introduced to the mill and this modern advance would prove to be formative in the development of Lancashire as a centre of Britain's cotton manufacturing industry. Quarry Bank Mill was one of the first to invest in steam, which permitted further development of the productive capacity of the mill and got over the problem of low water levels halting production. By adopting this approach, Greg's investment heralded a change in the factory system since from then on production could be situated near to markets and a labour force, rather than having to be built to take advantage of water power. In this regard, mills began to be established across the Lancashire region and very quickly it became a heartland for cotton manufacture since it had both sea ports and an existent spinning community, which could now be brought into the new mills and harnessed to machines so as to raise production to greater heights. Indeed, one of the first to take advantage of this mechanical revolution was Samuel Greg himself who built a steam powered spinning mill in Manchester.

A Level Exam-Style Question Section A

Study Source 15 before you answer this question.

Assess the value of the source for revealing the benefits of Greg's apprentice system for the apprentices themselves and the impact of the system on the working of the mill at Styal.

Explain your answer, using the source, the information about its origin and your own knowledge about the historical context. (20 marks)

Tip
When answering this question, you should consider the different people who stood to benefit from the system – does the source offer a broad idea as to who benefited?

ACTIVITY
KNOWLEDGE CHECK

The impact of Quarry Bank Mill

1 Using the data in Figure 4.1, draw a graph showing the growth in value of that market. While the data that we have may offer us the big picture, why might they not always provide the whole picture? Look at the profits generated from the Quarry Bank Mill in Figure 4.2.

2 Draw up a short list of the ways in which Quarry Bank Mill might have influenced the development of the cotton industry in Lancashire.

3 How far can we understand the development of a complex industry by looking at a single enterprise?

4 How significant do you think Quarry Bank Mill was in helping to shape the course of Britain's industrialisation?

Conclusion

Samuel Greg and Quarry Bank Mill were important aspects of the early stage of the Industrial Revolution. Greg bridged the gap between the pre-industrial domestic system of production and the arrival of the industrial cotton mill. Investment in production linked to technical advances in spinning attracted a range of entrepreneurs who thought there was money to be made in the textile trade. The venture at Quarry Bank Mill was substantial, but not the sole focus of Greg's business as Arkwright's had been at his mill in Cromford in Derbyshire. However, the opportunities afforded by a rapid rise in demand for yarn and the onset of the French wars led to greater investment in this arm of his business. The expansion of the mill also pointed to the complexities of the new factory system; it required knowledge of the technology, an understanding of how to organise labour and a sufficiently skilled workforce to operate the spinning machines. The undertaking also demanded capital and careful management to weather the fluctuations in the international market that had become the main focus for the British textile industry.

The need for water power to drive the machines in his factory had drawn Greg to Styal and its proximity to the River Bollin. However, the siting of the mill in a location remote from large concentrations of labour posed a problem. The need to provide a stable and skilled workforce forced Greg to invest more capital into providing accommodation and education for his operatives. It also led to the use of child labour to help sustain production. In doing so, Greg made full use of his knowledge of the Poor Law, not only to locate suitable candidates for his factory but also to help fund them. The growing population had put pressure on the local provisions for the poor and many parishes were only too keen to rid themselves of their pauper children. The use of child labour in the early Industrial Revolution was to become more controversial in the 19th century when factory reformers were moved to act to bring the practice to an end. Nevertheless, Greg was viewed by contemporaries, as well as later commentators, as an exemplary employer who attempted to look after the needs of his workforce, which was also of concern to his wife Hannah. While it is undeniable that Greg engaged in philanthropic acts both on a small and large scale, he was also a hard-headed businessman who could calculate the financial worth of a perceived act of kindness, particularly if it gave him greater control over his workforce.

Mary Rose has argued that for Greg the Quarry Bank Mill was just one of his many interests, yet it was to become one of his most consistently profitable. Attempts to exploit the transatlantic cloth trade proved disastrous for Greg's business as the complexities of managing such a complicated undertaking was far beyond his ability to manage effectively. Production on the other hand was a different matter and, though demanding of investment, it continued to provide returns to offset the losses elsewhere. As has been discussed in this chapter, it would be wrong to see the success of Quarry Bank Mill as in some way inevitable – the economies of scale created a product that was able to maintain profits in an ever more competitive market. It was a combination of access to capital, commercial knowledge and technical ability that maintained the business. Despite the demand for textiles, many firms went bankrupt as fluctuations in price and demand left them exposed to financial difficulties when trying to balance investment to expand capacity against market volatility.

The history of cotton is the history of a revolution, one that defined the industrial world. What had appeared settled was transformed rapidly, as factories replaced workshops and mechanisation supplanted domestic forms of production. The artisan gave way to the mill hand, and control of production passed to men like Greg who now ordered the worker's day and controlled how and when they worked. Lancashire was transformed into the cotton capital of the world as hundreds of textile mills spread across the county. Quarry Bank Mill was just one of many mills around Manchester. However, it was one of the earliest in the region and, after the arrival of Peter Ewart in the 1790s, one of the more advanced in its use of water and steam power. It marked the rise of a new class of mill owner and the old ways of commerce gave way to more specialised ventures in spinning mills, weaving sheds and calico printers. While the world did not change overnight, Samuel Greg and his mill were indicative of a new world that by the end of the 19th century would become all-pervasive as industrial capitalism shaped the destiny of Britain.

ACTIVITY
SUMMARY

Samuel Greg: cotton and cottages, 1784–1816

1 What made the cotton industry revolutionary? To help answer this, first draw up a mind map and put the question in the centre. Then go back through the chapter to look for evidence. You might want to group these under the headings of 'Innovation', 'Organisation' and 'Markets'.

2 Looking at your mind map, think about how these things came together to make a revolutionary change. Could one have existed without the other or did they have to evolve at the same time? Put your thoughts down as a series of short notes.

3 What would you say was Samuel Greg's main contribution to the revolution in the cotton industry? Consider your mind map and notes above and write a paragraph to answer this.

4 Considering the impact of the workforce on mill life, how might we view the human cost of the Industrial Revolution? Go back and look at how the organisation of production, the use of child labour and the conditions in the mill might be seen today. Write a short paragraph that reflects on how we should approach the issue as historians. Can we be objective or do values come into play?

WIDER READING

Ashton, T.S. *The Industrial Revolution 1760–1830*, Oxford University Press (1948)

Beckert, S. *Empire of Cotton*, Knopf (2014)

Galbi, D. 'Child labour and the division of labour in the early cotton mills', *Journal of Population Economics*, Vol. 10 No. 4 (1997)

Hanson, D. *The Children of the Mill: The True Story of Quarry Bank*, Headline (2014)

Knick Harley, C. 'Prices and profits in cotton textiles during the Industrial Revolution', discussion paper in *Economic and Social History*, University of Oxford, No. 18 (2010)

Mathias, P. *The First Industrial Nation*, Methuen (1969)

Murray, R. 'Quarry Bank Mill', *British Journal of Industrial Medicine*, Vol. 15 No. 293 (1958)

National Trust, Quarry Bank, www.nationaltrust.org.uk/quarry-bank/features/samuel-greg-of-quarry-bank

Rose, M. 'Diversification of investment by the Greg family, 1800–1914', *Business History*, Vol. 21 No. 1 (1979)

Rose, M. *The Gregs of Quarry Bank Mill: The Rise and Decline of a Family Firm, 1750–1914*, Cambridge University Press (1986)

Sekers, D. *A Lady of Cotton: Hannah Greg, Mistress of Quarry Bank Mill*, The History Press (2013)

Solar, P. 'The English cotton spinning industry, 1780–1840: as revealed in the columns of the *London Gazette*', paper given at the University of Warwick conference on Economic History, 2009.

Spartacus Education, Samuel Greg http://spartacus-educational.com/TEXgreg.htm

Ure, A. *The Philosophy of Manufactures*, Charles Knight (1835)

3.5 Isambard Kingdom Brunel: railways and ships, 1833–59

KEY QUESTIONS

- How far was Brunel's Great Western Railway an improvement on existing rail networks?
- How did Brunel use his design and engineering skills to solve engineering problems of the day?
- What was the impact of Brunel's work for passenger travel and goods transport?

INTRODUCTION

Brunel's obituary, in *The Engineer* on 23 September 1859, noted that, 'However brilliant may have been Mr Brunel's career, it was, in many respects, an unfortunate one; and we believe, no-one felt this truth more keenly than himself.' The legacy of Isambard Kingdom Brunel was complex, and illustrates both the attraction of his revolutionary approach to engineering and the difficulty and cost in realising its full potential. There was a fine line between innovation and novelty, with the latter bringing costs without advantage; a charge that was levelled at Brunel by his critics, such as the locomotive engineer George Stephenson and the shareholders in many of his projects.

From the start, Brunel, born in 1806, grew up in a house dedicated to engineering, with his father Marc Isambard Brunel being a well-known engineer. Marc Brunel was French by birth, but had fled the country after the French Revolution of 1789. In Britain, he had made his name, if not his fortune, with a machine that was able to cut rigging blocks for the navy, a task that had hitherto been done by hand, and subsequently he set up his own civil engineering practice.

Isambard Kingdom Brunel soon showed a talent for engineering, and under his father's direction was encouraged to make detailed drawings of buildings, which developed his powers of observation and assessment. He proved a good artist and draughtsman, and his skills would be invaluable in designing his ambitious engineering projects. When he was eight, Brunel began to learn Euclidian geometry, and developed a thorough understanding of mathematics and geometric construction. After a time at a boarding school in Hove, East Sussex, he was sent to France to finish his education, before being apprenticed to Louis Breguet, the leading French watchmaker of the time. There he developed his practical engineering skills on a much smaller scale than would become his stock in trade later in life; his works would be defined in terms of largest, fastest and longest. On his return to England in 1822, at the age of 16, he went to work for his father, who was involved in the construction of the first tunnel to be built under the Thames. The work was both dangerous and demanding as the project

1829 - Isambard Kingdom Brunel sends in four designs in for a bridge at Clifton, Bristol

1831 - Brunel's second design for suspension bridge accepted and work begins on the Clifton Suspension Bridge

1833 - Brunel appointed chief engineer to the Great Western Railway (GWR) Factory Act Government grant for education

1835 - Second GWR parliamentary bill receives royal assent

1825   1830   1835

1830 - Liverpool to Manchester Railway, the first purpose-built passenger railway, opens

1832 - Parliamentary Reform Act Riots in Bristol

1834 - First parliamentary bill for GWR rejected Tolpuddle Martyrs

1838 - GWR opens, linking London to the West Country SS *Great Western* makes first voyage across the Atlantic

encountered numerous problems created by the geological strata below the river. Despite Marc Brunel's innovative design for a tunnelling shield to protect the workings – variants of which are still in use today – flooding remained an ever-present danger. Such an incident occurred on 12 January 1828, when Brunel was inspecting the workings for his father. A wall of water rushed into the tunnel and he was lucky to survive, as he noted in his diary. He was pulled from the water by some workmen before he drowned. The experience did not put him off engineering, and within a short time he was back at work. However, he had come face to face with the human cost of 19th-century civil engineering, where workmen's lives were often cut short by poor standards of safety.

EXTEND YOUR KNOWLEDGE

The Thames Tunnel
The tunnel was finally completed in 1843, after many delays due to a shortage of funds and flooding. When it was opened, it was described as the eighth wonder of the world, being some 396 metres long at a depth of 23 metres below the river. It was only open for foot passengers, as there was not sufficient money to build the ramps necessary to transport goods by horse and cart. In 1865, it was bought by the East London Railway and opened for rail transport by steam train in 1869. It would not be until 1913 that the line was electrified and made part of London Underground, where it is the oldest tunnel on the oldest underground system in the world.

HOW FAR WAS BRUNEL'S GREAT WESTERN RAILWAY AN IMPROVEMENT ON EXISTING RAIL NETWORKS?

The opening of the Stockton and Darlington Railway in 1825 marked a new era in transport innovation. Iron rails and steam power were to provide an efficient and rapid system to move vast amounts of goods and numbers of people across the country. In the decades that followed, a massive network of individual railway projects would be joined up into a national network of interconnected lines.

The role of Brunel

In 1833 in Bristol, the leading merchants of the city decided to set up a committee to plan for the construction of a line from Bristol to London. This line would be the longest stretch of rail track constructed, at 118 miles. A number of the project's backers suggested that the committee organise a competition to find the best engineer for the job, though it was not decided who would be competent to judge it. Brunel, whose reputation had been established in Bristol by providing the winning design for a suspension bridge at Clifton, saw that this was an opportunity to make his fortune, but he rejected the idea of competition. Brunel wrote to the committee, 'You are holding out a premium to

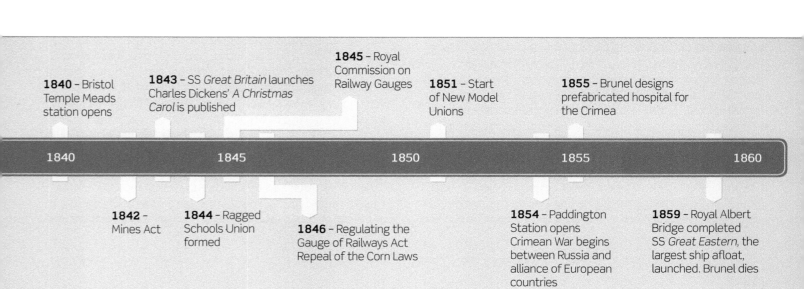

1840 – Bristol Temple Meads station opens

1843 – SS *Great Britain* launches Charles Dickens' *A Christmas Carol* is published

1845 – Royal Commission on Railway Gauges

1851 – Start of New Model Unions

1855 – Brunel designs prefabricated hospital for the Crimea

1840   1845   1850   1855   1860

1842 – Mines Act

1844 – Ragged Schools Union formed

1846 – Regulating the Gauge of Railways Act Repeal of the Corn Laws

1854 – Paddington Station opens Crimean War begins between Russia and alliance of European countries

1859 – Royal Albert Bridge completed SS *Great Eastern*, the largest ship afloat, launched. Brunel dies

the man who will make you the most flattering promises', which was a bold move for a man just into his thirties and with few commissions to his name. Brunel suggested to them that he would provide the best route for the line, not necessarily the cheapest. In support of his case, he lobbied leading members of the board such as Charles Saunders and William Sims. The tactic proved successful and he was appointed the engineer for the project on 7 March 1833 by a majority vote of the board of directors of the railway. The decision was all the more remarkable as Brunel had no previous experience of railway building. For historians such as L.T.C. Rolt and Steven Brindle, it is seen as a triumph put down to Brunel's sheer force of personality, and it also points to one of the more overlooked of Brunel's talents – that was as an effective lobbyist for his own cause.

SOURCE

1

From a letter by Brunel to Mr George Whatley, a solicitor to the committee formed to promote the railway between London and Bristol. The letter points to Brunel's force of personality and his method of lobbying for support.

Dear Sir

A survey is about to be made of the line of railway between Bristol and London – I hope to be employed in making it. The committee meets to decide the question on Wednesday next. Of four gentlemen who comprise the sub-committee there are two – both of the Society of Friends – to whom I am only known by reputation and not personally. It is possible that Mr Stourge, who took an active part in our Gloucester & Birmingham Railway, may be acquainted with them and if Mr Stourge formed a favourable opinion of my activity on that occasion his writing to those gentlemen may be of great use to me. Their names are Mr J. Harford of Harford & Davies wine merchants, and Mr Tothill. The latter to be of real use ... I have the less hesitation in asking as I think your Committee owes me some consideration – in asking you to exert yourself for me I must trust to your kindness...

The Great Western Act

To build a railway required a **Private Act of Parliament**, which in the case of the Great Western Railway (GWR) met with much opposition. After the second reading of the bill, it entered the committee stage, where for a record 57 days it was subject to a barrage of criticism. The stagecoach operators and the canal companies made their opposition felt, as did landowners and farmers close to London, the latter fearing that the new railway would bring in cheaper produce to the capital. Brunel had to defend his chosen route before the scrutiny of the parliamentary committee, and a number of engineers were called by the line's opponents to give their opinion on the suggested route and offer alternative proposals. Where the line came into London, there was particular criticism from landowners worried about the railway's impact on their properties. Yet Brunel was able to answer this opposition and show the advantages of his plan for the GWR. He even had support from George Stephenson, later a critic of his broad gauge, who on giving evidence commented, 'I can imagine [he said] a better line, but I do not know of one so

good.' Much was made of Brunel's insistence that the line be as straight as possible so as to increase speed, and where possible no more than a 1 in 1,000 incline. This would necessitate additional **viaducts** and bridges to be constructed, as well as building the longest tunnel then attempted, at Box, just outside Bath, all of which would significantly increase costs. The bill, however, was defeated at the committee stage, in the House of Lords. Despite this setback, Brunel and the Great Western Company raised new capital through a share issue and brought the bill back to parliament the following year. A better-organised lobbying campaign this time proved successful in the face of continued opposition to the plan, and it finally received the royal assent in 1836.

KEY TERMS

Private Act of Parliament
An Act sponsored by an individual or group where the interests are of that individual or group. A Private Act of Parliament for the building of a railway or canal is necessary to put in place legislation enabling the compulsory purchase of land and the bridging of rivers. The Act would also regulate what the petitioners were entitled to do and set limits on when they should do them.

Viaduct
An elevated section of railway track used to cross low ground to keep the line level and not increase gradients. These were an expensive necessity where a line followed a more direct route rather than following the contours of the landscape.

Broad-gauge railway

Until the construction of Brunel's Great Western Railway, rails had been set at a distance of 1.435 metres apart. George Stephenson, a locomotive engineer, had chosen this gauge for the Stockton and Darlington Railway and this had become the standard for subsequent lines. For Brunel, ever the innovator, this appeared absurd, as a wider distance between rails would mean carriages could be built with larger wheels at the side, offering a lower centre of gravity, which had the potential to provide greater stability and higher speeds. Wider carriages would also mean more passengers, with travellers sitting four abreast rather than three, as encountered on the standard or, as it was often referred to, the narrow gauge. His adoption of a 2.14 metre gauge, which became known as broad gauge, offered the potential for greater efficiency and a smoother ride, yet it also posed issues of increased costs due to the width of the line. Such engineering innovation and its potential advantages in terms of speed, comfort and economy were not without their technical challenges, as well as additional costs. For Brunel, the challenge was to not only solve the engineering problem but to make the GWR into a model for future railway expansion.

Though Brunel had commenced construction of the railway, one of the earliest problems encountered was that the locomotives he had designed lacked power and were mechanically unreliable. Far from providing a fast service, the railway was also noted in the popular press for the discomfort experienced by its passengers on the sections of the line that had been opened and were running a regular service. Critics of the scheme were quick to pick up on these failings and dismiss the practicality of the broad gauge. One of the most notable was Professor Dionysius Lardner. Lardner was an academic and promoter of popular science through publications and lectures. In his opinion, the greater wind resistance of the broad-gauge locomotives meant that they had to carry more fuel to power them, the additional weight of which added to the problems of power and speed; these arguments he presented to the public though articles in the press. Lardner's assertions based on the initial difficulties of Brunel's engines would be proved false when Daniel Gooch, an apprentice engineer with experience of locomotive design, was taken on by the Great Western Railway.

Daniel Gooch

Daniel Gooch was a locomotive engineer who had worked for George Stephenson. He was persuaded to join the GWR in 1837 to work on development of engines and rolling stock (railway carriages and goods wagons). Gooch was more conservative in his approach to the construction of his engines than Brunel, starting with an analysis of what worked then moving to see how it could be improved. He abandoned some of the novel innovations attempted by Brunel in the armament of boilers and tenders for carrying coal and went back to basics. He persuaded Brunel to purchase two locomotives from George Stephenson, standard-gauge engines called *North Star* and *Dog Star*, which were then converted to run on broad gauge. Rather than using Brunel's method of starting with nothing then constructing what you want based on a vision of the end product, Gooch chose a more empirical approach, building on experience and refining the locomotives available into something more suited for the task intended. For Gooch, the focus was on developing more efficient boilers and arrangements of axles and tenders, and his work resulted in the Firefly class of locomotives. By the mid-1840s, speeds of 60 mph had been achieved by Great Western with their Firefly engines, far in excess of their standard-gauge rivals. The importance of speed for the GWR was key to the marketing of the Bristol–London project. Not only were such speeds possible, they were regularly achieved. The straightness of the line and the power of the locomotives permitted engines to travel faster and not have to brake constantly to deal with bends in the track or cope with steep inclines.

Gooch was to go on and develop many classes of engine at the Swindon railway works, set up by the Great Western Railway in 1841.

SOURCE
2

From Daniel Gooch's evidence to the Parliamentary Gauge Commission in 1846. The evidence presented clearly shows the superiority of the broad-gauge locomotives. What is also of note is the amount of rolling stock that the engines could pull, which was greater than narrow or standard engines could pull.

Question	Will you state what the speed of the various descriptions of passenger trains is, including and excluding time lost in stopping and specifying the load in each case?
D. Gooch	On the Great Western the average trains, excluding the third class and the quick, are timed to 26 ½ miles an hour, including stoppages. Of course they are frequently running at 50 miles an hour; 45 is probably their average running speed; but that much depends upon the dimensions: if they are long they are obliged to run more quickly. We can, with 120 tons, do 45 miles an hour.
Question	What is your average weight of passengers per train drawn by one engine, or average number?
D. Gooch	I do not know exactly. We have brought in as many as 16 or 17 carriages, besides private carriages, well-filled by passengers.
Question	With one engine?
D. Gooch	With one engine. We have brought in passenger trains frequently with 120 and 130 tons of weight with one engine. We did that frequently during the summer months. I have an account of some actuals trains that were worked. One of our engines brought in 122 tons, a passenger train, and the speed upon that was 45 miles an hour, the highest speed attained. The way in which we got at the speed was this: I was making experiments with the consumption of water and coke.
Question	Was that at Ascot Races?
D. Gooch	No, it was an ordinary train. I ascertained the weight for the purpose of making experiments.

EXTEND YOUR KNOWLEDGE

Daniel Gooch (1816–89)

Historians such as L.T.C. Rolt and R. Angus Buchanan have argued that without the aid of Daniel Gooch, the whole Great Western broad-gauge project would have failed. His role was key not only in finding engineering solutions to the problems of creating broad-gauge locomotives, but also in protecting Brunel's reputation and legacy. Gooch was elected Conservative MP for Cricklade in 1865, and was persuaded to join the board of the Great Western Railway in the same year, becoming its chairman. He saved the railway from near bankruptcy as the cost of transferring goods between different gauges had affected the economic viability of the company. He remained a staunch supporter of Brunel's broad gauge and it was only in 1892, after his death, that all lines were converted to the 1.435 metres standard gauge. He was also responsible for using Brunel's ship the SS *Great Eastern* to lay the first transatlantic telegraph cable. He was granted a baronetcy in 1866 in recognition of this work.

In 1846, the Great Western produced its Iron Duke class of locomotives, which were to set the benchmark for all others in service, with an estimated top speed of 80 mph and an average between 53 and 59 mph. Though the GWR continued to expand with the building of the Oxford, Worcester and Wolverhampton Railway, and the acquisition of smaller lines, increasing traffic became a problem with the break of gauge. Despite these difficulties, Gooch, who became chairman of the company in 1865, continued to defend the advantages broad gauge until his death in 1889. By the end of the 19th century, standard-gauge locomotive design had improved and could challenge the best of the broad-gauge machines, while the costs of transferring goods between different widths of track increased as the volume of trade expanded. In 1892, the GWR finally abandoned broad gauge. Broad-gauge railway continued to exist, however, in Ireland, Russia and India, though in all these cases the distance between the rails was never as great as Brunel's Great Western.

SOURCE

3 Iron Duke class of locomotives first developed in 1848. These engines continued in service, though modified as the Rover class, until 1892.

ACTIVITY
KNOWLEDGE CHECK

Designing and building the Great Western Railway

1 What reasons are given for Brunel's choice of route and width of track? Make a list.

2 What problems did the line face in terms of opposition and technical difficulty?

3 What advantages was the GWR able to offer in the end? Make a list.

4 Look at your notes and write a short paragraph in support of the statement that the Great Western Railway represented a revolution in rail transport.

Brunel and his critics

The construction of the Great Western Railway did not proceed smoothly for Brunel. Though it was not uncommon for such large civil engineering undertakings to overrun in time and cost, the perceived novelty of his design linked to increasing need for investment led to questions being raised by shareholders. His methods were questioned by many of the backers of the project and he became reliant on the then-chairman of the board, Charles Russell, to defend his reputation. Still, Brunel was called before the board on a number of occasions to defend his management of the construction of the line.

SOURCE 4

From Brunel's report to the directors of the Great Western Railway in August 1838. By this date, Brunel was losing support among the directors and shareholders in the company as questions were raised over rising costs and the poor performance of the locomotive rolling stock. Here Brunel mounts his customary robust defence of his abilities and the need to maintain support for the project.

Gentlemen,—As the endeavour to obtain the opinions and reports of Mr. Walker, Mr. Stephenson, and Mr. Wood, prior to the next half-yearly meeting, has not been successful, I am anxious to record more fully than I have previously done, and to combine them into one report, my own views and opinions upon the success of the several plans which have been adopted at my recommendation in the formation and in the working of our line; and in justice to myself and to these plans, and indeed to enable others to arrive at any just conclusion as to the result which has been attained, or as to the probable ultimate success or advantages of the system, it is necessary that I should enter very fully, I fear even tediously, into a recapitulation of the circumstances, peculiar to this railway, which led to the consideration and the adoption of these plans, which some call innovations and wide deviations from the results of past experience, but the majority of which I will undertake to show are merely adaptations of those plans to our particular circumstances.

It will be necessary also that I should refer to all the numerous difficulties which we have had to encounter, which have necessarily prevented the perfect working of these plans in the first instance, but which have been overcome, or which are gradually and successively diminishing; and, finally, I am prepared to show that, notwithstanding the novelty of the circumstances, and the difficulties and delays which at the outset invariably attend any alteration, however necessary, or however desirable, from the accustomed mode of proceeding, and notwithstanding the violent prejudices excited against us, and the increased difficulties caused by these prejudices, the result is still such as to justify the attempt which has been made, and to show that in the main features, if not in all the details, the system hitherto followed is good, and ought to be pursued.

In the end, the main line went well over budget, costing around £6 million rather than the £2.5 million first proposed. The GWR, however, paid a dividend of three percent in 1841 and continued to pay a dividend over the next decade of between three and eight percent. Though the cost per mile was higher than that of standard-gauge railways, the difference was not that great. The historian Steven Brindle suggests that it cost £56,300 a mile to build the GWR, while the equivalent for the London and Birmingham standard-gauge railway was £53,100 a mile. While the engineering of the GWR might have been without compare, and its achievements in terms of speed and comfort set the standard for other operators, the long-term economics of the business were not always as soundly based as the board and Brunel might have hoped.

The reasons for the 'battle of the gauges'

Broad gauge failed to win many supporters among the established railway companies. Early railways such as the Stockton and Darlington, and Liverpool and Manchester Railway companies, which had been engineered by Brunel's rival George Stephenson, had set the standard with narrow-gauge track. They were followed by other railways, such as the Leicester and Swannington Railway in 1832, designed by George Stephenson's son Robert, and the Eastern Counties Railway Company in 1837, which ran between London and Ipswich. The matter of the cost of conversion tended to dissuade others from experimentation as widening track might entail new construction of bridges and tunnels to accommodate the larger locomotives and rolling stock. The historian L.T.C. Rolt points out that by 1845, there were only 274 miles of broad-gauge track, while there were some 1,901 miles of Stephenson's narrow-gauge standard track. Brunel's design had numerous critics, both from the engineering community, such as George Stephenson, and among investors. The anonymously published pamphlet, 'Railway eccentrics: Inconsistencies of men of genius exemplified in the practice and precepts of Isambard Kingdom Brunel', in 1846 was one such attack on the engineer's competence and the ability of his schemes to return a profit due to cost overruns because of what was perceived to be Brunel's over-ambitious designs.

Although the Great Western engines might have been more efficient in terms of fuel consumption, speed and comfort for the passenger (after Gooch's redesign of the locomotives), at the point standard-gauge and broad-gauge lines joined difficulties arose. In 1844, when the GWR became involved in the Bristol to Gloucester railway, the two gauges met for the first time. The break of gauge at Gloucester meant that passengers had to suffer the inconvenience of carrying their luggage across

---

A Level Exam-Style Question Section A

Study Source 4 before you answer this question.

Assess the value of the source for revealing the difficulties Brunel faced in the building of the Great Western Railway and how far it might be seen as an insight into the shortcomings of Brunel's innovative design.

Explain your answer, using the source, the information about its origin and your own knowledge about the historical context. (20 marks)

Tip

Remember that all major civil engineering projects tend to face delays and challenges that were not always foreseen. The question is to what extent these are the sort of issues that any engineer would have faced building a railway line or do they point to underlying problems with Brunel's plan? Certainly, his critics would point to the latter, while his many supporters would suggest that here was a man rising to meet the challenge of what was, at the time, the largest railway construction in the country.

the platform from one train to another in order to complete their journey. The problem was more serious for freight that had to be loaded from one gauge of wagons to another, which took much effort and increased costs.

In 1845, the question of the width of track became of national importance with the establishment of a royal commission by parliament, which would take evidence from all interested parties and make recommendations regarding the different gauges of track. George Stephenson and most of the railway companies were critical of the broad gauge and considered the narrow gauge more than adequate for their needs. In response, Brunel felt that it necessary to challenge this opposition to innovation in the form of a practical demonstration, a tactic that he would use to great effect on a number of other occasions, such as the steamship race across the Atlantic between his SS *Great Western* and the SS *Sirius*.

Brunel's demonstration proposal was to run a race between two locomotives over a set distance to demonstrate the advantages of the broad gauge. As it proved impossible to run on the same stretch of track, it was decided to run separate speed trials. The broad gauge train would travel from the terminus at Paddington to Didcot, a distance of 53 miles and the narrow-gauge locomotive would travel from Darlington to York, which was 44 miles. Gooch selected the engine *Ixion* to demonstrate the advantages of the GWR. To champion the cause of the narrow gauge, two locomotives were picked, 'Engine A' and the *Stephenson*. In the trial, the *Ixion* averaged between 50 and 60 mph, pulling loads of 80, 70 and 60 tons. Engine A managed a maximum of 53 mph when pulling only 50 tons between Darlington and York. An attempt to pull 80 tons had to be abandoned due to bad weather. The *Stephenson* had even less luck, running off the rails and overturning after just 22 miles.

The royal commission of 1845 and the Gauge Act 1846

With the demonstration proving that the broad gauge was technically far superior to the narrow gauge, Brunel felt that the report would be favourable. It was with considerable dismay then that when the commission published its findings, they were far from sympathetic to the broad gauge. While in the body of the report it was generally acknowledged that the broad gauge offered certain mechanical advantages over the narrow gauge, the commission felt that this did not overcome notable disadvantages of having two gauges of rail.

SOURCE

From the report of the royal commission in 1846. The recommendations of the commission were passed into law the same year and restricted the building of any new broad-gauge track. While the report accepted that Brunel had constructed a railway that was technically far in advance of its competitors, the existence of two different gauges undermined the economic case for it.

Such appear to the Commissioners to be the advantages which the broad gauge at present offers; and although they cannot consider them sufficient to compensate the evils attendant on two gauges, if it were now possible to obtain uniformity of gauge, yet, as two gauges are established...

[T]he Great Western Railway was fairly opened: and achieved in theatrical phrase, a great success. The carriages – that is to say, the -first-class carriages – were luxuriously roomy and airy. The breadth of gauge admitted the construction of a conveyance of her Majesty truly royal; the road was smooth and the pace swift...

So long as the two systems remained apart, and the public had neither the means of comparing the effects of the two gauges upon fares, nor of enduring inconvenience from their contact, all was well. While the whole innovation was a novelty...

It was soon found that merchandize did not flow so smoothly and continuously over this route as over the Grand Junction, the London and Birmingham, the Midlands and other lines where no interruption of gauge occurred. Passengers walked across the platform with all their small baggage, in order to change from broad to narrow, from four abreast carriages to three abreast carriages, and vice versa. This was unpleasant in the night-time, and in cold weather, and highly inconvenient to mothers with families, to the lame and the blind.

After a lengthened investigation, which commenced in August 1845 and an examination of witnesses... in January 1846 they made a Report which concluded with the following results and recommendations: first that the gauge of four feet eight and a half inches be declared by legislation to be the gauge to be used in all public Railways now under construction or hereafter to be considered in Great Britain...

The recommendations were that the existing broad-gauge railways should remain. Broad-gauge schemes that had been given parliamentary approval but were not in operation, such as the Birmingham and Oxford Junction Railway, would be required to build mixed gauges (in these cases, an extra rail was added so narrow-gauge rolling stock could run on the broad-gauge system). All new railways in England would be required to be the standard gauge of 1.42 metres. Though following the report there was much discussion of its findings, with Brunel mounting a strong defence of the broad gauge, in 1846 the Regulating the Gauge of Railways Act was passed. The legislation followed the recommendations of the royal commission, preventing the building of any further broad-gauge railways in England.

Why Stephenson's narrow gauge became the standard

The issues that troubled the commission most were the problems posed by the break of gauge, particularly the effect this had on costs, a matter that would prove to be a particular drawback for the Great Western in its later years. For the GWR, the success it had in attracting freight onto its track had to be balanced with the strain it placed on the railway when goods had to be reloaded where there was a break in gauge. Though the inconvenience of the travelling public was emphasised in the report, it was the fear expressed by manufacturers regarding delays and additional expenditure in transporting goods that were perhaps the most persuasive. Given the fact that there was only 274 miles of broad gauge track in operation by 1845, whereas 1,901 miles of narrow-gauge railway had already been constructed, in essence the decision was down to cost and capital already invested. This has led to some historians, such as Rolt, to speculate that if the GWR had been built ten years earlier, broad gauge might have become preferred. However, the height of the railway building bubble was 1846, with 272 railway bills brought before parliament that year, representing a proposed 9,500 miles of new track. Apart from the proposals for the extension of the GWR to Oxford and lines in South Wales, the vast majority were for the standard gauge.

Figure 5.1 The state of the completed railway network in 1845. As can be seen, broad-gauge railways only made up a small percentage of the total amount of track completed. From *The Transport Revolution from 1770* by Philip Bagwell (1974).

115

A Level Exam-Style Question Section B

How accurate is it to say that connectivity – in terms of preventing breaks in gauge – was more important than construction cost and technical superiority in influencing the royal commission's decision to adopt Stephenson's narrow gauge? (20 marks)

Tip

Think about the reasons given by the commission and the economic implications of the change. If they accepted that Brunel's system was, in engineering terms, superior to that of Stephenson's, why did they not just get the existing lines to upgrade to broad gauge?

ACTIVITY
KNOWLEDGE CHECK

The battle of the gauges

1 Write down the three reasons why having two different gauges of track would have been such a problem as the railway system expanded.

2 Now make a list of the advantages that the broad gauge had over the narrow gauge.

3 With a partner consider the statement, 'Brunel placed more emphasis on speed and comfort than on building a national railway network.'

4 To what extent was the whole broad-gauge enterprise reliant on the practical skills of Daniel Gooch rather than the vision of Brunel?

HOW DID BRUNEL USE HIS DESIGN AND ENGINEERING SKILLS TO SOLVE ENGINEERING PROBLEMS OF THE DAY?

Brunel undertook his first major construction project when he entered a competition to build a bridge across the gorge at Clifton in Bristol in 1829. It is remarkable that at so early an age, being just 23 years old, he demonstrated his confidence in his own skills by proposing the construction of a suspension bridge, which would have been the longest single span ever attempted at that time. The money for the project was provided in part through a bequest by a Bristol merchant, William Vick. However, the more substantial part of the cost had to be raised by public subscription. In many ways, the Clifton project set a pattern for Brunel's later work – it was ambitious and pushed the boundaries of what was possible, there was difficulty in raising funds for the project and there were numerous cost overruns. Yet it also showed Brunel's abilities as a visionary in terms of design, and his strength of personality to drive such works forward despite any difficulties encountered, which is why his work has become an icon of the achievements of mid-19th-century civil engineering.

EXTEND YOUR KNOWLEDGE

The Clifton Bridge competition
It had been decided to hold a competition to seek designs for a suspension bridge, with a first prize of 100 guineas. Brunel saw this as an opportunity to make his mark as an engineer and submitted four possible designs. The eminent engineer Thomas Telford (1757–1834) had been appointed to judge the entries and select the most promising. To the surprise of all concerned, Telford rejected all the designs claiming (without providing any evidence) that it was impossible to build a single span of a suspension bridge over 183 metres. Though he considered Brunel's design 'very pretty and ingenious, [it] would most certainly tumble down in a high wind' as its span exceeded what he believed to be the maximum possible. On rejecting all the other designs, Telford then made his own proposal for a bridge supported by two enormous towers that would run from the foot of the Avon gorge to the top of Clifton downs, a height of 101 metres.

The cost and impracticality of Telford's design resulted in a rerun of the competition in 1830, to which Brunel submitted a modified proposal, shortening the span of his bridge to 214 metres. The committee eventually accepted this as the winning entry and appointed him the engineer to the project.

Clifton Suspension Bridge
The Clifton Suspension Bridge was not finished in Brunel's lifetime. It proved difficult to raise finance for the bridge, particularly in the aftermath of the Bristol riots in 1831. It was not until 1836 that work began on building the two large abutments on either side of the gorge. These masonry supports and their accompanying towers were eventually finished at a cost of some £14,000. By 1843, costs had exceeded the available capital and a further £30,000 was needed. The project had also run out of time, as set out in the Act of Parliament governing the construction of the bridge, and Brunel was told to close the site and dispose of unused materials. The bridge was to be the first of Brunel's many disappointments, in this case his great engineering ability and vision outstripping the funds available to realise his ambition. It was not until 1860, a year after Brunel's death, that members of the Institute of Civil Engineers came together to complete the work as a tribute to the great man, under the direction of John Hawkshaw and William Barlow. The bridge was eventually opened on 8 December 1864.

Although Brunel was not there to see his work completed, he did play a part. The chains to support the span of the bridge came from his Hungerford Suspension Bridge across the Thames, which was dismantled to make way for the present Charing Cross railway bridge.

Problem-solving during the GWR line construction

The final stretch of the Great Western Railway, between Chippenham and Bath, required the construction of a tunnel some 2,950 metres in length. When finished in 1841 it was the longest railway tunnel of its day in England and an engineering marvel, exceeding the record held by the Kilsby Tunnel, which was 2,224 metres long. From the start, there had been concern expressed regarding what some felt to be a 'most dangerous and impracticable tunnel', as it was described by supporters of a rival Basingstoke to Bath line. Brunel's plan for the GWR was to construct the straightest and flattest route to maximise speed and improve comfort for the passenger, which necessitated the building of additional bridges and tunnels. It was proposed that any gradient would be no more than 1 in 1,000 yards, though at Box the line would be forced to take on a 1 in 100 incline. This particular project took innovative engineering ability, additional capital and a considerable cost in human life, with the death of at least 100 workmen in the construction of the tunnel.

Building the Box Tunnel

The Box Tunnel was part of the last, and probably the most difficult, stage of the construction of the Great Western Railway. Work began on this section as early as 1836 with the sinking of six permanent and two temporary **shafts** to provide ventilation for the construction project that were 8.53 metres in diameter, with the longest being 91.44 metres deep. Flooding proved to be a problem and, in November 1837, a second 50-horsepower pump had to be installed. Work dropped behind schedule, and in 1840 Brunel decided to make more resources available to speed up completion. From that point on, 4,000 men and 300 horses were employed around the clock on the project. Blasting took place while workmen were still in the tunnel so as to save time, a practice that proved to be extremely hazardous and was in part responsible for the 100 accidental deaths that occurred in the building of the tunnel.

To cut the time needed for completion, it had been decided to dig from both ends of the tunnel at the same time. George Burge was to be the contractor overseeing the construction from the western (Bath) end of the tunnel and two local men, Brewer and Lewis, were to manage the project from the eastern end of the tunnel, at Box. There had been anxiety among the directors of the GWR about this approach. It was with some relief, therefore, that when both ends met in 1841, they were less than two inches out of alignment, which was put down to Brunel's skill as an engineer.

SOURCE

From a letter by Brunel to Lewis and Brewer in 1838 regarding the difficulties encountered in the construction of the Box Tunnel and his loss of patience with his contractors. The management of contractors was always an issue with Brunel and he often took a very hard line with those he considered were not ready to meet their full commitments.

Gentlemen

I have so repeatedly and earnestly expressed my opinion of the necessity under the present circumstances and particularly after the great delay which has taken place… of getting rid of the water in Shaft No 7 that I had expected great exertions would have been used to attain this object. I need not say how much I am disappointed and surprised at your neglect to attend to this – I am compelled to believe that you have either deceived me as your intention of prosecution this necessary work of that delay arises from the greatest apathy and negligence and a total disregard of my orders and your own real interest. It is now 2 months since the water was pumped out of the shaft and you promised that immediate steps should be taken to proceed as rapidly as possible with the sinking… Since then, although every hour is of the greatest importance, nothing has been done or so little that it is not worth mentioning…When I visited the works on Tuesday morning the progress made and indeed the whole mode of proceeding appeared to me ridiculous… I can no longer delay taking most decisive measures. Unless the whole shaft is sunk 12 feet or at the rate of 4 feet per day between the present time and Saturday night, I shall on Monday morning proceed with that part of the work at your expense and I have directed that men may be ready for that purpose and I shall also feel it my duty to request the Directors to levy the penalties due upon this contract and to continue to do so until the work is placed in a satisfactory state. I regret exceedingly that such a course should be necessary, but the total neglect shown to my repeated cautions and the utter want of energy displayed leave no alternative.

> **A Level Exam-Style Question Section A**
>
> *Study Source 6 before you answer this question.*
>
> Assess the value of the source for revealing the difficulties Brunel had in constructing the Box Tunnel and what it says about the complexities of managing a project where work has been subcontracted to a number of firms.
>
> Explain your answer using the information given about its origin and your own knowledge about the historical context. (20 marks)
>
> **Tip**
> *Although Brunel was the consulting engineer on the Great Western Railway, he had to rely on subcontractors who were given targets to meet and then left to get on with it. Was Brunel too heavy-handed in the way he acted or did he need to assert his authority? What were the problems he faced? Was it just a question of looking at progress charts or was it a case of constantly dealing with crises as the work progressed?*

Controversy over design

The east end of the tunnel managed by Brewer and Lewis had been cut through clay and blue marl, so this section of the tunnel had to be lined with bricks for stability. In all, some 30 million were used in completing the structure, being supplied from the local Hunt brickyards. At the west end, Burge had to drive the tunnel through half a mile of solid Bath stone. Brunel considered the geological strata strong enough not to require lining. In this, he was opposed by the eminent geologist Dr William Buckland, who asserted that the vibration of the trains would cause a collapse. Brunel replied that, '[Though, I] might be ignorant as I may probably be myself of the science of geology… I ought now to possess a more thorough and practical knowledge of this particular rock.' Concern continued and the directors asked for the tunnel to be illuminated to reassure the public. This was rejected and a survey by the **Board of Trade Inspector** General for Railways found there to be no safety fears about the tunnel. Yet this did not prevent the more nervous travellers for a time breaking their journey at Corsham or Box and taking the stagecoach into Bath.

The completion of the line between London and Bristol was not the final act of the GWR, as in 1844 an extension of the broad-gauge line to Exeter was completed by the Bristol and Exeter Railway company. The line was engineered by Brunel in two sections: from Bristol to Taunton the line ran straight and level, in the manner of the Great Western; however, between Taunton and Exeter it was forced to take on greater gradients as it went into Devon. At this time, Brunel claimed a conflict of interest arose between his work for the Great Western and the Bristol and Exeter Railway, resigning as chief engineer on the project to extend the line. It is not immediately clear what he considered this conflict of interests to be, but the decision might be related to tensions with board members of the Great Western.

Innovative design of bridges and stations

The Maidenhead Bridge and the Wharncliffe Viaduct at Hanwell

One of the first bridges to be built on the Great Western Railway was at Maidenhead, where it crossed over the Thames. The river at this point was some 88.39 metres wide so Brunel had originally planned a three-arch bridge with supports going down to the chalk **bedrock**. When it was found that the chalk was too soft for the foundations, Brunel decided to build on the hard gravel layer above the chalk. He also decided to reduce the number of arches to two, so as not to impede the flow of the river and so prevent flooding.

The new design presented a number of challenges for the engineer. It would require arches some 39 metres wide, a record for the time. Brunel proposed to flatten his arches, leaving just a rise of 7 metres, preventing the need for the proposed bridge to be raised in height. This would mean that there would not have to be an incline as the rail line crossed the Thames. The arches were constructed of concrete with brick facing, and their shape added to the strength of the structure, reducing the amount of masonry support needed and adding to the graceful design of the bridge. The novelty of the design caused the contractor for the project, Thomas Chadwick, to fear that it would collapse once the wooden supports were removed. In the end, Brunel convinced him by the use of geometry in a set of diagrams that the bridge would stand.

At Hanwell, the line had to cross low-lying ground, and to keep it level it was necessary to construct what became known as the Wharncliffe Viaduct. The finished structure was 270 metres in length with eight semi-elliptical arches supported on revolutionary hollow piers. The arches were also an innovative design, with the use of cast-iron girders to provide support for the arched spans between the piers. However, the Wharncliffe Viaduct at Hanwell experienced problems with cracks appearing in the cast-iron girders after a fire in 1847 damaged the original cast-iron supports. This led Brunel to experiment with different designs of girder so as to find a more effective replacement.

SOURCE

From a letter by Brunel to the board of the Great Western Railway on 18 April 1849. He explains to the directors his reasons for changing the design of the viaduct and why he felt this was worth the extra expense involved. For some, the experimentation represented innovation and improvement; for others, it was seen as a novelty that did nothing but increase costs.

Cast-iron girder bridges are always giving trouble, from such cases as the Chester Bridge, and our Great Western road bridge [viaduct] at Hanwell, which, since 1838, has always been under repair, and has cost its first cost three times over, down to petty little ones, which, either in frosty weather or from other causes, are frequently failing. I never use cast iron if I can help it; but, in some cases it is necessary, and to meet these I have had girders cast of a particular mixture of iron carefully attended to, and I have taught them at the Bridgewater foundry to cast them with the flange downwards instead of sideways. By these means, and having somebody always there, I ensure better castings, and have much lighter girders than I should otherwise be obliged to have.

Dissatisfaction with cast iron led Brunel to experiment with wrought iron in the 1840s. Wrought iron was more expensive than cast iron as it needed to be smelted then rolled into girders. However, wrought-iron construction meant that larger girders were able to be manufactured, and with the addition of flanges they could be made stronger than cast iron. Brunel also developed a range of designs for fabricated girders that added strength to the design. Wrought iron was to be used in a number of his bridge-building projects, such as the Chepstow railway bridge in South Wales and the Royal Albert Bridge at Saltash in Cornwall. The latter of these was perhaps one of his greatest civil engineering triumphs and the last one he was to see completed.

The Royal Albert Bridge

A crossing over the Tamar, at Saltash, was first considered in 1844 as part of the extension of the Cornwall Railway. The original proposal was for a ferry, but Brunel rejected this idea in favour of a 340 metre wooden viaduct across the river using six spans of approximately 32 metres each to support a double track. In 1847, test bore holes were made to see how deep supports would have to be driven into the ground to secure the bridge on bedrock. Due to objections from the Admiralty, who wanted a wider passage for shipping, the plan had to be modified. Brunel rose to the challenge. However, it was not until 1852 that a fully revised plan was submitted, which was approved by the Admiralty in 1853.

Brunel then abandoned the idea of a wooden viaduct, as it would be far too difficult to construct one that gave sufficient width of span and height to permit the passage of large ships up the river. In its place was to be a wrought-iron bridge. The plan had been for double track, but a single-track design was eventually proposed as a way to save money, as the cost of the project had increased markedly. The bridge would consist of two 138 metre spans fastened to a central pillar; the railway would be carried some 30.5 metres above the highest spring tides so as to permit free passage on the river. The central support was to be a great cylinder constructed on the riverbank and then floated on pontoons on a rising tide before being sunk into position. Some delay was caused in cutting through a bed of oyster shells that lay beneath the silt. Workmen had to go through an airlock into a pressurised section that prevented the water rushing in as they dug. Though not a new idea, it was engineered by Brunel, who entered the airlock himself to monitor the workings. By February 1855 the great cylinder rested on bedrock and work could begin on the construction of the bridge. Two years later the two spans were floated out to the construction site, pulled by HMS *Ajax* and then slowly raised by **hydraulic lifts** as the end towers were built. These lifts were constructed out of wrought-iron tubes designed to provide extra strength and stability. The bridge was finally opened by Prince Albert in May 1859, four months before Brunel's death. As a monument to his reputation, his name and initials were affixed to one of the great towers that hold up either end of the bridge.

KEY TERM

Hydraulic lift
A lift that is powered by a pump that compresses liquid so as to raise or lower an object. Instead of using a pulley and rope, a telescoped ram is placed under the lift and liquid is forced into it to raise the platform. Such a method permits the raising of large, heavy objects with less effort than trying to winch them using winding gear. The only drawback is that such systems are only effective over a relatively limited distance as it becomes difficult and expensive to build very long hydraulic rams.

The construction of the Royal Albert Bridge at Saltash in 1857, showing the second span soon after it was floated onto the piers and had been jacked up the first 12 feet (3.7 m) towards its final position. The photograph clearly shows the scale of the task faced by Brunel in raising the bridge as well as the huge piles that had to be built to hold the two massive iron spans.

ACTIVITY
KNOWLEDGE CHECK

Application and theory

1 In the case of the Box Tunnel and the Wharncliffe Viaduct at Hanwell, how did Brunel learn about the materials he was working with?

2 What would you say were the main challenges faced in building the Box Tunnel? Draw a spider diagram of the issues that you have identified, then consider how they might be related.

3 How might you respond to the statement, 'The Great Western Railway was the product of ambition over necessity'?

The great stations of Temple Meads and Paddington

KEY TERM

Hammer beam
A peculiarly English form of roof truss design dating from the Middle Ages. Where buildings were so wide that it became difficult to support the roof timbers with a single cross-beam, shorter beams were used then fixed to the roof beams, creating the stepped effect known as a hammer beam.

Brunel described the Great Western Railway as 'the finest work in England'. It was not only to be marked by innovative engineering but also in architectural opulence. Temple Meads station in Bristol and Paddington station in London stood at either end of the original Great Western line and represented the grandeur of Brunel's vision. The Bristol terminus was opened in 1840 and resembled a Tudor mansion with turrets and 16th century-style windows. The design was a way of linking the modernity of steam to the historic city of Bristol. Inside, large iron columns, a product of the industrial age, supported massive **hammer beam** roof supports, originally a medieval design, for a roof truss that Brunel decided to use for this project. The building consciously linked the traditional with the modern, with the stone clad exterior and medieval-inspired hammer beams resting on cast-iron pillars supporting a great glass canopy. The station was to be a statement emphasising the triumph of the railway. As the line was above the level of the surrounding ground, as it entered the city on a viaduct across what had been low-lying marsh land, Brunel introduced a hydraulic lift at the station to raise and lower wagons from ground level up to the height of the line. While Temple Meads was completed in the early 1840s, the London terminus of the Great Western at Paddington was not started until 1849 and not finished until 1854.

Before the building at Paddington, the Great Western had a temporary station on the site, but the company wanted a grand building in order to make an unequivocal statement about the ambition of the railway and emphasise its greatness. The station at Paddington was even more ambitious than Temple Meads, though its exterior would not be as impressive – only the entrance could be seen from the road, as the level of the track was below that of the surrounding buildings. The area for the station was large, some 213 metres long by 73 metres wide. Into this space Brunel introduced two rows of iron columns supporting a gigantic arched roof modelled on Joseph Paxton's design for the Crystal Palace of the 1851 Great Exhibition. The influence of the Crystal Palace was important, as in many ways it was the first modernist building. Its form and function were closely linked and, though it was impressive in terms of scale and design, it was the industrialisation of its prefabrication that was in many ways most impressive. The construction was innovative in its use of glass and iron to create a temple of light. If Temple Meads had been a Tudor mansion of the industrial age, Paddington was a cathedral of glass dedicated to the railway traveller. There was much less ornament than at Bristol, giving the station a much more modern look.

SOURCE 9

The newly developed Paddington Station in London, 1854, as designed by Brunel.

EXTEND YOUR KNOWLEDGE

Prefabrication of buildings

Joseph Paxton (1803–65) was head gardener to the Duke of Devonshire at Chatsworth and his work on greenhouses for the duke led him to develop a system of prefabricated construction with metal and glass. Paxton's design for a glass palace to house the Great Exhibition of 1851 demonstrated the potential for large-scale prefabrication of buildings. His techniques were to influence Brunel in his construction of Paddington Station as well as the design of his Crimean hospital; Paddington featured a standardised arrangement of uprights and girders that could be rapidly assembled. Though a flamboyance of decoration tended to define mid- to late-19th century architecture, the use of prefabrication pointed to a modernist approach to construction, where industrial processes replaced artisan skills and there was more emphasis on form and function than adding ornamentation.

Design of prefabricated hospital for the Crimean War

In 1854 war broke out between Russia and an alliance of European powers that included Britain. The Crimean War was the first major conflict on the continent since the end of the Napoleonic Wars in 1815, and was to be remembered chiefly for the lack of clear military leadership and the inadequacies of organisation and supply. For the British forces sent to the Crimea, this resulted in 16,323 men dying of disease, while only 2,755 were killed in action. The war had prompted Brunel to offer his services to the Admiralty with a proposal for a floating gun platform, which was not met with enthusiasm. A year later, the appalling conditions at the main British medical facility at Scutari were made public by Florence Nightingale, who lobbied government for a new hospital to be constructed. One of her particular targets for criticism was Sir Benjamin Hawes, who was married to Brunel's sister Sophia. Hawes was seen as part of the incompetent chain of supply that was responsible for the disasters in the Crimea. Brunel was approached by Hawes, who was the parliamentary under-secretary at the War Office, and asked to provide plans for a 1,000-bed hospital that could be quickly fabricated in England and the parts shipped out to be assembled where it was required.

The project represented the combining of a number of Brunel's skills, not only as an innovator and designer, but also as someone who could utilise existing technologies. As Rolt comments in his biography of Brunel, much of what was done appears obvious to us today, but at the time it was all new. The plan was to construct a hospital made up of a collection of standard units, wards, accommodation and toilets, joined by linking corridors. Each ward had a fan to help with air circulation and a stove powered by candles for heating water for washing, which was a major contributor in helping to control infection. Looking at the availability of lavatories, it was found that cheap designs used by workhouses could be utilised as they needed little water in their operation, which was a decided advantage as water in Turkey was at a premium and it needed to be used sparingly. An iron-built kitchen was also provided, as was a similarly constructed laundry.

With the completion of the fabricated parts in Britain, the issue of transporting the 11,500 tonnes of equipment and stores demanded the services of 23 steamers and sailing ships. The first shipment arrived in May 1855, and the last in December of the same year. It was not until early 1856 that the hospital was fully assembled by the newly formed Corps of Royal Engineers at Renkioi, in Turkey, and ready for use just as the war ended. Nevertheless, it provided much improved facilities for 1,331 patients, with only 50 fatalities, representing a death rate of around 3.8 percent. This was an improvement in raw figures over Scutari, the hospital overseen by Florence Nightingale, which had a death rate that averaged 14 percent.

SOURCE
10

From the report of Dr Parkes to the War Office in 1857. Dr Edmond Parkes was put in charge of the hospital at Renkioi and would later become a leading campaigner for greater attention to hygiene in medical facilities.

Although the hospital was ready for 300 patients on July 12th, 1855, we were not called on to receive sick till October 2nd. From that time till February 11th, eleven ships arrived from Balaclava and Smyrna... The total number of military patients who were received from these ships was 1,244 and, in addition, 87 soldiers were admitted, either from the guard at Renkioi or Abydos, from transport ships which touched at Renkioi.

The construction of the hospital was admirably adapted for the men recovering from illness. As all the wards were on the ground, as soon as a man could crawl he could get into the air, either in the cool and sheltered corridor or in the spaces round the hospital

The anticipations we had formed of the health of the spot and of its adaptability for a hospital were quite confirmed by the experience of more than a year. The winter was mild and the climate seemed especially adapted for pulmonary complaints, of which we had a large number. The changes of temperature, it is true, were very sudden and great: but as the men had warm wards, these changes were not felt and there were few days in all but the most delicate and consumptive patient could not get out into the sheltered corridor for a short time during the day.

ACTIVITY
KNOWLEDGE CHECK

Building and prefabrication

1 What are the contrasts between the construction of Bristol Temple Meads station with that of Paddington? Draw up two columns, one labelled Temple Meads and the other Paddington and list the key aspects of these buildings.

2 What was required for the prefabrication of Brunel's hospital?

3 Look at the notes you have made and write a paragraph explaining why prefabrication would have proved to be a useful way to control costs in construction.

WHAT WAS THE IMPACT OF BRUNEL'S WORK FOR PASSENGER TRAVEL AND GOODS TRANSPORT?

While the Great Western Railway would secure his legacy in terms of bricks and mortar, Brunel was also looking to use his talents in other areas and saw a potential to apply his knowledge of civil engineering in the construction of seagoing vessels. The 19th century had seen an increase in both passenger and freight transport by sea, with thousands emigrating to Australia and the USA. Here it would seem that there might be rich pickings for an engineer who could exploit the rising demand for shipping.

From rail to sea: transporting the public

At a difficult and argumentative meeting of the Great Western Railway's directors in 1835, Brunel was recorded as responding to a question about the length of his preferred route from London to Bristol by suggesting that they might consider extending their interests across the Atlantic to New York. The idea, on all accounts, was met with uneasy laughter, but one member of the committee, Thomas Guppy, took it seriously, and after the meeting spent the evening discussing the possibility of building a steamship to cross the ocean. Under Guppy's direction, the Great Western Steamship Company was formed to construct and operate a vessel that would run regular crossings between Bristol and New York. This ship was to be called the SS *Great Western*. As a business proposition, the setting up of a transatlantic connection from Great Britain to America appeared to offer many attractions. However, it also presented a challenge to develop the technology so as to meet the demands of an ocean-going steamship service.

The SS *Great Western* takes the railway across the Atlantic

Many thought that the venture was folly. Brunel was not known as a naval engineer and there was a great deal of doubt about his proposal that a steamship, unaided by sails, could make a crossing of the Atlantic. In a lecture at Bristol in 1835, Dr Dionysius Lardner postulated that it was impossible to construct an ocean-going steam-powered ship using the current technology. He argued that the size of vessel capable of a crossing would be caught in a trap – that however much capacity was increased to carry fuel, this would see a further increase in water resistance against the hull, and so would prevent the ship from travelling further. Though Lander's assertions caused some to question the wisdom of the enterprise, Brunel was adamant that his calculations were correct and that they demonstrated it was possible to design a steam-powered ship that could carry sufficient coal, but without adding to the resistance of the hull against the water, and so avoid Lardner's dilemma of size counteracting power.

Following the start of construction of the SS *Great Western* in 1836, two other companies emerged to compete for the passenger and mail trade to New York, the British and American Steam Navigation Company, based in London, and the Transatlantic Steamship Company, from Liverpool. It would now be a race to see who could cross the ocean first and establish their reputation.

Knot
A nautical measurement of speed, with 1 knot equal to about 1.15 miles an hour. So Brunel's *Great Western* at 8.5 knots travelled at just under ten miles an hour.

Clipper
A type of fast sailing ship developed in the middle of the 19th century. Clippers were most famously used for the transport of tea, but they also carried other goods such as spices and even opium. They were far faster than the early steamships, but depended on favourable winds, so they were not always as reliable.

When completed, the *Great Western* was 71 metres in length and two steam engines drove the paddles on either side of the ship, with a speed of 8.5 **knots**. Though a good speed for a steamship, it was still only about half that of the fastest **clippers**, which under sail could reach 14 knots when the wind was in their favour.

For the 1830s, the *Great Western* was one of the largest ships afloat and could carry 128 passengers and 60 crew. It was finished in 1837, and began sea trials before its maiden voyage in 1838. It appeared that Brunel had stolen a march on his rivals, as neither had a ship ready to start a service. However, the Transatlantic Steamship Company decided to charter the SS *Sirius*, a much smaller ship, and rip out much of its accommodation to provide space for extra fuel. Disaster struck the *Great Western* in March 1838, during the sea trials, when fire broke out in one of the engines. While the damage was minimal, in the confusion Brunel had fallen 20 feet and had to be taken ashore. While the *Great Western* was in dock for repairs, the *Sirius* sailed out of Cork with 40 passengers on board, giving her four days' head start. Despite this advantage, the *Sirius* still faced a challenge from Brunel's ship, which was more powerful and was soon gaining on its challenger. The *Sirius* arrived in New York on 22 April 1838, but had to be brought into port due to its supplies of coal being exhausted as well as any other combustible material on board. The following afternoon, the *Great Western* steamed into the harbour with 200 tonnes of fuel left in its bunkers. Despite the *Sirius* arriving first, it was the *Great Western* that was judged the winner as it had arrived under its own steam.

SOURCE

11 The welcome received by the *Great Western* on its arrival in New York was recorded by one of its passengers and later reported in the first biography of Brunel. It shows the interest generated by the race and the way it grabbed the popular imagination.

Myriads were collected, boats had gathered round us in countless confusion, flags were flying, guns were firing, and cheering rose from the shore, the boats, and all around loudly and gloriously, as though it would never have been done. It was an exciting moment, a moment of triumph.

The ship started its return journey on 7 May and took just 14 days to arrive in its home port of Bristol. To cross the Atlantic in 14 days was a considerable feat. At the time, the average for sail was around 19 days, although the packet ship *Dreadnought*, skippered by Samuel Samuels, made the trip from New York to Liverpool in just ten days in 1859, setting a new record. The *Great Western* was to complete another 60 transatlantic voyages, proving popular with passengers. However, the company made very little profit on these sailings as most of its earnings were eaten up in the construction of Brunel's next ship, the SS *Great Britain*. In 1845, the *Great Western* ran aground and the company, being short of funds to refloat it, decided to sell it to the Royal Mail Steam Packet Company in 1846, where it became one of their best vessels. In 1857, the *Great Western* met its end when it was broken up by Messrs Castle of Vauxhall, where Brunel went to witness the end of his famous ship.

Brunel's design was to influence all future paddle steamers and set the benchmark for transatlantic travel in terms of comfort and speed until the arrival of the *Great Britain*. It also enhanced his reputation and showed him to be more than just a railway engineer.

The SS *Great Britain*: innovation that set the standard for a generation

The relative success of the *Great Western* led to the ordering of a second ship for the company, to be known as the *Great Britain*. It was to be bigger and faster than its predecessor and, when completed, would be the largest passenger ship in the world, until Brunel's next venture. Plans for the ship were drawn up by Brunel and construction started in 1839. It had not been originally intended to use iron in the construction of the *Great Britain*, but the visit to Bristol of the iron-hulled SS *Rainbow*, a steamship built by John Laird of Birkenhead, so impressed Brunel that he was won over to the possibilities of the material in ship design. Iron did not rot or suffer from woodworm, it was stronger than wood and permitted the building of larger ships without massively increasing weight. The cost of iron was also falling as the cost of wood was on the rise. A year later, the plans for the ship were changed again after the arrival in Bristol of the SS *Archimedes*, the first ship in the world driven by propeller, designed by Francis Pettitt Smith and owned by the Ship Propeller Company. The original design of the *Great Britain*, which had included paddles, was scrapped, leading Brunel to redesign the engine and layout of the ship, which resulted in further delays in construction and an increase in expense. In a report prepared for the steamship company, he outlined the advantages of **screw propulsion**, making the case for its greater efficiency and power and, though the changing of the plans did not go without comment, Guppy and Brunel were able to carry a majority of the board. In 1845, this propulsion system was demonstrated, rather dramatically, by a contest between HMS *Rattler* and HMS *Alecto*. The *Rattler* was a converted paddle steamer that the Admiralty had offered Brunel to demonstrate the possibilities of propeller propulsion. In a test of strength, the two ships were chained together and a tug of war was held between them. The *Rattler* triumphed over the *Alecto*, towing the paddle steamer to the shore at 2.8 knots.

SOURCE 12

From Brunel's report to the Great Western Steamship Company about the screw propeller, 1840. This report argued for a change in design of the *Great Britain*, replacing its paddles with a screw propeller. Brunel sets out the technical advantages presented by the innovation and why it would be of use on the often stormy Atlantic crossings.

[The] great regularity of motion is naturally consequent upon the screw being unaffected by the rolling of the ship, and upon its being immersed and not exposed therefore to blows from the sea, and except in the case of its being lifted out of water, the resistance... is perfectly smooth.... [The] extent of the variation could never approach to that to which paddles [steamers] continually expose an engine... A heavy sea or a deep plunge will occasionally bring the engines nearly to a stand; while at other moments, if the engineers are to be believed, the paddles are left free and the engines run away at a fearful speed. I am inclined to think this description of the effects somewhat exaggerated; but certainly the screw cannot be... exposed to the same variations as the paddles—it cannot be stopped by the action of the sea, indeed, being wholly immersed, the resistance cannot be increased at all, while under no circumstances can it be relieved to the extent to which paddles are, which are both on some rare occasions quite out of the water; and therefore whether the resistance of the screw is so constant as I believe it to be, or not, yet as compared with that offered by paddles, it is certainly all but perfectly constant.... the effect upon the steerage is singular, the mass of water put into motion by the thrust of the screw is thrown directly upon the rudder, and the consequence is not only that when the ship is going at any given rate, the rudder is passing through the water at a greater rate, and consequently is more sensible, and acts more powerfully upon the ship; but even when the ship has no way, but the screw is at work, the rudder is acted upon by water moving perhaps at two or three knots per hour, and the vessel is still under command—this must be a most important power to possess in a ship, and must materially diminish many of the greatest dangers arising from a strong head wind and sea, and at the same time and under the same circumstances must increase the speed by improving the steerage. And lastly, her diminished breadth of beam. Important as this alteration would be to any vessel, it is peculiarly so as connected with Bristol...

Despite the technical advances represented by the *Great Britain*, the first propeller-driven iron ship, in many ways it was not to prove a success. Though the *Great Western* had led the way in ship design, the transatlantic service from Bristol was not a commercial success. Since the 18th century, Liverpool had replaced Bristol as the main port for Atlantic trade. The *Great Britain* marked the end of the dream to extend the Great Western Railway to America, as the *Great Britain* would operate out of Liverpool. Though the launch of the *Great Britain* in Bristol was accompanied by much celebration in 1844, on its completion it could not undergo sea trials until the following year, as the dock gates were not wide enough to permit it to leave the port. It had been up to the Bristol Docks Board to arrange the alterations. However, it had not promoted the special Act of Parliament that was needed to permit the alterations and so additional delay was added to the project.

When the *Great Britain* steamed out of Liverpool in July 1845, it became the largest passenger ship in the world at 98 metres in length, with room for 252 first- and second-class passengers and 130 crew. However, on this maiden voyage across the Atlantic it only carried 45 passengers, although the hold had a full 600 tonnes of cargo. It took just 14 days and 21 hours to reach New York, but it was found the ship tended to roll even in relatively calm seas as the keel was too small. On its second voyage, heavy seas damaged Brunel's six-bladed propeller and it was decided to revert to a four-bladed design that had been used in the *Archimedes*, which proved to be more reliable. In 1846, further misfortune befell the *Great Britain* when it ran aground in Dundrum Bay, Ireland. The robust design of the double hull prevented any serious damage and it was refloated in 1847 at a cost of £34,000. But by now the shareholders had run out of money and the ship was sold to Gibbs, Bright & Company for £25,000. The *Great Britain* was then refitted to provide a regular passenger service between

KEY TERMS

Propeller/screw propulsion
The use of a propeller, or screw, is the most commonly encountered form of propulsion in modern shipping. The propeller sits below the water level, and so unlike paddles is not exposed in rough seas, making it a more efficient and effective way of driving a vessel through the water.

Liverpool and Melbourne, Australia, for emigrants to the colony. In 1854, there was an interruption to this trade when the ship was chartered by the War Office to transport troops to the Crimea. From 1870, the *Great Britain* no longer carried passengers but became a cargo ship carrying Welsh coal to San Francisco. In 1886, it was wrecked off the Falkland Islands.

The SS *Great Eastern*: scale beyond utility

In 1851, Brunel was approached by the Australian Mail Company to consult on a design for a ship to travel between Britain and Australia for the delivery of mail. Brunel suggested that they needed vessels of 5,000 to 6,000 tonnes that would require one refuel of coal when passing the Cape of Good Hope in South Africa. His suggestion was accepted and two ships were ordered the following year, the SS *Victoria* and the SS *Adelaide*, to be built at John Scott Russell's yard at Millwall, with Brunel as a consulting engineer. Brunel then set about developing one of his most grand schemes, the one that would prove to be his last. He proposed building a ship that was capable of steaming around the world, which would not have to refuel and so cut down on the costs of maintaining coaling stations. Such a radical idea did not, however, appeal to the Australian Mail Company, possibly because of the scale and cost of the undertaking, as well as the fact that they had just ordered two new ships. Yet Brunel was able to convince one of his old friends from his Great Western Railway days, Christopher Claxton, and John Scott Russell to consider the venture and the Great Eastern Steam Navigation Company was born. However, as with Brunel's other projects, things did not run smoothly. The idea was to be part of the expanding passenger and mail traffic to India, China and Australia, but in 1852 the British government granted an exclusive mail licence to the Pacific and Orient Steam Navigation Company. The ensuing resignations from the board of the Great Eastern Steam Navigation Company and lack of capital meant that work was delayed until 1854 when sufficient investors were found. More problems occurred in 1856, when Russell's ship building yard went bankrupt and creditors attempted to seize the half-completed ship and sell it to cover his debts. Fortunately, they were prevented from doing this and construction resumed again once the yard had come out of administration. However, debts continued to increase and in 1858 the Great Eastern Steam Navigation Company was dissolved and the ship was bought by the newly formed Great Ship Company which oversaw the final construction stage of the vessel.

When launched in 1858, the *Great Eastern* was by far the largest ship ever built: one could have fitted both the *Great Western* and the *Great Britain* inside her hull. It was 211 metres in length and its gross tonnage was 18,914 tonnes. The ship was powered by two massive engines: one linked to paddles, the other to a screw propeller. The rather cumbersome design was necessary, as the available technology did not permit sufficient power to be generated to drive such a vast ship by propeller alone. The ship had room for 4,000 passengers and 418 crew. After its fitting-out, the ship was ready for its maiden voyage to America on the 9 September 1859. Sadly, Brunel was not there: he suffered a stroke on 5 September and died ten days later . Though it had been designed for Far Eastern trade and to travel long distances without refuelling, there was never sufficient work for the *Great Eastern* there and it never sailed around the Cape of Good Hope. The owners instead gave the ship over to the transatlantic passenger trade between the UK and the United States. Here its size was a disadvantage, as it was not as fast of the other carriers. The maiden voyage only had 35 paying passengers. However, it gained a government contract for the next trip, carrying 2,144 officers and men as well as 200 horses to Quebec, Canada. Though the ship made some small profits, it was badly damaged in a great storm in September 1861 and ran aground the following year, all of which placed heavy costs on the Great Ship Company, causing it to run out of capital. The investors lost confidence in the venture and the ship was put up for auction in 1864. However, the auction failed to attract much interest and the ship was offloaded in a private sale for just £20,000. The *Great Eastern* now entered a new life as a cable layer, its great size and manoeuvrability making it ideal for this task. In 1866, at the second attempt, it laid the first telegraph cable from Ireland to Newfoundland. Later it was involved in laying cables from France to America and from England to India.

SOURCE

13 Brunel standing against the launching chains for the SS *Great Eastern* at the Millwall docks in 1857. This famous image of the great engineer, with his trademark stovepipe top hat, shows the scale of the project of the *Great Eastern*, as he is dwarfed by the massive launching chains.

A Level Exam-Style Question Section B

How far could it be argued that Brunel's ships had an important impact on the transatlantic passenger trade? (20 marks)

Tip

Think about the innovations that Brunel made to his ships and how they increased speed and comfort, and contrast them with the mixed financial success that these ventures had.

ACTIVITY
KNOWLEDGE CHECK

Innovation and economics

1 Make a list the innovations that Brunel brought to the design of his ships, both in terms of technical advancement and scale.

2 What were the three most important reasons for the lack of profits form Brunel's shipbuilding schemes. Compare your answers with a partner and decide on your combined top three.

3 In terms of finding a market and servicing the needs of the travelling public, assess the idea that Brunel was more an innovator than an entrepreneur. Consider the evidence for and against this assertion.

EXTRACT

From *Brunel: The Man Who Built the World* by Steven Brindle and Dan Cruickshank (2006), a popular work on Brunel and his creations.

In the end Brunel was a man of his time: to see him as a modern figure is to diminish as well as misunderstand him. In his qualities, both his vices and virtues, he was decidedly un-modern. The last man in the world to listen to subordinates jealous of his pre-eminence, a harsh manager, bullying and intractable to contractors and seemingly careless of safety... Always willing to use new ideas, even on very large projects.

EXTRACT

From *The Annals of Bristol* by John Latimer (1887). Latimer was a chronicler of the history of Bristol in the 19th century and had very firm views on the contribution Brunel made to the city.

A history of the Great Western Railway is not within the province of this work, but a few facts concerning an enterprise so closely connected with the city may not be out of place. The time has long passed away since there was any difference of opinion as to the deplorable error of the original board in neglecting the sober-minded, practical, and economical engineers of the North, already deservedly famous, and in preferring to them an inexperienced theorist, enamoured of novelty, prone to seek for difficulties rather than to evade them, and utterly indifferent as to the outlay which his recklessness entailed upon his employers. The evil consequences of his pet project, the 'broad gauge' system, on the commerce of Bristol will have to be noticed hereafter. For the present it will suffice to show the fallaciousness of Mr. Brunel's estimates. The original share capital was fixed by his advice at £2,500,000. Before the line to London was completed, the directors had to ask for votes bringing up the expenditure to £6,300,000, which did not include any part of the outlay for the permanent station at Paddington. In 1844 this vast sum was increased to £8,160,000, inclusive of loans. As may be suspected from the figures, the directors were even more imprudent than was their subordinate. For several successive years there seemed to be no limit to their aggressive designs.

EXTRACT

From *Brunel: The Life and Times of Isambard Kingdom Brunel* by R. Angus Buchanan (2006). Buchanan's work looks critically at Brunel's contribution to engineering and places it in a historical context.

We do not need to argue further the case for Stephenson here, but so far as Brunel is concerned it is important to assess his stature as of the greatest heroes of British engineering. In the first place his reputation endured well. The broad gauge has gone, having arrived too late to convince public opinion... but the bulk of Brunel's dramatic civil engineering on the GWR survives... The Clifton Bridge and the Royal Albert Bridge, the great brick viaducts and the bridge over the Thames are still in fully working order. However it is necessary to qualify any hero-worship.... it is necessary also to assess Brunel as a man, to see how he fulfils the heroic role that posterity has thrust upon him. There interesting indications of his desire for the recognition of others in the revealing personal diary of his early years. He confessed that: 'My self-conceit and love of glory or rather approbation vie with each other which shall govern me.' Nevertheless, he established a strict discipline and daily regime for himself that reveal his determination to give priority to the demands of his profession.

THINKING HISTORICALLY Evidence (6b)

The strength of argument

Answer the following:

1 Read Extract 1.
   a) What is weak about this claim?
   b) What could be added to it to make it stronger?

2 Read Extract 2.
   a) Is this an argument? If yes, what makes it one?
   b) How might this argument be strengthened?

3 Read Extract 3.
   a) How have they expanded their explanation to make the claim stronger?
   b) Can you explain why this is the strongest claim of the three extracts?

4 What elements make a historian's claims strong?

Conclusion

In many ways, it is hard to give a definitive evaluation of Brunel's record as an engineer, as much depends on where one stands. His conduct in the competition for the Clifton Suspension Bridge and over the route for the Great Western Railway demonstrate his confidence in his own abilities and high level of self-belief. In terms of innovation, he could claim responsibility for pushing the boundaries of what was thought possible and, in many ways, revolutionising civil engineering in terms of vision and method. His designs for bridges and tunnels looked to the use of new materials and showed a great inventiveness in planning and construction. The Royal Albert Bridge and the Box Tunnel were triumphs of organisation and innovative engineering that are still in use today, yet there is a question mark hovering over his reputation and what he really contributed. The Great Western Railway was a project that in many ways points to the ambiguity of his legacy. It was of advanced design and set standards for later railway projects in terms of speed and comfort, but costs constantly increased, and in the end, though it made money, investors questioned the amount of return in comparison to investments in other railway companies. Brunel's dogmatic adoption of the broad gauge was to prove an error, as others did not follow and he was unable to see that the problem of competing gauges outweighed the possible superiority in speed. Inexperience could also prove to be a problem, as in the innovative design of the SS *Great Britain*, which rolled in mild seas due to the original keel being too small to stabilise the ship. However, he was also capable of successfully completing vast engineering projects that would have defeated lesser men; contemporaries always make reference to his energy, which must have been substantial to have overcome the opposition he often faced. His ventures into maritime construction set the benchmark for what was to follow. He demonstrated the possibilities for steam power to replace sail for ships crossing the ocean, for iron to replace wood as a form of maritime construction and the screw propeller to replace the paddle. However, his ships, like his railway, made little if any money for investors. It was not that they did not work, but that the trade that they were to serve was not there. The vision of London to New York via Bristol was an enticing one, but the port of Liverpool had become dominant in the transatlantic trade, and the demand for a crossing from Bristol to America was not sufficient to support his venture. Likewise, the SS *Great Eastern* never fulfilled its promise as a passenger steamer that travelled the globe, and it was only after its sale, at a knockdown price, that it came into its own as a cable-laying vessel. Was it then that Brunel was a genius of innovation who was just a little short on luck when it came to making a profit?

ACTIVITY
KNOWLEDGE CHECK

Building Britain

1 In pairs, discuss the contribution Brunel made to engineering in the 19th century. Decide on your top three.

2 Looking at the three choices that you have made, list the reasons why you think that they were so important.

3 To what extent could it be said that Brunel built Britain? Plan an essay that supports your assertions.

ACTIVITY
SUMMARY

Brunel's legacy

The legacy of Isambard Kingdom Brunel is complex and there are differences of opinion held by historians as to his impact and influence on society.

1 Draw up a balance sheet with three columns.
- In column 1, write down Brunel's failures.
- In column 2, write down his successes. You might want to discuss with a partner what is meant by 'success' and 'failure'.
- In column 3, write down all the things that he was either a leader in or the first person to do.

2 Looking at your balance sheet, think about the lasting impact his successes have had on the society we live in today.
a) Write a paragraph arguing that Brunel's ideas and engineering ability have shaped the modern world.
b) Reflect on Brunel's failings and write a paragraph arguing that he was not always a hero to his contemporaries.

3 Write a short biography of Brunel of no more than 500 words for a popular publication. How might you sum up his legacy?

WIDER READING

Brindle, S. and Cruickshank, D. *Brunel: The Man Who Built the World*, Weidenfeld & Nicholson (2006)

Brunel Online Archive www.ikbrunel.org.uk

Buchanan, R.A. *Brunel: The Life and Times of Isambard Kingdom Brunel*, Bloomsbury (2006)

Cavendish, R. 'Birth of Isambard Kingdom Brunel', *History Today*, Volume 56, Issue 4 (2006)

Rolt, L.T.C. *Isambard Kingdom Brunel*, Penguin Books (1990)

3.6

John Kemp Starley: cycles, cycling clubs and emancipation, 1885–1901

KEY QUESTIONS

- What was the significance of the Rover safety bicycle?
- How did the adoption of the safety bicycle impact on leisure pursuits?
- What was the significance of the safety bicycle for women?

INTRODUCTION

Before John Kemp Starley's safety bicycle, cycling (or 'velocipeding' as it was often known) had been a fad for an elite few. However, in a few short years after his simple invention, the bicycle had become a massive international craze, from France to England and across the Atlantic to the US, which would have significant effects economically and also on social attitudes and behaviours.

The bicycle bridged the gap between the steam age, which had provided a transport system for conveying the multitude, and the arrival of the motor car, and its vision of the freedom of the open road, with consumers able to travel where they liked. It was pedal power that would define the later decades of the 19th century, creating a new world of leisure, fashion, political activism and personalised transport; as well as giving rise to an industry that employed thousands and exported its product round the globe. The bicycle would make its mark in the emergent socialist movement as well as being an iconic symbol of female emancipation, changing the way women dressed and promoting ideas of independence. It also gave people the chance to explore the countryside, as well as being used for more mundane tasks, such as to travel to work.

It was not the invention of the bicycle that was to be the catalyst for this social revolution, which had its origins in the early part of the century, but the refinement to that design. The 1880s witnessed the final transformation of Baron von Drais's 1817 invention of 'the running machine' into the bicycle we are familiar with today. To arrive at that point, the evolution of the bicycle went through a number of phases, incorporating arrangements of pedals, levers, gears and wheel alignments before the appearance of the 'safety bicycle' in 1885, the origin of all modern bicycles.

1885 – Rover safety bicycle is unveiled at the Stanley Bicycle Show

1887 – Pneumatic tyre is developed by Dunlop and replaces solid rubber tyres in bicycle design

1884	1885	1886	1887	1888	1889	1894

1884 – Prototype of the Rover safety bicycle is developed

1886 – London to Brighton race to publicise the speed of the Rover bicycle

1887 – Dunlop develops pneumatic tyres

1894 – First Clarion Cycle Club is formed

WHAT WAS THE SIGNIFICANCE OF THE ROVER SAFETY BICYCLE?

The inventor of the safety bicycle, John Kemp Starley (1854–1901), came from a dynasty of cycle manufacturers who had based themselves in Coventry. His uncle, James Starley, had made his money from the invention of the 'Ariel' high-wheel bicycle in 1870 – better known today as the 'ordinary' or penny-farthing. The rider sat above the large front wheel, which was driven by pedals. The bicycle was not easy to handle as it required a running start before the rider leapt on the machine. However, it was a significant improvement on earlier designs and proved to be a great success commercially, particularly among the more athletic cyclists. In 1877, it was followed by the development of the chain-driven **differential gear** to aid the efficiency of the machine, an innovation still present on bicycles today.

James also produced a popular tricycle known as the 'Salvo' for cyclists who wanted to travel at a more leisurely pace. His son, William ('Big Bill') Starley, carried on the family business, assisting in the development of the **lever-driven** ladies' tricycle. This permitted women in long skirts to use their arms to drive the machine rather than face the danger of their skirts becoming tangled in the pedals.

The Starley family, originally from Essex, came to Coventry in the 1850s. James was involved in the setting up of a sewing machine manufacturing business, and had moved to the town to take advantage of the skilled labour employed in the watch trade, which had begun to decline due to competition from imported Swiss watches. In 1869, the Coventry Sewing Machine Company, prompted by the growing bicycle craze, decided to diversify into cycles. It obtained a contract for the manufacture of 400 '**boneshaker**' bikes for export to France.

James Starley began modifications to the boneshaker and the following year set up his own bicycle business with William Hillman. Later, in 1876, it became Starley Brothers when Hillman left to form his own company. The venture proved successful, manufacturing high-wheel bicycles as well as tricycles. The high-wheel bicycles, such as the penny-farthing, attracted the young, moderately well-off, athletic male customer. They were attracted to the speed of the machines and were keen to race their bicycles. The youth of this group and the focus on racing met with social disapproval. The popular press worried about the safety of the public and the term 'cads on castors' was coined to describe the brash young men who rode the penny-farthing. The design of the 'ordinary' bicycle, with the seat over the large front wheel, was not only hazardous for the male rider, but prevented women, with their long skirts, from using them as they would be unable to get onto the bicycle and, even if they did, their clothing might well become tangled in the pedals. For women, the tricycle was the preferred option, if they had the finances to purchase one. However, these machines were not always considered appropriate for ladies; especially, the 'social tandem', a side-by-side arrangement of seats that in mixed company was considered to encourage inappropriate socialising. Attitudes changed in the early 1880s when it became known that younger members of the royal family had purchased special tandem tricycles – royal patronage gave them acceptance into respectable society. However, it remained a world of gender separation: the bicycle represented masculine values of strength, speed

KEY TERMS

Differential gear
The arrangement of wheels and chains found on a modern bicycle that can be used to change the ratio of rotation to power the rear wheel, making the machine faster on the flat and easier to ride when ascending an incline or hill.

Lever driven
A machine that could be worked by hand to power the wheels, similar in design to those found on a modern cross-trainer.

Boneshaker
An early design of bicycle with solid iron-rimmed wheels and pedals attached to the front wheel. There was a partially sprung frame to which a saddle was attached in an attempt to increase the rider's comfort. The bicycle's construction reflected earlier German machines that had undergone further development in France in the 1850s.

1896 – John Kemp Starley forms the Rover Company
The bicycle famine, where demand far outstrips supply

1904 – The Rover company begins car manufacturing

1895	1896	1897	1898	1899	1900	1904

1897 – The bicycle boom peaks

1898 – The Great Slump, as demand for new cycles falls
Starley Brothers goes out of business
Formation of the National Dress League

SOURCE

John Kemp Starley, inventor of the safety bicycle, outside his factory in Coventry in 1895. The bicycle illustrated here is the modified version that went into mass production. It has all the features of a modern bicycle, such as the chain-driven rear wheel and the handlebars linked to the front forks, though the curved frame would soon be replaced by the diamond shape of most modern bikes.

and independence, while women had to make do with the tricycle. Though women might be able to experience some independence of travel at this time, society still worried about the propriety and moral hazard that such a form of transport presented.

John Kemp Starley and the design of the safety bicycle

It was on the recommendation of James Starley that John Kemp Starley joined the firm of Haynes and Jeffries, a small builder of cycles under licence to Starley Brothers. John Kemp Starley, however, was to prove as ambitious as his uncle and began to think about how to improve the cycles on which he was working. He wanted to increase the driving power and improve the safety of the machine by changing the centre of gravity away from the rider sitting over the drive wheel to being seated between the wheels, as had been the case on the boneshaker. As his ideas evolved, Starley began to look for a business partner to share the risk, help raise funds to pay for development and set up production. This he found in William Sutton, the owner of a haberdashery in Coventry who was a keen cyclist as well as a lover of fast horses. Sutton's contacts in the business community, along with Starley's family connections, helped raise the capital for the new venture of Starley and Sutton. Starley's attempt to redesign the bicycle were not carried out in isolation; a number of other small manufacturers were looking at ways to improve on the 'ordinary'. This in part explains the secrecy that surrounded Starley's prototype, which was tested on the country roads outside Coventry.

By 1884, the first prototype of the safety bike was ready. It had a 19.44 cm front wheel, coupling-rod steering with handlebars, a braced single-backbone type frame and a chain-driven rear wheel with gears of a style to be found on modern bicycles.

It was called a safety bicycle because the rider was now positioned between the wheels and lower to the ground rather than mounted above the large front wheel of the 'ordinary'. The arrangement gave greater stability as well as making it easier to ride. In changing the centre of gravity and adding a rear-wheel brake, there was less chance of the cyclist being thrown face first onto the ground, should there be a need to brake sharply. The new machine was christened the Rover. It was not until the following year, 1885, that it was publicly unveiled at the annual Stanley Bicycle Show in London. However, Starley's cycle attracted opposition from the athletic riders of the penny-farthing racing bikes, who treated his bike with contempt, calling it 'crawler' and 'beetle' and suggesting that it was an option for the older cyclist. At the show, it was the Starley Brothers new tricycle, the 'Psycho', that was to gain the most attention. Despite the Rover's muted reception, this was the design that would change the cycle industry. In a lecture given 14 years after the unveiling of the Rover, Starley reflected on his motivations and the effectiveness of his design (see Source 2).

SOURCE 2 From a guest lecture given by Starley to the Royal Society of Arts, in London in 1898. Starley was an active member of the Royal Society of Arts, which was founded in 1754 to promote practical solutions to social challenges.

I felt the time had arrived for solving the problem of the cycle... I therefore turned my attention solely to the perfection and manufacture of the Rover bicycle.

The main principles which guided me in making this machine were to place the rider at the proper distance from the ground; to connect the cranks with the driving wheel in such a way that the gearing could be varied as desired; to place the seat in the right position in relation to the pedals, and constructed so that the saddle could be either laterally or vertically adjusted at will; to place the handles in such a position in relation to the seat that the rider could exert the greatest force upon the pedals with the least amount of fatigue; and to make them adjustable also.

I had been considering what a man pedalling a bicycle could be compared to... it largely resembled walking up a ladder, but... whereas the pedals went down in the former; the man went up in the latter. I therefore had to determine where the handles should be placed to enable him to bring the whole of his weight on to the pedals.... It was... the handle-bar which compelled me to adopt the present form of machine, as I could not get it sufficiently forward by the other type. It will be seen by the position of the handle-bar on the Ordinary [high-wheeler] bicycle, that it was utterly useless and imperfect for this purpose.

... my aim was not only to make a safety bicycle, but to produce a machine which should be the true Evolution of the Cycle, and the fact that so little change has been made in the essential positions, which were established by me in 1885, prove that I was not wrong in the cardinal points to be embodied to this end.

SOURCE
3

The prototype Rover bicycle. As can be seen, it differs in style from modern bicycles. The handlebars are set back and not over the forks of the front wheel, the frame is not the diamond shape of a modern bicycle and the rear wheel is smaller than the front.

Promoting the safety bicycle

The safety bicycle did not have a monopoly on the market and Starley and Sutton faced competition from William Hillman, who had originally been in partnership with Starley. He produced a model called the Kangaroo, in part based on a design by Otto and Walis, with a geared front-driven wheel, rather than the rear wheel drive found on the Rover. Hillman was quick to promote his model and in 1885 organised a 100 mile race from Twyford in Berkshire to Norman Cross, Huntingdonshire, the object being to demonstrate the superiority of the Kangaroo over other cycles of the day. Reports of the race caught the public imagination and sales of the Kangaroo subsequently increased. The road race did not go without adverse comment, however; there were letters to the press criticising the reckless behaviour of racing on the public highway with suggestions that it might put lives at risk.

The moral panic was such that the authorities issued a statement prohibiting such activities, though it was far from clear what they could do or what particular laws had been broken.

In the face of such competition, Starley was eager to demonstrate the qualities of his machine too. In the cycling papers, he announced a race to be run from London to Brighton and back again, a distance of 100 miles, on 25 September 1885. However, the actual starting point had to be kept secret until the last minute as there were worries the Metropolitan Police would try to stop the event. There were no spectators, therefore, to cheer the riders on their way as they sped off. Starley and Sutton arrived at the finishing point in Brighton in good time and waited anxiously for the first rider to appear. It was with great satisfaction that when George Smith, an established cycling veteran, crossed the finish line, a look at their watches told them that he had beaten the record set up by Hillman's Kangaroo. With the ensuing publicity, sales of John Kemp Stanley's Rover machine rose sharply and success seemed assured.

Unfortunately, Sutton did not live to see the triumph of the Rover, as he was killed in a road accident the following year. With his death, the partnership was dissolved and a new company created known as J.K. Starley and Company Limited. A further name change was made to the Rover Company Limited in the 1890s. The decision to rebrand the company was in part a response to the phenomenal success of the Rover, to the point that the word for bicycle in Polish was Rover (Rower), and partly to prevent any confusion with his late uncle's firm Starley Brothers.

The safety bicycle would go through a number of further developments after 1886 and, though most were minor, there were two important ones. The first was the adoption of **pneumatic tyres** developed by John Boyd Dunlop in 1887, replacing the solid rubber tyres of earlier bicycles. These revolutionised cycling, lightening the weight of the machine as well as making for a smoother ride. The letter in Source 4 from John Boyd Dunlop is indicative of Starley's attraction to innovation and improvement in design.

KEY TERM

Pneumatic tyre
Developed by John Boyd Dunlop, the pneumatic tyre had an inflatable tube. These gave a smoother ride than the solid rubber tyres used previously and helped the bicycle go faster, though there was always the danger of punctures due to the poor state of the roads.

SOURCE

From a letter by John Boyd Dunlop to John Kemp Starley in 1897. It provides evidence of Starley's forward thinking and his appreciation of the potential of the development of the pneumatic tyre, a refinement that meant that all solid-tyre cycles were now out of date, given the superior performance of the inflatable tyre.

Dear Sir

Everybody knows that you set the fashion in the introduction of the rear-drive safety, but few know that you were the first gentleman in England to appreciate the pneumatic tyre.

Long before the Pneumatic Tyre Company was floated you sent hubs and spokes to Edlin & Co., Belfast, to have wheels built and fitted with pneumatic tyres.

It was my intention to make the wheels when built, over to you with the view to a flotation. Edlin was in a small way very busy and therefore unable to complete the wheels in a reasonable time, hence the project fell through

Yours

J.B. Dunlop

The second innovation was the adoption of the diamond-shaped frame that can be seen on modern bicycles today. This was first used on the Royal Rover model of 1904. The frame was constructed from straight lengths of tubular steel brazed or welded together, unlike the curved frame of earlier models. The new design increased the ease of manufacture as it was no longer necessary to bend the tubular frame, and it added strength to the machine by securing the seat to the front forks of the bicycle by means of a crossbar.

Starley and the invention of the safety bicycle

1 'John Kemp Starley was an innovator more than an inventor.' Look at Sources 3 and 4 and consider how far you think they confirm or challenge this statement. Make a list of points for and against.

2 Draw up a list of reasons why Starley's innovations in bicycle design were more important for the long-term success of cycling than those made by his uncle.

The economic importance of the safety bicycle

Cycle production increased rapidly in the latter part of the 1880s, and included not only the new safety bicycle, which dominated the trade, but also older designs and tricycles, which remained popular among some groups of cyclists. However, growth was not without its setbacks. In the early 1890s, a slump hit the industry as demand fell for bicycles with solid tyres in favour of Dunlop's pneumatic design. Producers were left with unsold stock and production dropped among many of the manufacturers. This particular drop in trade was short-lived and by late 1894 demand increased sharply after an increase in rubber production permitted the universal adoption of pneumatic tyres. Trade increased so much that in 1896 there was the famous bicycle famine, as the public's appetite for cycling outstripped the capacity of the domestic producers to supply the market. The Coventry press was full of stories, many exaggerated, of purchasing agents with vast sums of money scouring the town looking for machines. The journal *The Armature Wheelman* talked in April of that year of bicycles seen everywhere but not one to be bought.

The cost of cycling

One constant in the growth of the industry was price. As production grew, the cost of new cycles tended to fall. However, they did not necessarily fall sufficiently to enable all classes to purchase them. Most cyclists in the 1890s tended to come from the middle class or sections of the skilled working class. Nonetheless, by the end of the century a growing second-hand market did extend ownership to an even wider range of consumers.

SOURCE

5 From the weekly *Scottish Cyclist* in 1904. It deals with the increasing importance of the second-hand market in widening bicycle ownership.

Proof of the effect on the second-hand market of the fall in prices. When the high grade [bicycle] cost on average 18 guineas, and the second grade [bicycle] stood at 13, our... private [second-hand] sales advertisements columns were many and voluminous... Today there is scarcely one column of these advertisements in 'Cycling'. The reason lies... in the fact that the second-hand cheap machine is not worth advertising to an expert or real cyclist. It is more easily sold through the local weekly at a price that represents a loss of about 50 per cent on the rider's first cost. The workman and the labourer becomes its owner and the mission of the cycle opens a further chapter for good.

The best bicycles remained expensive, at around £30 each in the 1880s (which would equate to around £3,000 today). However, lower-grade cycles such as the Swift Safety No. 2, retailed for just £16 10s in 1888. Though this was a marked reduction in price, it was still a considerable sum of money for a working-class household. An unskilled labourer in 1900 might be living on as little as 17 shillings a week, and such a purchase would represent a considerable amount of his yearly income. Even among the better-off skilled workers, who might be earning more than double the wages of the labourer, the cost of a new bicycle could be prohibitive. The historian Eric Hobsbawm suggests that the development of hire-purchase schemes was one way to help boost demand, and a series of credit agencies developed to cater to this, as had been the case for other consumer durables such as sewing machines. Manufacturers also became increasingly innovative in the way they promoted sales. One example of note was provided by William 'Big Bill' Starley, who introduced a practice whereby a bicycle could be had for a down payment of a guinea, followed by regular small payments, but if the purchaser could introduce another customer to the manufacturer then they would get a guinea back as a finder's fee. However, it was to be the constant refrain of cycling journalists that the market needed a high-quality machine for £10, at which price it was believed the joys of two-wheeled transport could be enjoyed by virtually anyone.

The impact of the cycle trade on Coventry

Though among some contemporaries it was known as 'cycle city', and there were a large number of cycle manufacturers there, Coventry did not have a monopoly on the industry in the early 1880s. Production was spread across the country, with important centres in the Midlands, Yorkshire and London. In 1881, the industry employed just 1,000 workers nationally, with 700 of those in the Midlands, of which 400 worked in Coventry. By 1885, there had been rapid growth in demand and of the 5,000 employees now engaged in the trade, 3,000 were in Coventry. By 1890, that had risen further, with 4,000 workers engaged in cycle manufacture in Coventry.

Year	Coventry	UK
1881	400	1,000
1885	3,000	5,000
1890	4,000	8,500

Figure 6.1 Data compiled from Board of Trade figures showing the number of people in employment in cycle manufacture for Coventry and the UK as a whole.

Employment continued to grow rapidly in the 1890s, as did the size of firms. For example, the Swift Cycle Company, based in Coventry, had 1,000 employees and was producing 700 machines a week in 1896. From 1894 to 1895, manufacturers in Coventry produced 20,000 cycles a year, rising to 40,000 in 1897, at the peak of the boom.

The increase in employment was linked with a growth of investment in the cycle trade as productive capacity grew. Nationally, capital invested in the larger **joint stock companies** involved in cycle production rose from £405,000 in 1888 to £1,019,000 in 1894, and to an enormous £19,594,124 by 1897, the peak of the cycling boom. Production nationally by the early 1890s was running at around 500,000 bikes a year, with many for export to France. It is interesting to note that, in the early part of the century, France had been far more important in the development of the cycling, but by the 1890s its industry had been eclipsed by that of Britain, which also saw off American and German competition. British cycles became dominant globally before the First World War, supplying Europe, the Americas and the Empire. By the end of the 1890s, Starley Brothers had set up depots to handle exports to Europe, America, Africa and Japan.

The expansion of production also saw changes in the way in which manufacture was organised. Larger batches of cycles were assembled using parts that became increasingly standardised and were interchangeable between different designs, which simplified production. In the larger factories, separate departments were set up to concentrate on the construction of particular parts of the bicycle, for example just focusing on the production of wheel rims. The whole process saw increasing focus on the division of labour so as to improve efficiency and speed up the completion. Skilled tradesmen in workshops produced components that would be assembled into finished products by semi-skilled labour, a technique that not only reduced cost but also improved the speed of manufacture. This pattern of production would later be a key characteristic of the car industry. The gender of the workforce also changed, with increasing numbers of women employed as enamellers to make company badges and as wheel builders. Mass production techniques were in many ways first encountered in the cycle trade, but it would be the motor industry, with its moving assembly line, that would finally perfect the continuous production of even more complex manufactured goods.

The Great Slump

As the boom grew, speculators were attracted to the industry, the most notorious being Ernest Terah Hooley. He had set himself up as a stockbroker with £35,000 left to him by his mother. Hooley encouraged companies to raise capital with public flotation of shares. The first to do so was the Raleigh Cycle Company, which raised £250,000; it was followed by sewing machine company Singer, which raised £600,000. The money was used to invest in new productive capacity and the trade grew rapidly. Between 1894 and 1897, investment capital rose massively, much of which was due to Hooley's speculative adventures. He became ever more ambitious, buying Dunlop's patent for pneumatic tyres – which had originally been sold for just £700 – for £3 million; then he quickly resold it for £5 million, pocketing a handsome profit. Big Bill Starley was mesmerised by the boom and speculated wildly in cycle shares, encouraged by Hooley. John Kemp Starley, on the other hand, was far more restrained and, though he sought to make the most of the boom, he resisted all invitations

> **KEY TERM**
>
> **Joint stock company**
> One that issues stock (shares) to raise capital for investment rather than borrowing money from banks. These shares entitle investors to part of the profits and can be traded on a secondary market such as a stock exchange.

KEY TERM

Over-capitalisation
Where a company raises more money than is needed and is either unable to invest that money efficiently or ends up creating productive capacity greater than the available market demands.

by Hooley to float his company. While he invested heavily, he did this from his own profits rather than raising share capital.

The boom turned to bust in 1898, as the massively **over-capitalised** industry found it had overproduced to the point that there was no longer a market for its products. The slump soon led to Hooley's downfall, as he was beset by creditors for payment for the bills he had run up in the boom years. Bankruptcy and disgrace followed. In his autobiography Hooley freely admitted to dubious practices and questionable dealings, though he was not prosecuted for them at the time. Another casualty was Big Bill Starley and the company of Starley Brothers, which went out of business. John Kemp Starley was able to ride out the storm as he was not in debt. However, the slump sharply reduced his company's profits and led to him looking for other market opportunities to rebuild his finances.

Though the cycle industry remained important in Coventry, by 1911 it accounted for just 26 percent of the workforce nationally, while at the height of the boom it had employed 49 percent of the those engaged in cycle production. While profits recovered by 1900, with the big manufacturers such as Rover (John Kemp Starley's company), Eagle Cycles, Swift and Triumph seeing substantial returns, competition between manufacturers in Coventry continued to be intense, which tended to reduce prices and put a squeeze on margins.

SOURCE

From a New Zealand newspaper, the *Poverty Bay Herald*, 12 November 1898. The scale of the slump is shown by the way in which it became news around the world. As far away as New Zealand, papers were discussing the impact of the slump and reflecting on its cause.

A Level Exam-Style Question Section A

Study Source 6 before you answer this question.

Assess the value of the source for revealing the impact of the slump at the end of the 1890s and the significance of the overcapitalisation of the industry in leading to its sudden decline.

Explain your answer, using the source, the information about its origin and your own knowledge about the historical context. (20 marks)

Tip
Think about why the news of the slump was being reported in a local paper on the other side of the world. Also think about how John Kemp Starley was able to survive the downturn in the industry while others went bankrupt.

The cycle manufacturing trade in England is just now under a big black cloud. No one would think it, if he judged by the great increase of cycling during the past two or three years, but the Secretary of the Cycle Workers' Union ought to know whereof he speaks, and he recently drew a most melancholy picture of the state of the trade. When it was at its height it kept 10,000 people busy in Birmingham in the manufactories alone; to-day there are not more than 2000 employed, and the factories are practically at a standstill. The rim department of one of the largest used to employ 200 men, now a man and a boy can do all the work required. .... The depression is said to be almost entirely due to the over stocking which took place when the boom was at its height, but the collapse of Mr Hooley and the effect that incident had upon some to the cycle companies he had promoted, is also the cause of part of the present trouble. The demand for cycles still keeps up, but even if it does not slacken it will not keep all manufactories going, and there is keen competition from foreign makers, especially from America. Coventry feels the present situation most keenly, but then Coventry for a number of years has always been either up in the 'seventh heaven of prosperity' or down in the dumps. Just now it is very much in the dumps, and its condition contrasts sadly with the state two years ago. Then workshops were going up all over the city, lodgings were at a high premium, work was plentiful for all, and labour was in insufficient supply. Now there are 2000 unemployed in the cycle trade in Coventry, besides numbers who have left the place, there are no occupants for the temporary huts which were erected for workmen, lodgers are no longer packed three or four to a room. 'After the boom the slump,' as the stockbroker's ditty has it. Efforts are now to be made in the North of England to reach a part of the community which has hitherto had to go without bicycles. Trust-worthy machines are to be turned out at a very low figure, depots will be opened all over the kingdom, and the cycles sold like sewing machines, on the time-payment principle, at about eighteen pence a week.

The consequences of the slump were to be long term and had a profound effect on the cycle trade in Coventry. As Source 6 suggests, there were attempts to produce for new markets. However, these were not sufficient to take up the spare productive capacity. The result was that a number of cycle manufacturers, such as Starley's Rover Company, Hillman and the Swift Company, decided to diversify and went into the production of motorcycles and cars. By the turn of the century, Rover had returned to profit. However, it was no longer based on the production of bicycles but on its increasing involvement in the motor industry.

From cycles to cars

The relationship between the speculation in the cycle trade and the rise of the motor car is exemplified by one of Hooley's key supporters, H.J. Lawson. Lawson bought the Daimler Motor Syndicate Limited in 1895. Though it was based in London, he decided to move its production to Coventry, taking over a disused cotton mill in the town. Lawson had been a leading advocate for the removal of the Red Flag Act, which had required that a person holding a red flag must proceed in front of a motor vehicle on the highway to warn of its coming. On its withdrawal in 1896, he organised the first London to Brighton Car 'Emancipation Run'. Lawson's apparent success in the motor trade attracted many cycle manufacturers into the industry at the time of the slump. The move into motorcycle and car production would provide a return to profitability for Rover and some of the other cycle manufacturers. Lawson, however, was not so lucky and after a number of business failures at the turn of the century, he was prosecuted for fraudulently obtaining money and was sent to prison in 1904.

ACTIVITY
KNOWLEDGE CHECK

The development of the cycle industry

1 What evidence do we have that Coventry was the centre of the cycle trade?

2 Working with a partner, come up with three reasons why cycling might have become more affordable at the beginning of the 20th century.

3 Look at Source 6. Why was the slump considered news on the other side of the world? Make a list of the effects of the slump on the cycle trade, then use this to answer the question.

HOW DID THE ADOPTION OF THE SAFETY BICYCLE IMPACT ON LEISURE PURSUITS?

From the 1850s there had been a steady increase in leisure time and a corresponding expansion of ways in which to spend it. Until the 1880s, this was mainly the prerogative of the middle class, who were able to enjoy visits to places of cultural improvement such as municipal galleries and museums, as well as participating in clubs and societies of various types. Leisure became more than a time when one was not working, it took on a form where individuals engaged in social activities that did not necessarily involve the family group. Leisure was something to be enjoyed; it was more than rest – it demanded activity. By the end of the century, even the working class was enjoying more free time. Social reform, such as the Shop Acts in the 1890s, had restricted the time retail outlets could open, reducing the hours worked by shop assistants. Trade union campaigns around the eight-hour working day demanded eight hours of work, eight hours of sleep and eight hours of recreation and rest. Another sign of the increase in leisure time was the expansion of music halls in the 1880s, which was in response to a growing demand for working-class entertainment. Even among the less well-off, time was increasingly spent outside the home and kinship networks, though for many working-class women the home remained the primary focus of their lives. These activities ranged from allotment associations to the expanding working men's club movement. By the 1890s, it would also include an array of cycle clubs that catered for a wide range of interests.

The cycling craze did not begin with the John Kemp Starley's safety bicycle, but it was the adoption of the safety bicycle that would see it reach its height. Cycle clubs began to appear in the last decades of the 19th century. The oldest, the Pickwick Bicycle Club, was formed in 1870 – a club of which Starley himself was an enthusiastic and active member. The Pickwick Club was rather exclusive, with each member adopting the name of one of Dickens' characters from his book *The Pickwick Papers*. By the end of the decade, groups with more mass appeal began to appear, such as the Cyclist Touring Club, formed in 1878. Though the Cyclist Touring Club catered for the fashionable and professional classes, it could still boast over 60,000 members by 1899. Among the ranks of its enthusiastic members were some 200 serving MPs, which gave it considerable political influence. It has been estimated that, in the last decade of the 19th century, there were around 2,000 cycling clubs founded throughout the country. The Saturday or Sunday club runs became a significant leisure activity, with group outings to the countryside and places of interest. The public's infatuation with the bicycle even led Thomas Cook to promote cycling tours of the continent for the better-off.

These included maps, itineraries and recommended routes. To keep the enthusiast informed, a cycling press evolved. Regular columns devoted to the joys of the bicycle began to appear in many of the national and local newspapers. Specialist magazines, such as *Cycling Weekly*, first published in 1891, had 41,000 readers by 1900. It was a market that appeared to just grow and grow, attracting ever more comment and becoming a focus for increased commercial activity. Cycling mania by the 1890s gripped the globe and its influence would not only affect the way in which people travelled, but would have a profound effect on culture and politics.

Cycling clubs, community and respectability

By the late 1890s, there were about 1.5 million cyclists in Britain, out of a total population of 35 million. For the first time, many men and women were able to enjoy the freedom to go where they liked, to engage in leisure activities that did not revolve around family or local community. New associations emerged, with clubs offering the opportunity to meet people with similar interests and broaden one's experience of the world. These clubs grew up in wide variety of social spheres. There were church-based groups for different denominations, such as the St Christopher's Catholic Cycle Club in Leeds; work-based associations, as was the case with the Bourneville Cycle Club, formed by employees of the Cadbury chocolate factory in Birmingham; the Vegetarian Cycling and Athletic Club formed in 1887; and the Theatrical United Cycling Club. Clubs were also formed by political groups, particularly on the left, with the appearance of the Clarion Cycling Club in 1894.

Challenge of the open road

Not all welcomed the growing appetite for Sunday excursions into the countryside. There were numerous letters to the press complaining that other road users were constantly being menaced by cyclists. Lord Randolph Churchill raised the question with the Home Secretary regarding the way the new pneumatic tyres meant that cyclists could silently come up on someone and catch them unawares The press engaged in moral panics, focusing on reckless riders, as in the 1896 case of a Mr T. Harrington, MP, who was injured in a collision with a bicycle on a Dublin street. Popular disapproval of cycling in some quarters was evident by reports in the cycling press of 'roughs' pushing cyclists off their bicycles or placing lumps of wood on the road so as to unseat the unwary rider. Particular ridicule was reserved for women cyclists, who were seen as a menace to themselves and the public at large.

Such opposition did little to diminish the popularity of cycling. However, the state of the nation's roads was more of an issue for the cycling clubs. In the summer, cyclists got covered in dust from the unmade roads and, in winter, the roads were often impassable because of mud. Worse for the new pneumatic tyres were the flint chippings used to surface many rural and urban roads – these small, sharp stones became lodged in the tyres and caused punctures. The Cyclists Touring Club complained constantly about the poor maintenance of roads and in 1886 created the Roads Improvement Association (RIA). The group lobbied hard on behalf of road users and distributed pamphlets on improving road surfaces. Later on, the RIA would be taken over by the car lobby. The campaign did meet with some success in raising the issue of the state of the roads in parliament, and such debates brought the issue to public attention. One effect of this lobbying was that the Local Government Act 1888 included provisions for county councils to take over the responsibility for the maintenance of main roads, to be paid for out of local rates, though it remained up to the council to decide what it considered to be a main road.

When cyclists were not menaced by poor roads it was other road users who proved to be a danger. The congested streets of many British cities were hazardous to the cyclist. On cobbled streets, congested with horses and carts, the cyclists had to take care. Even on the less-congested road, accidents happened.

SOURCE

An example of the way in which the local press treated bicycle accidents, from the *Brecon and Radnor Express* in 1891.

Last week, Mr. Osmond Larkin met with a serious accident whilst proceeding along the Watton Road on his bicycle. He came into collision with Messrs. Jones Bros. horse and cart, with the result that he was knocked down and the wheel of the vehicle passed over his chest and arm. He also sustained injuries to the head. Mr. Larkin was promptly taken to Dr. Owen's surgery, where his injuries were attended to, and now we are happy to state he is out of danger and rapidly recovering. The bicycle was broken, and the horse's legs badly cut.

ACTIVITY
KNOWLEDGE CHECK

The development of the cycle industry

1 Using the material above, consider how you might define the word 'leisure'. What do you feel that it means in the context of the rise of the cycling club?

2 List the ways in which cycling had an impact on society as a whole. Think about the changes that it brought and how it shaped leisure activities.

3 Do you agree with the view that, 'Victorian society was far from at ease with the rise of the bicycle and this led to a moral panic in the press'? Explain your answer.

The Clarion Clubs

The **Clarion** Cycling Clubs were a particular phenomenon of the 1890s and represented an interplay between rising political activism, increased opportunities for leisure pursuits (at least amongst the skilled working class) and the mass popularity of cycling. The *Clarion* newspaper was founded in Manchester in 1891 on a capital of £400 by Alexander Thompson and Robert Blatchford, the latter formerly a journalist with the *Manchester Chronicle*, who had resigned from his previous position to start a paper to promote socialist ideas. Under the editorship of Blatchford, the paper rapidly grew in popularity and the famous Clarion vans would travel the locality distributing socialist propaganda. Groups were formed by readers to support the paper through leisure and educational activities. These included football teams, craft circles, cultural groups, choirs and, most famously, cycle clubs. The first club was formed in 1894 at a Labour Church in Birmingham by the Clarion representative in the Midlands, Tom Groom. It was originally known as the Socialist Cycling Club, but this was soon changed to the Clarion Cycling Club. Branches spread across the Midlands and the North, and by 1900 membership stood at over 8,000.

KEY TERM

Clarion
A clarion, or clarion call, is a strong statement or a demand for action in support of a particular cause.

EXTEND YOUR KNOWLEDGE

Labour Church
The Labour Church was a movement started by former Unitarian minister John Trevor. The first Church was founded in Manchester in 1891 and it rapidly spread to other industrial cities such as Bradford, Leeds, Wolverhampton, Birmingham and Nottingham. The Church focused its teachings on ideas of social solidarity and the emancipation of labour. With the departure of John Trevor in 1900, the organisation went into decline and had disappeared by the time of the First World War.

The *Clarion* was not the only socialist paper that gave space to cycling. Keir Hardie's *Labour Leader*, the paper of the Independent Labour Party, had a regular feature called Cycling News, while *Justice*, the journal of the Social Democratic Federation, carried reports of 'flying propagandists' touring the country on their bikes. The success of the Clarion Cycling Club even led to a Clarion bicycle being manufactured under licence by Swift Cycles of Birmingham. Not to be outdone, the Social Democratic Federation advertised its own brand of bicycle, Liberty, in the pages of its paper.

Nature, health and politics

Tom Groom would occupy a key place in the Clarion Cycling Club. Not only was he a founding member, he was also its national president. In the pages of the *Clarion*, he wrote the popular 'Cyclorama' column about the club's activities and interests. In his section, much was made of the idea of a return to nature and an appreciation of natural history. Socialism was not just about the redistribution of wealth, but was presented as a way to go beyond the material confines of industrial society and become a more whole human being. This idea of the liberation of the individual from the mundane that cycling provided is found in H.G. Wells' 1896 novel *The Wheels of Chance*. Wells, a socialist and supporter of the *Clarion*, described his main character's infatuation with the freedom of the open road and his need to get beyond the confines of his job as shop assistant.

SOURCE 8

H.G. Wells was a keen cyclist and socialist author. In his work *The Wheels of Chance*, published in 1896, he offers a description of how the urban dweller experiences the countryside on a bicycle and the ways in which this represents a new and exciting possibility for leisure and freedom from the industrial town.

In the background of his consciousness was the sense that about this time Briggs would be half-way through his window dressing, and Gosling, the apprentice, busy, with a chair turned down over the counter and his ears very red, trying to roll a piece of **huckaback** – only those who have rolled pieces of huckaback know quite how detestable huckaback is to roll – and the shop would be dusty and, perhaps, the governor about and snappy And here was quiet and greenery, and one mucked about as the desire took one, without a soul to see, and here was no wailing of 'Sayn', no folding of remnants, no voice to shout, 'Hoopdriver, forward!' And once he almost ran over something wonderful, a little, low, red beast with a yellowish tail, that went rushing across the road before him. It was the first weasel he had ever seen in his cockney life. There were miles of this, scores of miles of this before him, pinewood and oak forest, purple, heathery moorland and grassy down, lush meadows, where shining rivers wound their lazy way, villages with square-towered, flint churches, and rambling, cheap, and hearty inns, clean, white, country towns, long downhill stretches, where one might ride at one's ease (overlooking a jolt or so), and far away, at the end of it all, the sea....

It was perhaps half-way between Cobham and Ripley. Mr. Hoopdriver dropped down a little hill, where, unfenced from the road, fine mossy trees and bracken lay on either side; and looking up he saw an open country before him, covered with heather and set with pines, and a yellow road running across it, and half a mile away perhaps, a little grey figure by the wayside waving something white. 'Never!' said Mr. Hoopdriver with his hands tightening on the handles.

The Clarion Cycling Club provided fellowship for socialist cyclists, extending their horizons and linking leisure to the practice of politics. The idea of leisure also tied into socialist demands for a shorter working week and the idea that the time would be taken up by wholesome pursuits to promote health, rather than in the public house. Annual 'meets', social gatherings organised by local Clarion groups, attracted large numbers of cyclists to the Peak District towns of Bakewell and Ashbourne. At the 1899 Skipton 'meet', 400 delegates attended and the organisers ran out of beds.

The contrast between the freedom of nature and the wretchedness of many of the industrial cities was a focus of much of Tom Groom's critique of contemporary social conditions. He wrote about the way in which cycling in the countryside among nature was in sharp contrast to the squalor of most industrial towns and cities. He further suggested that these experiences led people to question the present political system and demand change. It was this aspiration to go beyond the bounds of what they knew that formed the basis of the Clarion's socialism. What had been accepted as the norm was challenged by the experience of the weekend cyclist. Socialism in this context was more than an ideology of the redistribution of wealth to create a more equitable society, it was also a cultural movement that focused on political change that would transform the social environment.

The Clarion Scouts and their political impact

The Clarion Scouts were formed in late 1894 as a group of active propagandists who could go from place to place distributing socialist leaflets and holding meetings. A monthly journal, *The Scout*, was founded to promote their work, and activists were encouraged to contribute to its pages. In an 1897 pamphlet outlining the duties of the Scout, it was set down that the Scout's duty was to 'teach socialism', which they were to do through 'good-humoured argument'. The writer Robert Tressell gave a fictionalised account of the activities of Clarion Scouts in his socialist novel *The Ragged-Trousered Philanthropists* (Source 9).

SOURCE 9

Robert Tressell's socialist novel *The Ragged-Trousered Philanthropists* was written in 1910, but not published until 1914, after his death. The story deals with the emergence of the early socialist movement and the difficulties it had in making its case. Below is a description of a propaganda campaign carried out by socialist cyclists and the opposition they experienced.

One Sunday morning towards the end of July, a band of about twenty-five men and women on bicycles invaded the town. Two of them – who rode a few yards in front of the others, had affixed to the handlebars of each of their machines a slender, upright standard from the top of one of which fluttered a small flag of crimson silk with 'International Brotherhood and Peace' in gold letters. The other standard was similar in size and colour, but with a different legend: 'One for all and All for one.' As they rode along they gave leaflets to the people in the streets, and whenever they came to a place where there were many people they dismounted and walked about, giving their leaflets to whoever would accept them. They made several long halts during their progress along the Grand Parade, where there was a considerable crowd, and then they rode over the hill to Windley, which they reached a little before opening time. There were little crowds waiting outside the several public houses and a number of people passing through the streets on their way home from Church and Chapel. The strangers distributed leaflets to all those who would take them, and they went through a lot of the side streets, putting leaflets under the doors and in the letter-boxes. When they had exhausted their stock they remounted and rode back the way they came. Meantime the news of their arrival had spread, and as they returned through the town they were greeted with jeers and booing. Presently someone threw a stone, and as there happened to be plenty of stones just there several others followed suit and began running after the retreating cyclists, throwing stones, hooting and cursing...

The cyclists rode away amid showers of stones without sustaining much damage. One had his hand cut and another, who happened to look round, was struck on the forehead, but these were the only casualties.

A Level Exam-Style Question Section A

Study Source 9 before you answer this question.

Assess the value of the source for revealing the way in which the cyclists were used by the early socialist movement to spread their ideas and the significance of the bicycle in promoting social change.

Explain your answer, using the source, the information about its origin and your own knowledge about the historical context. (20 marks)

Tip
Think about how the bicycle gave access to the wider world to different groups and the impact that new freedom might have on groups that saw the newcomers and alien outsiders challenging the established order.

Such activities sometimes met with opposition, and the pages of the *Clarion* mention incidents where groups of cyclists were dispersed by local police. In 1898, for example, the Cheshire Constabulary were concerned about the threat to public safety posed by a Clarion meeting to be held at Chester, leading to a large police presence at the gathering. On another occasion, a rally in the Borders was prevented by the actions of the authorities. Large gatherings always made the police and local political establishment nervous as they feared the possibility of public disorder. The speed that such groups could achieve in moving from place to place meant that they were hard to keep under observation if law enforcement were not also equipped with cycles. The Scouts also encountered hostility from disgruntled locals, who saw the cyclists as uninvited interfering outsiders. In Tressell's work, the residents of the fictional settlement of Mugsborough chase the Clarion cyclists out of town, telling them they do not want their socialism there. This is interesting as it points to the insularity of many communities, even in the late 19th century, and how mass transport might be viewed with suspicion.

EXTEND YOUR KNOWLEDGE

Socialist cyclists
The Clarion Scouts were not the first to carry out leafleting campaigns aimed at bringing the socialist message to new localities. William Morris' socialist paper *Commonweal* published an article in 1887 detailing a cycle ride where the participants distributed leaflets in the villages that they passed through.

The Social Democratic Federation and Independent Labour Party

The Clarion tended to divide between the Social Democratic Federation (SDF), formed 1881, and the Independent Labour Party (ILP), created in 1893. The SDF professed a form of socialism linked to a strict Marxist interpretation of society that focused on economics, emphasising the tendency of capitalism to concentrate wealth in the hands of the few. Its ideas were broadly redistributive, with a focus on changing the way the economy functioned. Its leader, Henry Mayers Hyndman, had a reputation for being authoritarian, which led to a series of splits in the organisation and weakened its long-term influence. The ILP was less dogmatic, focusing on a Christian Socialist moral critique of capitalism as lacking in its responsibility towards the poor. It was less about changing the economy and more about creating structures that were more equitable, with an emphasis on offering some form of progressive social security. The ILP accentuated the need for a more collective basis to society, where the issue of poverty needed to be addressed and the rights of workers could be advanced through trade unions. There were not only differences in terms of ideology between the two groups, but also in how they promoted the socialist cause. The SDF was more radical and less inclined to take a reformist position towards capitalism, seeking to replace it with a socialist society, though it still supported electoral politics. By contrast, the ILP focused on incremental steps, seeking to create change by political reform such as the extension of the vote or promoting the rights of trade unions. Both groups were affiliated with the Labour Representation Committees, which were the forerunners of the modern Labour Party. The committees consisted of groupings of socialist societies and trade unions based in a particular locality. The object of these bodies was to promote the adoption and election of working-class Labour candidates for local bodies, such as school boards and boards of Poor Law Guardians, as well as at national elections. Under Hyndman, the SDF disaffiliated from the organisation and went on to form the British Socialist Party in 1911. Tensions also developed in the Clarion clubs between the ILP and Robert Blatchford over the latter's jingoistic support for the First World War, with many ILP cyclists breaking from the movement to form their own ILP cycle clubs. Despite these schisms in the movement, the Clarion Cycle Clubs continued to function with a number of groups still active in the north of England, such as the Stockport Clarion.

Cycling and popular culture

The popularity of cycling can be observed through the growth of cycling literature. In the 1890s, there were a number of novels on the theme of cycling. In other works, such as Tressell's *The Ragged-Trousered Philanthropists* (see Source 9), cycling might not be the focus of the narrative, but it played a symbolic role to signify modernity bringing the idea of socialism to the backwaters of Britain. Other works, such as H.G. Wells's *The Wheels of Chance* (see Source 8), tell the story of the transformative power of cycling. For writer Jerome K. Jerome, the bicycle was the chosen means of transport in his sequel to his bestselling *Three Men and a Boat. Three Men on the **Bummel***, published in 1900, chronicles the misadventures of his protagonists on a bicycle holiday to the Black Forest in Germany. The work is indicative of the growing popularity for touring holidays abroad among sections of the better-off middle class. As well as literature, the romantic aspect of cycling was encountered in popular song. In 1892 Harry Darce's 'Daisy Bell' caught the mood of the day.

> **KEY TERM**
>
> **Bummel**
> Said by Jerome K. Jerome to be German for a journey, short or long, that one has to return from within a given set of time.

SOURCE

From Harry Darce's 'Daisy Bell: A Bicycle Made for Two', 1892. It was a very popular music hall song supposedly inspired by the affair between King Edward VII and the Countess of Warwick, Daisy Greville. The chorus shows the young man's romantic intentions and the invitation to marry and cycle together on a bicycle made for two.

Daisy, Daisy, give me your answer do
I'm half crazy all for the love of you
It won't be a stylish marriage
I can't afford a carriage
But you'll look sweet upon the seat
Of a bicycle built for two

Courtship and cycling introduced yet another dangerous dimension to the cycling craze. Respectable middle-class Victorian society was concerned with propriety and could easily be scandalised by the suggestion of women asserting any sense of independence outside the home. Substance is provided for the image of young people becoming romantically engaged while cycling in 'Daisy Bell' by the historian P.J. Perry's work on out-of-parish marriages in Dorset villages from the 1880s. He argued that it was the growing popularity of cycling that meant that young people travelled beyond the bounds of their village and which led to a marked increase in marriages between couples from different parishes. Such a change in its own small way represented a change to the established social order, as even in the most rural of areas the bicycle could extend one's horizons.

> **ACTIVITY**
> **KNOWLEDGE CHECK**
>
> **Socialism and cycling**
>
> 1 Read through the section above and create a mind map of the social and political impact of cycling. Start with a bubble in the centre labelled 'Social and political impact of cycling'.
>
> 2 Why do you think that early socialists appear to have been so attracted to the Clarion Cycling Club? Was it just for the political meetings?
>
> 3 Look at Source 9 and consider the fictional depiction of a socialist propaganda event. What do we learn about the use of the bicycle as a tool of the activist? Why might the locals see the activists as outsiders and react aggressively towards them?

WHAT WAS THE SIGNIFICANCE OF THE SAFETY BICYCLE FOR WOMEN?

Before the advent of the safety bicycle, cycling had been a predominantly male pastime. There had been a masculine emphasis on speed and power that was used to promote the activity, which was seen as inappropriate for feminine physiology. Yet the safety bicycle was to take on a far more feminine character when increasing numbers of women joined the cycling craze. The smaller wheels and the lower seating position of the safety bicycle permitted women in their long skirts to ride. By 1890, a third of the membership of the middle-class Cyclists' Touring Club were women. In 1896, it is estimated that a third of the bicycles ordered were for women, a massive increase from 1893, when it stood at around one in 50. Despite the popularity of cycling, questions were raised about how appropriate it was for women to be cyclists. Late Victorian society found itself ill at ease with the role of women, and with the shape of the growing political campaign for female suffrage and the socially challenging ideas of what became known as the 'New Woman'. An increase in secondary education among middle-class women and a rise in employment outside the home in this group defined the New Woman as independent in thought and someone who could actively shape her own destiny. Victorian society struggled to come to terms with women outside the home and their participation in leisure activities, particularly worrying about the mixing of the sexes in cycling clubs.

Impact on mobility and independence

The vast majority of female cyclists were not radicals, in the sense of promoting a particular political agenda; they were, like their male counterparts, attracted to the freedom offered by the bicycle. They wished to travel from town to country, to be more social and break the spatial confinement of women to the home and expand their experiences of the world. The presence of women feminised social spaces, and what had been seen as exclusively masculine was subject to a female aesthetic, bringing the domestic to the public sphere. Tearooms and roadside hotels began to reflect the tastes of their female clientele. The raucous and rowdy behaviour that had been a characteristic of all-male groups was confronted by female respectability. While the public bar might remain male territory, the lounge became a place where more wholesome refreshments might be found. The historian Ruth Iskin has noted that many of the posters advertising bicycles for women tapped into the idea of a new freedom and a quest for mobility. Women were shown to be participating in the reshaping of their identities, emphasising the ideas of independence and mobility. The image of the female cyclist would become that of the New Woman of the 1890s as she asserted her independence and identity beyond the domestic realm.

The New Woman of the 1890s

The so-called New Woman was a construct that attempted to classify what was seen as a new, and in many quarters disturbing, phenomenon of a woman politically engaged, physically active beyond the home, educated and pushing against the prevailing conservative attitudes towards her gender. She stood for social and economic equality between the genders and for the emancipation of her sex. In a time when married women had only just been given property rights and none were able to vote in national elections, the New Woman was celebrated in the radical sections of the press, and in novels such as H.G. Wells' *Ann Veronica* and Ella Hepworth Dixon's *The Story of a Modern Woman*. In Wells' *Ann Veronica*, the protagonist contemplates how far the new age has emancipated women, and while she agrees that cycling has freed her sex from some of its restrictions and given it new horizons, she worries that all that has happened is that women are now held on long ribbons rather than tethered to the kitchen. These themes were also taken up in the cycling press, particularly in the magazine *The Lady Cyclist*.

An advertisement from the 1890s for Rover bicycles with an emphasis on selling to the female cyclist. It is also interesting to note that the riders are depicted not in 'rational' dress (see page 148), but in everyday wear.

EXTRACT

1 From *Representations of the New Woman in the 1890s* by Clare Mendes (2013 PhD thesis). Mendes reflects on the representation of the New Woman in the magazine *The Lady Cyclist* and how the magazine depicted cycling as a way both to personal health and social emancipation.

The Lady Cyclist, a publication for female cyclists, made the connection between cycling and the New Woman in August 1896 at the same time that Fenwick Miller began to include more articles about exercise for women. The Lady Cyclist claimed that cycling not only provided a new freedom for women to broaden their minds, but it also adapted woman to the responsibilities of suffrage, already having the experience of venturing into new territory. Following the mould of her character sketches, Fenwick Miller acknowledged famous women who had been known to cycle, encouraging readers to take up the sport. In June 1897, she reported that the novelist Henrietta Eliza Vaughan Stannard claimed cycling to be a 'blessed means of relaxation and relief from the many cares which do and always must beset the lot of women'. Stannard's observation reinforced Professor Mosso's reflections on gymnastics by stressing the mind and body link: whilst still desiring a room of their own, they could at least have an activity of their own, through which good health would bloom from the connection between a satisfied mind and, in turn, a satisfied body.

While the New Woman of literature only really represented a small group, often from the better-off, she acted as a trailblazer, questioning the status quo and challenging convention. The bicycle had opened up new opportunities to participate in the world, expanding geographical, social and political horizons. For feminist intellectuals of the day, such as the Austrian philosopher Rosa Mayreder, cycling was seen as a giant step towards the emancipation of women. The scale of the reaction in the establishment press to the New Woman is indicative of the threat that she was seen to pose to traditional values and the stability of the family. What society found disturbing was that women had been able to enter what until the 1880s was a closed masculine sport. They dared to go beyond the confines of the domestic world to assert their identity, something the journalist and author Eliza Linton found particularly distressing (see pages 148–49). And it is in this context we should see the New Woman, not so much as a fearless individual taking on a male establishment, but as a more general tendency among a particular generation who began to question the social norms of high Victorian society.

Radical women

For the women's suffrage movement, the bicycle played a part similar to that of the *Clarion*. Groups of activists were able to travel from place to place spreading suffragist propaganda. Women cycled both for the cause and as a social activity, enabling them to experience the world beyond the domestic sphere. Many of the leading figures of the movement were also keen cyclists. Millicent Garrett Fawcett, leader of the National Union of Women's Suffrage Societies, which remained committed to non-violent action in support of votes for women, organised women's cycle outings and picnics. She also encouraged readers of the magazine *Wheelwoman* to donate their old bicycles to working-class women so that they could participate in cycling events. Perhaps the most avid radical cyclist was Christabel Pankhurst, the daughter of Emmeline Pankhurst, the leader of the more militant Women's Social and Political Union.

EXTRACT

2 From *The Suffragette Movement* by Sylvia Pankhurst (1931). Pankhurst describes the challenges of cycling and the way in which her sister, Christabel, saw the bicycle as a form of exercise to improve her physical well-being in an age that often saw women of the middle and upper class as almost semi-invalids afflicted by 'women's problems'. It also hints at the unease that even progressive families might feel about their daughters gaining such freedom.

Thenceforward, every available day was spent in cycling. Though the journeys were often too long for me, and I would scarcely pedal the last miles, the Sundays with the club were pleasant. It was delightful to be out in the country, and the men were kind in helping push one up the steepest hills. It was when riding alone with Christabel that I endured a veritable torture. My crimson face and gasping breath were the wordless answer to her impatient 'Come on!' Afraid of being considered a nuisance, I would strain and strive till it seemed that my heart would burst. Finally she would disappear from me, climbing some hill, and arrive home somehow an hour before me. I remember being thrown over the handle-bars and rising up so shaken that I had to walk for some distance before I could remount, while she rode on, not noticing that I had ceased to follow. She delighted in hill climbing, and was proud to be able to mount the noted steeps which some of the men in the club essayed in vain. Dr. Pankhurst accepted, but obviously regretted this craze for cycling, which took us away from home every Sunday and seemed to be drawing us away from the public interests so dear to him.

A Level Exam-Style Question Section B

To what extent did the development of the bicycle in the 1880s change women's experiences of the world? (20 marks)

Tip
While not everyone could afford a bicycle, large numbers of people could. Reflect on how far it changed the image of women, their agency and remade their social world.

Impact on fashion

The New Woman pioneered a new cycling dress code: **rational dress**. Women cyclists had been held back by their long skirts, which often caught in the chain or the spokes of the wheel. Accidents were common and there were calls for a style of dress that would be more appropriate for cycling. Men had adopted trousers that tucked into long socks to prevent them becoming entangled in the gears of the bicycle. The rational dress that evolved for women comprised split skirts, bloomers or knickerbockers that like the male counterparts were tucked into long socks. Short jackets were also in evidence, as well as functional footwear. Such dress was symbolically breaking the norms that were considered appropriate for female dress and behaviour. Though by modern standards the outfits might appear rather formal, in comparison to the female clothing of the 1890s they were simple and functional. The problem was that simplicity and functionality were not seen to be feminine traits but masculine virtues, which often resulted in vocal opposition to the fashion. The late 19th century would witness a struggle between the craze for tight corseting, which restricted the body to the point that women fainted due an inability to breathe properly, and rational styles of dress that rejected the corset for a more natural body form. By 1910, the time of the corset as a mainstay of women's fashion was on the wane as less tight-fitting clothes became popular, in part influenced by ideas of rational dress, though long skirts and pompadour hair styles continued to restrict movement.

The broader movement for rational dress pre-dated the cycle craze and had links to the American Amelia Bloomer and her followers, who in the mid-19th century attempted to promote a more practical form of dress for women in the form of baggy trousers, known as bloomers. The Rational Dress Society was founded in 1881 under the presidency of Florence Pomeroy, Viscountess Harberton, a keen cyclist. It was followed in 1898 by the Rational Dress League, which attempted to promote the wearing of rational dress among women cyclists through the pages of the *Rational Dress Gazette*. Despite the high profile given to the design, only a minority of female cyclists dressed that way, with most continuing to wear long skirts.

The year 1898 was to see one of the most well-known clashes over rational dress. The Hautboy Hotel, in Oakham, Surrey, refused to admit Lady Harberton to the coffee room while she was dressed in knickerbockers. As the hotel considered her dress masculine, she was directed to the common bar. Lady Harberton took her case to the Cyclists' Touring Club to have the hotel taken off recommended club itineraries. After much debate, the club supported Lady Harberton and the Hautboy lost its place in the club handbook. A subsequent court case was not so successful and compensation could not be gained from the business for its refusal to permit Lady Harberton to enter its coffee room. However, the action of the Cyclists' Touring Club encouraged other businesses such as the White Horse in Dorking to remove their ban on knickerbockers lest they be deprived of the patronage of such a prestigious cycling club. Even so, many establishments remained opposed to rational dress and continued to discriminate against women so attired.

EXTEND YOUR KNOWLEDGE

Florence Pomeroy, Viscountess Harberton (1844–1911)
Viscountess Harberton was an active member of the Central Committee of the National Society for Women's Suffrage, and later joined the Women's Social and Political Union, the suffragettes, as well as being an enthusiastic cyclist and political radical who challenged social norms. When she died in 1911, she gave strict instructions that no one was to appear at her funeral in mourning as this was not how she wished to be remembered.

Opposition to the female bicycling craze

In the face of what was seen as such provocation, others rallied to defend traditional values against this vulgar impostor. One of the most consistent critics of the New Woman and all her works was the journalist Eliza Linton. In her 1883 essay 'The Girl of the Period' she takes to task all ideas of women shaping their own destinies.

SOURCE

From 'The Girl of the Period' by Eliza Lynn Linton, published in 1883. Linton was highly critical of the idea of the New Woman and her comments are descriptive of the gendered culture of the late 19th century and how challenges to such social norms were seen as unwomanly and unattractive to men.

The marvel in the present fashion of life among women is, how it holds its ground in spite of the disapprobation of men. It used to be an old-time notion that the sexes were made for each other, and that it was only natural for them to please each other and to set themselves out for that end. But the Girl of the Period does not please men. She pleases them as little as she elevates them; and how little she does that, the class of women she has taken as her models of itself testifies. All men whose opinion is worth having prefer the simple and genuine girl of the past, with her tender little ways and pretty bashful modesties, to this loud and rampant modernization, with her false red hair and painted skin, talking slang as glibly as a man, and by preference leading the conversation to doubtful subjects. She thinks she is piquante and exciting when she thus makes herself the bad copy of a worse original; and she will not see that though men laugh with her they do not respect her, though they flirt with her they do not marry her; she will not believe that she is not the kind of thing they want, and that she is acting against nature and her own interests when she disregards their advice and offends their taste

SOURCE

This illustration appeared in the satirical magazine *Punch* in 1895 and shows the contrast between rational dress and the long skirts common in the 1890s. The humour of the print suggests that such dress was more a statement than just practical attire and fits with the general depiction of women in rational dress in the popular press.

Gertrude. "MY DEAR JESSIE, WHAT ON EARTH IS THAT BICYCLE SUIT FOR!"
Jessie. "WHY, TO WEAR, OF COURSE."   Gertrude. "BUT YOU HAVEN'T GOT A BICYCLE!"
Jessie. "NO; BUT I'VE GOT A SEWING MACHINE!"

Women did not only experience hostility from the business community and establishment figures but were frequently shouted at in the street. Kitty Jane Buckland, an advocate of rational dress, recalled in a letter to her brother in 1897 how children would yell and shout at her as she cycled past them. Many of the comments were crude and questioned her gender and femininity.

Another female cyclist noted that as she cycled past a barber's shop in the East End of London the proprietor shouted after her, 'Come here and I'll cut that hair for you'. The hostility faced by advocates in part explains the decline in the popularity of rational dress by the beginning of the 20th century. The fashion had tended to be confined to the more middle- and upper-class cyclists and even among them was not widespread. The cost of the outfits was quite high and well out of the range of most working-class women unless they made the outfits themselves. Most women stuck to their long skirts and managed the best that they could. Developments such as covered chains helped and by 1914 skirts had become a little shorter, which went some way to preventing them catching in the pedals.

A Level Exam-Style Question Section B

To what extent did the cycle craze challenge accepted ideas of femininity? (20 marks)

Tip

Think about the criticisms of the New Woman, particularly from other women, and how they focus on a particular female role. Contrast this with the evidence that cycling built strength and offered the opportunity for women to exercise and abandon the restrictive corsetry that was part of 19th-century fashion.

ACTIVITY
KNOWLEDGE CHECK

Cycling and its effect on women's lives

1 With a partner write four sentences detailing the ways in which cycling changed how women lived their lives.

2 Using your sentences above as the basis of a mind map, consider what it is about those changes that might have provoked hostility.

3 'The New Woman was every woman.' What are the arguments for and against this statement?

THINKING HISTORICALLY   Interpretations (6a)

Ever-changing history

Our interpretations of the past change as we change. This may be because our social attitudes have changed over time or perhaps a historian has constructed a new theory or perhaps technology has allowed archaeologists to discover something new.

Work in pairs.

Make a timeline that starts with the invention of the safety bicycle and ends 50 years in the future. Construct reactions that illustrate the point that time changes history. In the future box, you can speculate how people might react to the event in 50 years' time. Here is an example:

1884	1884	1904	1960	2066
Event: The invention of the safety bicycle by John Kemp Starley	John Starley: 'The Rover: safer than a tricycle, faster than any bicycle…' The press: 'Cads on castors. It is a pastime for young men with money to spend.'	Scottish cyclist: 'The workman and the labourer become its owner and the mission of the cycle opens a further chapter.' Popular journalism: 'A popular pastime and increasingly a way to commute.'	National survey: 'The number of people travelling to work by bicycle drops below that of the number travelling by car.' Planning officer. 'Cycling is no longer a priority in the development of the road network.'	?

Answer the following questions.

1 Identify three factors that have affected how the development of the safety bicycle is interpreted over time, or might affect it in the future.

2 If a historian was to write a book proposing a radically new interpretation of social impact of the bicycle, how might other historians react? What would affect their reaction?

3 How will the future change the past?

Conclusion

John Kemp Starley's safety bicycle was a simple device, comprising an arrangement of wheels, pedals, gears and tubular frame. Given our modern perspective, it is often hard to conceive how revolutionary it was in the world of the 1880s. What had been a fad for the middle-class male became a pastime for both sexes and saw ownership spread to parts of the working class. Although a bicycle industry had existed since the 1870s, the development of the Rover bicycle transformed it. The market for the new design appeared to be limitless as the cycling craze made the fortunes of many in Coventry. In the decade between the development of the safety bicycle and the great slump, a new consumer society began to emerge, with mass markets for goods that fulfilled needs that had not previously been considered. In this sense, the bicycle was unlike other industrial goods, which tended to be versions of the previous hand-crafted ones. The bicycle had more in common with modern society, where new technologies take hold almost overnight; gramophones, televisions, computers and smartphones were a break with the past, and they were new things looking for a market and were rapidly taken up by the masses. Though the bicycle mania of the latter part of the 19th century was short-lived, the bicycle continued to be an important form of transport well into the 20th century. Even after the crash in the 1890s, the cycle industry managed to maintain its position in Coventry until it was supplanted in the early 20th century by the car trade. Many former cycle manufacturers would become involved in the production of cars; for example the Rover car company emerged from the Rover cycle company.

Starley's design was not only to transform the cycle trade, but it would also have a significant social and political effect. The culture of the cycle club and the freedom of the open road extended the horizons of hundreds of thousands of enthusiasts. Weekends became a time for leisure and jaunts into the countryside. These outings stood in stark contrast to the grime and overcrowding of many of the industrial cities of the Midlands and North. The bicycle became more than a form of transport – it offered a chance of transformation, a way to experience the world beyond the family, neighbourhood or factory. Such freedom attracted those with ideas of social emancipation and the early socialist movement. Though the Clarion clubs found the bicycle a valuable way to spread their message, it also was a way to celebrate community and envision what a new society might be like. The bicycle grabbed the imagination of a nation and for a time became a focus for popular culture celebrated in songs and novels. However, not all were enthusiastic and there were instances of moral panic over the new craze in the mainstream press. Particular animosity was expressed towards women, whose adoption of the bicycle was seen as a direct challenge to their allotted place in society. The New Woman was emancipated, achieved things through her own agency and looked for meaning outside of home and hearth. Considered even worse than that, some adopted rational dress as a way of participating more fully in society, no longer hamstrung by the fashion for long skirts. These women wanted to be viewed as equals in all spheres, including the right to vote. Starley's Rover bicycle became a tool for social change and what made him wealthy also helped reshape social attitudes among significant parts of the population.

ACTIVITY
KNOWLEDGE CHECK

Cycling and society

1 With a partner discuss what you believe to be the key impacts of the invention of the safety bicycle on society; together decide upon a list.

2 Thinking about the list you have produced, draw up four headings, 'Culture', 'Politics', 'Economics' and 'Gender'. Consider which headings the items in your list come under.

3 Look at Extract 2. What do we learn about the way in which the bicycle affected the life of Sylvia Pankhurst? Why might this have been indicative of a broader change in society?

ACTIVITY
SUMMARY

John Kemp Starley: cycles, cycling clubs and emancipation, 1885–1901

1 What was it that made the Rover safety bicycle such a success? Draw up two columns and in one list what made the design a success and in the other write down what impact that had on the market for bicycles.

2 Look at the criticism levelled at the cycling community. Did this change as the different groups became involved in cycling?

3 Consider the phrase 'cads on castors' and then look at the way in which Eliza Linton treats the issue of women cyclists. Write a short paragraph comparing and contrasting the two views.

4 Look at Sources 8 and 9. What made cycling radical? Write a short paragraph contrasting the images of Wells and Tressell. Consider the question, 'Is politics just about leaflets or can one further a political ideal in other ways?'

WIDER READING

Green, B. 'The new woman's appetite for riotous living', in A. Ardis and L. Lewis *Women's Experience of Modernity: 1875-1945*, John Hopkins University Press (2003)

Horton, D. 'Social movements and the bicycle', https://thinkingaboutcycling.files.wordpress.com/

Horton, D., Rosen, P. and Cox, P. (eds) *Cycling and Society*, Ashgate Publishing (2007)

Rubinstein, D. 'Cycling in the 1890s', *Victorian Studies*, Vol. 12, No. 1, Autumn 1977

The Victorian Cyclist, https://thevictoriancyclist.wordpress.com

Thinking About Cycling, https://thinkingaboutcycling.com

Williamson, G. *Wheels within Wheels: The Story of the Starley's of Coventry*, Geoffrey Bles (1966)

3.7

Herbert Austin: creating and adapting to market forces, 1905-28

KEY QUESTIONS

- To what extent did Austin's skills as an industrialist lead to the success of the Longbridge works?
- How successful was the development of the Austin Seven in changing the fortunes of the Longbridge plant?
- In what ways did the growth in Austin Seven ownership impact on British society?

INTRODUCTION

The growth of the motor trade in Britain has been characterised as one of both innovation and entrepreneurial vision. For the industrialist Herbert Austin, the former was the seen as the key stumbling block for the development of the car industry in the UK. As early as 1897, he put his opinions down in the columns of the *American Machinist*, complaining bitterly of the innate conservatism of British engineers compared to their American contemporaries. In Austin's view, a reluctance to modernise was what was holding back manufacturing in Britain. It was, therefore, his intent to promote innovation and flexibility to meet the challenges of the emerging new economy, where mass production of complex consumer goods was supplanting textiles and heavy engineering as a driving force for economic growth. However, one might question how far innovation by itself was the answer in Britain and whether it was also important to adapt production to meet the challenges of emerging consumer markets quite different to those in the United States. It might be the ability to adapt to the demands of the UK market that marked Herbert Austin out as one of the leading industrialists of the automobile age as much as his enthusiasm for engineering novelty. Modernised design could play a part, as in the case of the Austin Seven; in the interwar period, that secured the financial position of the Austin Motor Company. Of equal importance was the capacity to exploit new markets, which would prove crucial in transforming the British car trade. As car ownership grew in the interwar period, the Austin car became the icon of a changing Britain, where mass motor transport would have profound long-term implications for society, the economy and the physical environment. The epoch of the motor car had arrived.

1905 – Herbert Austin establishes the Austin Motor Company at Longbridge, Birmingham

1914 – Austin Motor Company stops car production and expands to produce armaments

1905	1910	1915

1913 – Production at Longbridge reaches 1,500 cars per year

SOURCE

Herbert Austin in the original Austin Seven in 1922. This was Austin's iconic contribution to the world of interwar motoring in Britain.

Herbert Austin was born into a British middle-class family in 1866, and as a young man had gone to Australia to undertake an apprenticeship in engineering at Messrs Richard Parks & Company. While there, he became acquainted with Frederick Wolseley, who was a pioneer in the use of sheep-shearing machinery. Austin was interested in the development of the technology and proposed a number of improvements. In 1893, he returned to England to take over the management of the Wolseley Sheep Shearing Machine Company located in Aston, Birmingham. Things did not go well for the undertaking as components supplied by outside companies proved to be of poor quality. Austin took it on himself to buy back the faulty merchandise and try to rescue the reputation of the company. These actions marked him out as a manager who knew the need to maintain the customers' faith in the product. It also pointed to his later tendency to be mistrustful of suppliers, which in the early days of his business led him to try to control quality by in-house production.

1921 – Government imposes horsepower tax Austin's company goes into receivership

1928 – Over 24,000 Austin Seven cars a year produced at Longbridge

1920   1925   1930

1919 – Cancellation of government armaments contracts
Setting up of first production line

1922 – The Austin Seven produced, a low-cost family car that has an immediate impact on family leisure pursuits

With the damage done to the Wolseley company's reputation by the marketing of inferior goods, and the reluctance of sheep farmers to mechanise, it was decided to try to diversify into other areas. By 1895, the Wolseley company had become involved in the production of machine tools to be used in the cotton industry, and components for cycle manufacture. The following year, Austin obtained an agreement from the directors to invest £2,000 in plant to build motor vehicles. More capital was needed, however, to start car production and in 1901 the armaments firm Vickers, Sons & Maxim went into partnership with Austin and Wolseley, investing £40,000. By 1913, Wolseley would be one of the leading British car producers and the venture marked Austin out as one of the pioneers of British automobile development and set him on a path that would shape the rest of his life.

TO WHAT EXTENT DID AUSTIN'S SKILLS AS AN INDUSTRIALIST LEAD TO THE SUCCESS OF THE LONGBRIDGE WORKS?

The partnership with Vickers did not last long as a disagreement over engine design in 1905 led to Austin being asked to resign. Austin's reaction was that he vowed that he would not make the same mistake again and be subordinate to others when it came to decisions over design. He decided to set up his own car manufacturing business at Longbridge, Birmingham, where he was joined by a large section of the skilled workforce from Wolseley, who he was able to persuade to join his new venture.

The role of Herbert Austin

Longbridge was on the outskirts of Birmingham, but was linked by road and had a railway station nearby; it also had plenty of open space for expansion should the venture prove successful. Austin had raised £37,000 capital and was able to negotiate the purchase of an empty printing works for £7,750. Much of the money came from Austin himself, as well as a loan from Frank Kaiser, and later Harvey du Cross Jnr, of the Swift Cycle Company, who also invested in the new undertaking. At the end of 1905, he had produced plans for his first car, which were shown at the Olympia Motor Show and advance orders were taken. The first Austin model was the 25 horsepower (hp) Endcliffe Phantom, which cost

£650; 120 were manufactured and sold in 1906. Austin's ability to set up production so quickly was in part due to the multiskilled nature of his workforce.

Setting up production at Longbridge
While Austin had done much to increase productivity and efficiency at Wolseley, traditional methods persisted at the Longbridge plant. Teams of workers would assemble cars, rather than individual workers performing a single task on an assembly line. Batch production, as it was known, offered certain advantages over the forms of mass production being developed in the USA. It required limited capital investment to begin manufacturing and it was easy to introduce modifications or change the design. It was ideal for short runs and could be easily adjusted to meet fluctuations in demand. On the downside, productivity could be low and was heavily reliant on having a skilled workforce. Austin was therefore fortunate to have sufficient skilled labour readily available at the plant who had the flexibility to perform the range of tasks necessary for car production. Expanding output, however, showed up problems with the batch system as it became harder to manage the growing number of workers and the range of models being produced.

Financing the new business
A shortage of capital for investment was also a problem in the early years. Though there was rapid growth in demand, there were limited funds to finance an expansion in production. As Austin was unable to find investors, he became reliant on extended overdraft facilities from the Midland Bank to maintain the cash flow of the business. While the company made money, the time between producing a car and being paid for it meant that the firm was often short of cash to buy new materials to continue production. By 1913, more long-term investment had been secured when mortgage and **debenture** loan capital rose to £103,000. However, this also increased the company debt (i.e. the more it borrowed, the less there was left to reinvest and the more it had to pay out to service its loans).

Pre-war car production

Though there were hundreds of small manufacturers, the motor trade in Britain before the First World War had already tended to concentrate on certain geographical centres. In the north, Manchester and later Liverpool became important for Ford, first as a point for the importation and assembly of cars, but later they were the focus for actual manufacture of cars for the British market. In the south, Cowley in Oxfordshire was chosen by the Morris Company to be the centre for its ambitions. Yet it was Coventry, Birmingham and the Black Country that would see the greatest concentration of car companies, where there were many firms involved in the metal trades that proved a draw for many of the early entrants into the motor industry. Some, like the Rover company, grew out of the cycle trade, but most had links to the light engineering that dominated the region's manufacturing industry, and were able make use of the plentiful supply of skilled labour.

Models and design

Before the war, Austin manufactured luxury cars, in a range of chassis and bodies up to 60 hp. Though there was a short-lived experiment with commercial vehicles, by 1914 the focus was back on the car market. Production increased and employment expanded going from 270 in 1907 to 2,300 employees in 1914; though this was still smaller than at his former employer Wolseley, which had 4,000 workers by 1913. The company began to build a reputation for reliability and innovation – Austin led the way in switching from the **open-topped landaulet** to the **closed limousine** body of the modern car.

Austin criticised fellow manufacturers, saying their conservatism in design and their resistance to standardisation of chassis manufacture were the reasons the British car industry was lagging behind that of France. Cars were often built in relatively small runs by most British manufacturers and there was a tendency to change design between runs. However, while short runs increased unit costs, there was little evidence that there was a mass car market at this time, so it is unclear how far reduction of cost would have been that advantageous. His bestselling model, introduced just before the First World War, was the four-cylinder Austin Twenty, which retailed for approximately £580 in 1913, which at that time was a considerable sum of money. Like other manufacturers of the day, he experimented with light cars for a wider market, and in 1906 he had produced a single cylinder, 7 hp car to be jointly manufactured with the Swift Motor Company. Four years later, in 1910, he created the Austin Ten, which had a four-cylinder engine but only produced 10.1 hp and was half the price of the Austin Twenty. It did not sell well before the war, with only 295 being sold in 1913, as it was considered underpowered and there did not appear to be a ready market for such medium-priced small cars. This is significant as there has been much discussion by historians as to how far price sensitivity was important in the pre-war British car market. A lack of price sensitivity suggests that such items were objects of prestige and status rather than utility, i.e. just a means to get you from A to B.

Even after the war, there was evidence that price was not as much an important deciding factor on purchase as the status given by car ownership.

The Austin Marlborough landaulet from the *Illustrated London News*, 1913. The Marlborough landaulet design shows the separation between the comfort of the passengers in the back with the more basic provision for the driver. The design was modelled on the popular landaulet horse-drawn carriage, which had a hood that could be raised or lowered for the comfort of the passengers. The market for such machines was confined to wealthy people who could afford a chauffeur and wanted to be seen about town.

The reputation of Austin's cars was enhanced after 1908 by their performance in international motoring events, where they competed successfully against those of other manufacturers. An added boost to the firm came when the then world boxing champion Jack Johnson bought one of the 100 hp sports car models. Even in these early days, the image of the car was important; it was considered to be more than just a utility vehicle, it was something that could bestow social status on its owner. Celebrity endorsement and sporting success were important elements in the pre-war marketing strategy. As sales increased, the firm took the lead in establishing showrooms, first in Norwich in 1910, then Manchester in 1911, and by 1912 it was operating in London's West End. These provided a range of services; as well as sales they included repairs, hire cars and use of an Austin owners' clubroom. Though demand increased, the complexity of production led to a reduction in the number of models available from six to three in 1913.

For Austin, the years before the First World War proved to be successful, with steadily expanding sales, though rates of profit started to decline after 1912. Profits in 1912 were running at a high of 14 percent of turnover but dropped to a low of around four percent of turnover in 1914. The decline in the rate of profit was linked to the need to invest in the business to expand production and pointed to one of the problems faced by Austin – finding the capital needed to meet the demand for vehicles. Figure 7.1 clearly shows the bottleneck in production and profits experienced by the company before the outbreak of war.

Year	Net trading profit	Sales turnover
1906	£5,308	£14,772
1907	£1,393	£84,930
1908	£14,915*	£119,744
1909	£18,439	£169,821
1910	£26,111	£209,084
1911	£34,062	£276,196
1912	£50,533	£354,209
1913	£31,399	£425,641
1914	£30,302	£633,186

*For eleven months

Figure 7.1 Net profit and turnover for the Austin Car Company before First World War. It is interesting to note that though sales continued to increase year on year, net profits fell back after a pre-war peak in 1912. This might point to increased costs of production as well as having to service rising company debt that was taken on to expand manufacturing capacity. Adapted from *Herbert Austin: The British Motor Car Industry to 1941* by Roy Church (1979).

The pre-war car market

Before 1914, the market for cars in Britain was undergoing a rapid transformation. The Society of Motor Manufacturers and Traders estimated that between 1909 and 1913 there was a threefold increase in production, with about 34,000 cars being manufactured by the outbreak of war. Historians continue to debate whether or not the car had gone beyond being the plaything of the rich at this point to become a consumer item of the middle class. S.B. Saul (see Extract 1) was particularly critical of Austin's performance in technical and business matters, calling them uninspiring. Austin certainly maintained the common practice of not laying down a chassis until an order had been received and a deposit paid. While productivity was not high at this stage, Roy Church (see Extract 2) suggested that Saul's criticism was unfounded and that within the range of motor manufacturers of the time (excluding Ford), Austin's workforce were more productive than most and it was consistent in turning a profit, which was more than could be said for Wolseley. Church has questioned the assertion that there was a mass market in Britain for large quantities of small, inexpensive automobiles, and that the choice to limit production was a wise one given the market possibilities and the availability of investment capital.

EXTRACT 1
From *The Motor Industry in Britain to 1914* by S.B. Saul (1962). It deals with the issue of how far pre-war car production was advanced or held back by the use of traditional methods of car production.

A considerable amount of hand finishing was still to be noted at the Austin works in 1914... the industry was quite unable to release itself from the traditional ways of engineering.... The industry remained the domain of mechanics rather than production engineers.

EXTRACT 2
From *The Rise and Decline of the British Motor Car Industry* by Roy A. Church (1995). Church takes a contrasting view to Saul on how advanced British car production was.

The larger British vehicle manufactures were using American and British machine tools designed for repetitive assembly. Typically production occurred in small batches, compared with the sequential flow production system in use in the large American factories. Where Saul took these as evidence of conservatism... the British system's flexibility suited... producing a variety of models for a limited and socially stratified market.

The case of Ford was in some ways an exception to the rule. In the US, a mass car market did exist, which Ford was able to supply from its Detroit base. It was from here that parts were shipped to the Britain to be assembled at the company's northern plants. As can be seen in Figure 7.2, Ford was by far the largest single supplier in the UK car market.

The top ten British car producers	Output in 1913
Ford*	6,139
Wolseley	3,000
Humber	2,500
Sunbeam	1,700
Rover	1,600
Austin	1,500
Singer	1,350
Arrol-Johnston	1,150
Belsize	1,000
Daimler	1,000

* At this time the American producer Ford imported cars that were assembled in Manchester.

Figure 7.2 Output by the top ten British car producers in 1913. It is interesting to note that Ford is by far the most successful of the pre-war car manufacturers, followed some way behind by Wolseley, while Austin comes sixth. From *The Motor Industry in Britain to 1914* by S.B. Saul (1962).

Source 3 is taken from an article on the Austin Motor Company. It is interesting to note the marketing strategies that Austin used to promote his product before the First World War. He not only tried to build what would be called today a brand identity by promoting the Austin Club, but he was at pains to emphasise the prestige of his vehicles by focusing on his leading clients. He was not alone in this latter tactic, with other manufacturers drawing attention to the purchase of their automobiles by the rich and the titled.

SOURCE

3 From an article in *The Times*, 9 February 1914, on the Austin Motor Company. It discusses the Longbridge plant, the cars in production and the leading people who were buying them.

The Austin Car has many characteristics not found in other cars, improvements which have been invented and perfected in the Austin Works. These are exemplified in the Austin cars which were shown at the last Motor Exhibition at Olympia.... [The London Sales room] near Marble Arch [is] convenient for the many customers of the company in Mayfair. Here also are... the clients' smoking room the chauffeurs' club room the hire department, where a large number of cars are always ready for service... The clients' rooms, which extend across the entire front of the building, are furnished and decorated in much the same style as the lounge in a modern club, the walls being panelled in oak, the furniture of pleasing old design and the floors laid with handsome rugs. The chauffeurs' room is furnished with billiard and reading tables and with every comfort and well-being of the men... There are depots in Manchester and Norwich though not as large, are furnished with a similar dignity... Among the purchasers of Austin pleasure cars have been HIH The Grand Duke Gavril Konstantinovitch, The Grand Duchess Marie Pavtonvna, HH The Rajah Kishori Lall Joswami, HE Princess Colonna, Marquis Del Merito, the Foreign Minister Madrid and Minister of the Interior...

ACTIVITY
KNOWLEDGE CHECK

Car production and the market for motor vehicles before 1914

1 Critically assess Source 3. Consider how far this is a marketing strategy as against a true representation of the key market for Austin cars.

2 Drawing on the evidence from Figures 7.1 and 7.2 dealing with the expansion of car production at Longbridge and the level of pre-war production in Britain, what factors might suggest that car ownership had gone beyond just the very rich but had not yet found a mass car market?

3 Look at the evidence and assess the argument that Herbert Austin failed to take advantage of the expanding market for automobiles.

Questions and answers

Questions that historians ask vary depending on what they think is important. It is the questions that interest us that define the history that is written. These questions change with time and place. Different historians will also come up with different answers to the same questions, depending on their perspectives and methods of interpretation, as well as the evidence they use.

Below are explanations provided by three historians to explain why British car manufacturers did not adopt mass production methods that were used in the USA.

S.B. Saul	Roy Church	Sue Bowden
Mass production was held back in the UK by a tendency to rely on traditional systems of production and an overemphasis on engineering products rather than production.	Mass production was held back as the market was not yet there for a cheap, low-horsepower car. Traditional methods were sufficient to supply the existing market and provided flexibility.	Mass production was held back by too many manufacturers in a relatively small market. If there had been fewer car makers then they might have been able to take advantage of economies of scale.

Below are some key events in the development of mass car production.

Henry Ford introduces the continuous assembly line before First World War	Wolseley becomes the largest UK car manufacturer in 1913	Herbert Austin introduces the assembly line at Longbridge in 1919
Wolseley starts manufacturing cars in 1896	In 1913, UK car market is around 34,000 vehicles	By 1914, there were 113 companies manufacturing cars in the UK
Wolseley continues using batch production after the First World War	The Model T Ford is the most successful car in the UK before 1914	In 1913, Ford produces 168,220 cars in the USA

Work in groups of between three and six.

1   Which of these events would have been of most interest to each historian? Explain your answer.

2   Each take the role of one historian and devise a question that would interest them about each of the events.

3   Discuss each event in turn. Present the questions that have been devised for each historian and offer some ideas about how they would have answered them.

4   For each event, decide as a group which question is the most interesting and worthwhile of the three.

Answer the following questions in pairs:

5   Identify the different ways that each historian would approach writing an account of Herbert Austin's not introducing the assembly line at Longbridge until 1919.

6   In what ways would Church and Bowden differ in their explanations of the significance of Ford's production of 168,220 cars in the USA in 1913? What would be the focus of their arguments?

Answer the following questions individually:

7   All three historians may produce very different accounts and explanations of the same piece of history. Of the three historians, whose account would you prefer to read first? Explain your answer.

8   Do the differences in these accounts mean that one is more valid than the others?

9   Explain why different historical explanations are written by different historians.

10 Explain why different explanations of the same event can be equally valid.

The impact of the First World War

The First World War was both an opportunity for the Austin company and a danger to its long-term survival. The demands of wartime production led to the expansion of the business, but also saw capital investment in plant and machinery that would prove to be a drain on the firm's resources in the post-war period and present a challenge to Austin's management. New works were built on the Longbridge site for the production of munitions and aircraft. The expansion of production was funded by the government, which provided the capital investment needed to increase output to the meet the demands of the war effort. By the end of the war in 1918, some eight million shells had been produced, 650 guns, 2,000 aircraft and 500 of the Austin-designed armoured cars, the latter being an order placed by the Russian government. The armoured car design consisted of the 30 hp 'Colonial' chassis with armoured plating and two turreted machine guns. After the revolution of 1917, the Russian market was lost, with later models being supplied to the British army. However, the vehicles already supplied saw service on both sides in the Russian Civil War (1917–22) and some were still in service in the late 1920s in the Polish army.

By 1918 the value of Austin's yearly production had risen to £9 million from £600,000 in 1914. The value of tangible assets went from £289,605 before the war to £1,837,853 by 1918. While turnover and the **asset base** of the company grew, profits were more modest, as shown in Figure 7.3. From a high of 10.3 percent of turnover in 1916, they dropped to around 3.7 percent of turnover in 1918, which was in the main due to excess profits duty being levied on the company after 1915. For Austin the war was important for improving the company's asset base, but did not help boost earnings.

KEY TERM

Asset base
The property, machinery and goods owned by a company. For Austin, the Longbridge works had been greatly expanded to meet the needs of the war. Government investments to improve production left the company in possession of assets such as the new North Works that had been developed for aircraft production.

Year	Net trading profit	Sales turnover
1914	£30,302	£633,186
1915	£63,909	£890,083
1916	£227,177	£2,208,187
1917	£262,642	£3,765,029
1918	£358,272	£9,535,680

Figure 7.3 Net trading profit and sales turnover for the Austin Motor Company, 1914–18. The data in this table contrasts with that in Figure 7.1 on page 156. From 1914 to 1918, both profits and turnover continued to grow year on year. However, the rate of profit remained low, in part due to government taxation, so that in 1918 on a massive turnover of £9,535,680 the company was only making around 3.7 percent net profit. Adapted from *Herbert Austin: The British Motor Car Industry to 1941* by Roy Church (1979).

The changing scale of production also necessitated innovation in the methods of assembly. Batch production, where groups of skilled workers worked together to assemble small numbers of cars, was replaced by more streamlined methods that utilised less-skilled labour to create a constant flow of finished goods. By 1919, the changing production methods saw the creation of a production line similar to that which Ford had pioneered in the USA before the First World War. The concept of the production line had developed in the late 19th century to improve worker productivity by breaking down the activities involved in the production of an item into a number of basic tasks to be endlessly repeated. What Ford had done was create a moving assembly line, where the item to be manufactured moved past the workers, who remained stationary at their workstation. The historian S.B. Saul was critical of the slow pace of adoption of this technique among British manufacturers, while Roy Church argued that it would not have been appropriate for the much smaller UK car market before the First World War. The added fixed costs and the need to maintain volume might well have pushed Austin's limited capital to breaking point. Despite the rise in output during the war, traditional methods were refined rather than replaced.

The war saw the supply of labour become a major issue for the company, and led to the building of the Austin village of 252 wooden bungalows, imported from Canada, to house some of the 22,000 workers at the Longbridge plant. There was also a fleet of 35 buses to bring workers to the plant. As skilled labour became harder to find, unskilled workers and women workers made up an ever-larger proportion of the workforce, necessitating changes to working practices such as providing job-based training and attempting to simplify the method of production. In 1917, Herbert Austin founded the Austin Technical Society, with the aim of promoting the study of engineering among his growing workforce, and to provide the skilled labour that the plant needed.

The Austin workforce

Despite the increasing numbers of semiskilled and unskilled workers, skilled labour remained an important part of the workforce, particularly in the manufacture of components for the production line. Austin was keen to maintain the quality of his workforce. As well as the Austin Technical Society, there was no apprenticeship premium charge, where apprentices would have to pay a fee to be accepted as an apprentice, which deterred many from becoming skilled workers. However, three months of wages were withheld until it had been established that the candidate was reliable, which was generous as some firms insisted that trainees work for nothing for the first 12 months. Accounts suggest that Austin held his apprentices in the highest regard and did much to encourage their development; he was well aware of the key role skilled labour played in meeting the challenges of production, which underscored his industrial paternalism. Austin himself considered his plant a 'democratic body' and he held weekly meetings with departmental heads; there was also a works council that discussed issues around production. However, Professor Stewart Clegg, an expert in business organisation, has described the relationship between management and workforce as despotic in the way Austin attempted to control his employees – a view shared by Roy Church, who felt that Austin's personality tended to dominate all such workforce communication. Austin's view of organised labour was not particularly positive and he was critical of unions, claiming that they hampered the ability of industries to compete. However, he was forced to negotiate with them as, though the union movement in the area tended to be weak, craft unions representing the skilled workforce were much stronger and well organised. In January 1918, the whole plant was brought to a standstill by a strike over the removal of the Works Committee chairman, Arthur Peacock, who had led a campaign for a higher weekly wage in lieu of bonuses. The highhandedness of Austin's actions was in part indicative of his management style, as was the later compromise to get the plant back to work – that Peacock would be reinstated pending an enquiry that seems to have never taken place.

The development of Longbridge and its economic importance to the West Midlands

The end of the war caught Austin by surprise, as he had confidently predicted in early 1918 that it would last another two years. Government contracts were cancelled and Austin was left with a massive new plant without orders. Carl R.F. Engleback, the Austin works manager, considered the plant at Longbridge as insufficient for the future needs of the business and that the arrangement of the building made it difficult for the plant to work economically. Yet the war had brought advantages. The mass production of armaments provided experience of how to restructure the plant's processes of assembly. Government investment had provided, among other things, a specialist metallurgy laboratory, construction of a hardening heat plant and the installation of huge sheet metal presses for car bodies.

Post-war strategies and challenges

In January 1919, the company claimed it had an order book worth £4 million in advance orders. Faced with these new circumstances, Austin outlined his production strategies. These were for a new car, the Austin Twenty; a 30 cwt (hundredweight) lorry; tractors; and electrical house lighting sets, to be produced over a three-year period. The aim was to build 100 cars a week, raise tractor production to the same level and manufacture 60 30-cwt lorries every seven days. This plan put a huge strain on the company's finances as, although it had profited by the war, it had to pay tax on these earnings leaving little to invest. Between 1919 and early 1920, £289,624 had to be raised to purchase new plant alone, and on top of this was a need for more operating capital to keep the business running. Austin's optimism was not without justification. The end of the war released much pent-up demand; the number of cars on the road had declined due to wartime rationing of petrol and the post-war boom offered a ready market. Other British manufacturers took a similar view, such as the Harper Bean group from Dudley and Wolseley, and it appeared to be a race to see who could get their products to market first. More threatening to Austin was the challenge from the US, as his Austin Twenty would be in direct price competition with Ford, which had not had to retool for the war effort. However, such optimism in a post-war boom was short-lived – the economy went into recession in late 1920. By 1921, the firm was in serious financial difficulty, with a deficit of £1.5 million. The slump saw asset prices drop, which left many manufacturers holding goods that were worth less than the cost of the materials that had been used to make them. Added to this, orders were cancelled as buyers faced financial difficulty, leading to major problems with cash flow, which was needed to service the company debt and pay suppliers. The firm was saved from receivership, but Austin would have to work with limited capital investment and was no longer in total control of the company.

 SOURCE 4   From an Austin Motor Company report, 3 February 1919. It details the company's continuing need to raise capital to meet the demands for a growing market for cars and other motor vehicles. Despite the optimism expressed here, the projected demand would evaporate by early 1921. © British Motor Industry Heritage Trust.

The Company has established depots in London and Manchester and controls a subsidiary Company in Paris. The production during the past year was over twenty times the pre-war turnover, entirely justifying the capacity of the personnel, the Staff, and Management of the Company.

This large output has been obtained without any additional Capital other than advances from the Government and the borrowings from the company's Bankers.

During this period of reconstruction a considerable output was maintained and profits made. To assist in carrying out this reorganization and extension, an issue of £1,000,000 in Preference shares was made in February, 1919, the Board of Directors considering that the provision of the larger amount of capital required to carry on the manufacture should be held over until the works were thoroughly in order, the various markets of the world properly tested, and a good number of the models in the hands of the public. The orders and contracts on hand at the present time are more 2.5 times the amount which was anticipated in January 1919, and an examination of the records show that an output of over £10,000,000 will be required to approximately satisfy the demands of the Company's agents and customers for the present year; an even larger amount is demanded for the succeeding years. This very large production is within the capacity of the works and organization, and the Directors have every confidence in asking for the subscription of the additional working capital outlined in the Prospectus, having satisfied themselves that it can be profitably employed in the business.

We are already turning out 75 Chassis and 25 Tractors per week, and confidently expect by gradual increase to reach by the end of June, the full schedule of output of 200 Chassis 100 Tractors and 60 Lorries per week besides our normal quantities of Electric Lighting Outfits and Spares.

To conserve the success gained by the Company's Agricultural Tractors in France, and to overcome the high duties and rates of Exchange, and the difficulties and expense of transport, and also to meet the natural desire of the French farmers to purchase tractors made in France, the Board decided during the past year to increase the capital of the French Company known as 'Société Anonyme Austin' to 10,000,000 francs, and to establish and equip a factory there.

A Level Exam-Style Question Section A

Study Source 4 before you answer this question.

Assess the source for revealing the strategy of Herbert Austin in developing his business for post-war markets and the ways in which the taxation of motor vehicles might have aided the advance of Austin over its rivals.

Explain your answer, using the source, the information about its origin and your own knowledge about the historical context. (20 marks)

Tip
Look at the issue in its wider context and balance the rise in cost of motoring for foreign importers with the need to produce a car for a new mass market. Remember pre-war motoring was not particularly price sensitive, but to what extent did this remain the case?

Economic importance of the Longbridge works

For the West Midlands the development of Austin's Longbridge works was indicative of an important economic change across much of the region. Though the metal trades were important employers in Birmingham, Coventry and the Black Country, they had tended to be concentrated around small-scale workshop production. There had been innovation in some sectors, as with the founding of the Birmingham Small Arms company in 1861, which became involved with the large-scale manufacture of guns, bicycles and eventually motorcycles at its Small Heath works in Birmingham, but this was the exception rather than the rule. The development of the motor industry after the First World War saw the building of new factories such as the Singer works in Birmingham and the Hillman factory in Coventry, both of which were custom-built plants for mass production. However, they were in the shadow of Longbridge, as it was here that assembly line production in the UK was pioneered. It would be Austin's innovation that would define the industry and provided the model to be followed by his British competitors. The development of continuous production also led to a growing demand for specialised components, which aided the growth of the region's component manufacturers. Companies such as Joseph Lucas Limited in Birmingham became specialists in the manufacture of headlights, while in Wolverhampton Rubery Owen supplied car frames as well as a range of other parts to the motor trade.

SOURCE
5 The Austin moving assembly line in 1920. This was a copy of Ford's model of a moving conveyor of cars. The assembly line offered the possibility to speed up production and streamline the process of fitting components to a car chassis. However, this came at a price. Assembly lines required large amounts of capital investment and had to run at a high volume to be profitable.

ACTIVITY
KNOWLEDGE CHECK

The impact of the First World War

1 Read Source 4. What challenges does this document suggest the Austin Motor Company faced after the First World War? What does it say about the opportunities for the company in the post-war world?

2 Make a list of the ways in which the First World War changed Austin Motors.

3 Was the First World War an opportunity or a challenge to the long-term development of the Austin Motor Company? Use your notes from the previous activities to draw up a table, placing the advantages in one column and the disadvantages in the other. Then write a paragraph summarising your conclusions.

KEY TERMS

Road Act 1920 and Finance Act 1921
The Road Act 1920 created the provision for a road tax fund, which was set in the Finance Act 1921 at a rate of £1 per horsepower. The idea was to create a hypothecated tax (money pledged by law for a specific purpose) that was to be used for the sole purpose of maintenance and improvement of the road network.

HOW SUCCESSFUL WAS THE DEVELOPMENT OF THE AUSTIN SEVEN IN CHANGING THE FORTUNES OF THE LONGBRIDGE PLANT?

The autumn of 1920 was a crunch time for Austin. His post-war strategy had been to concentrate on a single model but his choice of the Austin Twenty, which was a relatively expensive and high-powered car, brought him into direct competition with the American automobile manufacturers who supplied a similar product at an equally competitive price. By the July of 1920, he had sold 3,000 Austin Twenty cars, but the market was beginning to cool, as the **Road Act 1920** and the **Finance Act 1921** placed a tax on horsepower that added extra expense on such powerful machines, further limiting Austin's market.

The sudden drop in commodity prices as raw materials began to be available in greater supply after wartime shortages caused a fall in the stock market, resulting in a recession in 1921. Orders for new cars dropped sharply, which caused a crisis in the company's cash flow and forced it into receivership. All was not lost, however, as Austin was saved by the Midland Bank, which offered new capital, along with an issue of new shares to investors rather than a new debenture; the bank felt that this option favoured one set of investors over another. Though the company had been brought back from the brink of bankruptcy, capital remained limited and Austin had to adopt a different management style with his new finance director, Ernest Payton, who was appointed by the bank, and Carl Engelbach, as the works director. While Austin still remained at the helm, he was no longer in overall control of the company.

The post-war slump had a major effect on the Longbridge workforce. In 1919 there were 10,000 employees at the plant, but after the slump this rapidly declined, and in 1922 there were only 2,600 left. At the height of the war the need to bring in workers had led to the construction of a train platform by the factory that often was so packed it was hard to board the trains. However, in the immediate post-war years the flood had been reduced to a trickle. Things were to change markedly for the plant with the production of the Austin Seven. By 1926, the workforce had climbed to 25,000 and extra trains had to be put on from Birmingham and the Black Country to transport this vast army of workers. The small village of Northfield, close to the factory, began to grow rapidly. First, speculative builders built small groups of houses, but by the late 1920s large council estates were being constructed in the area that were soon filled with Austin workers and their families, though it must be noted that these dwellings were not intended to be lived in by car workers, but were built to address the problem of overcrowding in central Birmingham slums.

With the success of the new car the plant at Longbridge continued to expand. What in 1905 had covered just 2.5 acres had grown by 1928 to 220 acres, consisting of the North, West and South works. Keeping the production lines running required eight goods trains a day, with 120,000 tonnes of materials delivered annually. From the early 1920s there were extensions to the foundry at the North works followed by redevelopment of the chassis assembly line at the South works. Finally, in 1928 the North works were further extended for engine production, while the West works specialised in body construction and were the site of the paint shop. The pattern was one of specialisation and integration of production. By the end of the decade, increasing numbers of components were being brought in from local suppliers, such as Lucas and Rubery Owen, as Austin increasingly concentrated on car assembly rather than controlling all aspects of the production processes. The workforce also began to change, as among the skilled engineers there developed a strong trade union tradition that by the 1930s was to become more militant.

New thinking

On a trip to the US, it became obvious to Austin that the vast potential of the American producers meant that they could produce 20 hp cars far more cheaply and efficiently than he could. He felt that the concentration on the more powerful cars left a gap for a low-powered utility car that would face far less competition. The key strategy would, therefore, be to define a new untapped market for small cars rather than compete directly with Ford and Morris, who remained focused on producing larger cars.

In July 1922, test trials started for the new car and in November the Austin Seven was exhibited at the Olympia Motor Show. Austin had managed the design of it himself, taking on Stanley Edge, a draftsman from the Longbridge factory, to work with him on designs at Austin's home at Lickey Grange, situated in the Lickey Hills just behind the Longbridge plant. Edge convinced Austin to use a small four-cylinder side-valve engine that gave the car a 7.2 hp rating by the Royal Automobile Club (RAC). Though it was a small car, the relatively high power to weight ratio gave it a lively road performance and saw versions of it raced at Brooklands Small Car Handicap in 1923, where Austin's son-in-law Author Waite drove one to victory. However, Austin faced difficulties in bringing the new car to market. He had spent his own money in developing the initial design and had to pressure the board into agreeing to finance production.

Austin's idea had been to create a new car that would not be in competition with the **Model T Ford**, which had been the first mass-market car, but to break into the growing market for motorcycle and sidecar combinations. Ownership of these types of vehicles had grown rapidly after the First World

KEY TERM

Model T Ford
The 1908 Model T Ford was the first affordable mass-produced middle-class car. It defined the new era of motoring and was probably the most influential design of the first part of the 20th century.

War with 205,450 on the road by 1927. Church, however, has suggested that this is misleading, and that the market for the Austin Seven came from elsewhere. While he points out that the Austin Seven was only £25 more than a top of the range 1,000 cc Birmingham Small Arms motorcycle combination, relatively few of these were sold and the more common 350 cc to 700 cc were far cheaper than the basic Austin. Even with falling prices in the 1920s, slow income growth meant that it was among the middle class that a market was found. As can be seen in Figure 7.4, the price of an Austin Seven fell from £225 in 1922, to just £128 in 1928.

Year	Austin Seven annual vehicle production	Retail price
1922	178	£225
1923	2,409	£165
1924	4,800	£155
1925	8,024	£141
1926	13,174	£145
1927	21,671	£145
1928	24,247	£128

Figure 7.4 Austin Seven production and prices, 1922–28. The price of the Austin Seven fell as production increased and economies of scale helped to reduce costs. Adapted from *Herbert Austin: The British Motor Car Industry to 1941* by Roy Church (1979).

The Austin Seven gained a reputation as a reliable car that could fulfil many roles, from doctor's car to baker's van, and the Austin became a familiar sight in the interwar years. The car saved the Austin Motor Company, clearing the company debts and adding to its cash flow and capital. It was also exported and manufactured overseas, although some of the vehicle's shortcomings did detract from its reputation. In Australia, for example, there were complaints that it was too close to the ground and did not always perform well on the unmade roads of the outback. Despite these limitations, demand for the vehicle continued to grow in the 1920s. In 1928, the 24,247 Austin Seven cars manufactured represented just over 18 percent of the total UK car production.

A Level Exam-Style Question Section A

Study Source 6 before you answer this question.

Assess the value of the source for revealing the success of Austin's strategy of producing a small inexpensive car and his ability to bring it to a mass market.

Explain your answer, using the source, the information about its origin and your own knowledge about the historical context. (20 marks)

Tip

Consider how far the market might appear to have been price sensitive and the image of the Austin Seven as a vehicle for the family rather than work. You might also reflect on the size and scope of the UK car market in comparison to that of Europe and America.

SOURCE

6 Advertising notice for the new Austin Seven Light Car, issued 8 August 1922 by the Austin Motor Company. It not only provides technical specifications, but also paints a picture of providing ideal transport for a middle-class family living in the suburbs with limited garage space. The car is seen as an essential family item rather than a plaything of the rich. © British Motor Industry Heritage Trust.

There have been many attempts to design a car which would replace the motor-cycle and sidecar as a family conveyance. So far the latter type of machine has more than held its own. The Austin Motor Company are among the latest to attack the problem, and the outcome of the effort should be distinctly interesting.

The new Austin of seven hp is designed to carry a man and his wife and three children, and it is stated that in tests already made a speed of 52 MPH has been obtained, and that a consumption trial resulted in a satisfactory figure of 78 MPG. If the little car is soundly planned and constructed and the initial price is kept near £200 mark, as it is hoped that it will be, we shall certainly be nearer popular motoring than heretofore.

The model is orthodox in the general scheme, having a four-cylinder water-cooled engine which is specified to give off 10 HP at 400 RPM, a three-speed gearbox, rear live-axle and differential gear and torque tube, with a half-elliptical transverse spring in the front and quarter-elliptics at the rear, and adjustable worm and sector steering are among the principal chassis features.

The braking is done on all four wheels, and application of front and back sets is separate. The coachwork is arranged with two bucket seats in front, which are adjustable and detachable, and the rear seat is made for two or three children.

It will be readily seen from the above that the baby Austin is a car and not a compromise of makeshift, and this fact is also borne out by the body being fitted with a hood, the side curtains of which are full and open with the door. The road clearance is 9ins the wheelbase 6ft 3ins, the track 3ft 4ins, and the weight 6.5cwt, all important figures, especially for Colonial use and for popular motoring at home, where garage space is the baulking factor in the solution of many a would-be motorist's problem.

It is clear from the language used in Source 6 that the new car was to be both aspirational and practical in providing transport for the family. The image of domestic workhorse stands in stark contrast to the pre-war exclusivity afforded by the Austin Club and the list of aristocratic owners of Austin cars. Motoring was to be a new market that would make its mark on interwar Britain.

The Austin Seven proved to be the most popular model in Britain in the interwar period, with 375,000 built by 1939. Though this was not the company's only model, with the Austin Ten and the Austin Twenty still in production and aimed respectively at the medium and luxury markets, it was by far its most successful. Market share was increased, with Austin accounting for 25 percent of car production in the UK by 1929. This set it just below Morris, which maintained a 35 percent share, but it eclipsed Ford, which had 22 percent of the market in 1921 and had fallen to just four percent of UK car production by the end of the 1920s. However, the success of the Austin Seven and the growth of market share was not the whole story. Though Ford proved less successful than before the First World War against the competition in the British market, it is not clear to what degree Britain had a mass car market, especially in comparison with the USA (see Figure 7.5). What Austin achieved was to exploit markets that his competitors had not considered, such as for a small, inexpensive car for a middle-class market. The Austin Seven was not without competition, with the likes of the Rover Ten, a revamped pre-war design, and the Citroën 7 hp available. The Citroën model was more of a threat to the Austin Seven, and its contemporary design and competitive price led Austin to drop the price of its model to defend its market share.

Year	USA	Europe (including UK)	UK
1925	3,185,900	402,600	132,000
1928	3,815,400	486,500	169,600

Figure 7.5 The total output of cars in the USA, Europe and the UK, 1925 and 1928. This not only shows the contrast between European and American car production, it points to the differing rates of growth in production. Between 1925 and 1928, car production in Europe only grew by around 84,000, while in the USA the market sees another 629,500 cars, more than the total production of cars in Europe. From *Demand and Supply Constraints in the Inter-War UK Car Industry: Did the Manufacturers Get it Right?* by Sue M. Bowden (1962).

ACTIVITY
KNOWLEDGE CHECK

The impact of the Austin Seven

1 Looking at Figure 7.4, what two trends are indicated here regarding the success of the Austin Seven and the impact of mass production? Compare production of the Austin Seven in 1928 with the total production of motor vehicles in the UK for 1913 in Figure 7.2, just 15 years before.

2 Look at Source 6. Who did Austin identify as the key market for the new car? What evidence is there that the company was justified in this view? Make some notes and discuss them with a partner.

3 What evidence do we have that the Austin Seven represented a new world of mass motor transport? Look critically at the material above and reflect on how far we can talk of a mass market for cars before the Second World War.

IN WHAT WAYS DID THE GROWTH IN AUSTIN SEVEN OWNERSHIP IMPACT ON BRITISH SOCIETY?

That car ownership increased in the interwar period is not disputed – the production of new vehicles in British car plants expanded from 73,000 in 1922 to an interwar high of 379,000 in 1937. What is more difficult to ascertain is how far Britain become a mass car market, as was the case in the USA. The American automobile industry had seen demand for its product go beyond the confines of the middle-class consumer, with the car becoming an essential part of everyday life. In the US, it had been the Model T Ford that had been the herald of a new age of mass motoring. British manufacturers in the interwar period attempted to find a home-grown equivalent to bring motoring to the masses. However, despite the availability of cars such as the Austin Seven, Wolseley Hornet and the bull-nosed Morris Oxford, economic historian Professor Sue Bowden has suggested that in the UK the cost of motoring was possibly a more important factor in limiting the growth of the car market than the price of a new automobile. Professor Sean O'Connell, a historian of the motor trade, has argued that cars in Britain remained important symbolic goods that were primarily bought for leisure purposes. Even by the mid-1930s, sales to commercial travellers, doctors, farmers and professional and business users was estimated to be between 24 and 40 percent. Professor Raphael Samuel, in his work *Theatres of Memory*, pointed to an interwar anxiety of the middle class over their status and that to establish their place in the hierarchy symbols of position, such as motor car ownership, became increasingly important. And as motoring journalist Graham Robson has argued, it was seen that one should have the right car for one's station in life; a bank manager who drove a sports car might not be considered trustworthy. It can be argued that it was these factors of leisure, cost and status that define interwar motoring.

EXTEND YOUR KNOWLEDGE

Buying a car
The role of hire purchase was important in extending car ownership. Among the middle class, there tended to be a stigma attached to such agreements and consumers were shy of admitting to taking on debt. One of the main providers was the United Dominions Trust (UDT), which managed the market with a firm hand, discouraging the practice of no-deposit agreements and imposing credit rationing. All of these factors might well have limited the potential market for new cars.

Government policy

The growth in motoring resulted in an increasing demand for better roads. The state of Britain's road network had been a cause for concern since the 1890s and the boom in cycling. However, the government response had been limited. After the First World War, a greater emphasis was given to the issue with the formation of the Ministry of Transport in 1919 to oversee national transport systems. Its first task was to classify roads by usage, which was completed by 1921. Roads were ranked under three headings: Class 1 '**trunk roads**', Class 2 'link roads' and Unclassified.

KEY TERM

Trunk road
A main route that linked towns and cities.

EXTEND YOUR KNOWLEDGE

Road classification
The system of classification soon changed with Class 1 and Class 2 roads becoming A and B roads. To further distinguish one route from another, road numbers were added, for example the A1, A6, B225, etc. that is familiar to us today. The long-term effect of this was to aid road mapmakers and help the motorist with road signs that offered more than just the name of the next town.

County councils were given responsibility for the maintenance of Class 1 and Class 2 roads, but were not required to maintain Unclassified roads. Though there was some initial government funding immediately after the war, it was directed towards help to deal with unemployment rather than develop infrastructure. Long term, the upkeep of the network proved a strain on local resources, and the level of repairs and type of road surfaces varied from county to county. The Trunk Roads Act 1936 saw 4,500 miles of roads transferred from council responsibility to administration by the Ministry of Transport, which set national standards for road widths and surface layouts. However, the Ministry of Transport did little to upgrade roads through widening schemes and bypasses, concentrating instead on extending the amount of the road network with a tarmac surface. Though officials did visit Germany in the 1930s to see the *autobahns* (German motorways), such improvements were not seriously considered before the Second World War.

To help pay for the improvement of the transport network, a hypothecated tax called the Road Fund was established, paid for through an annual licence – motorists were expected to provide the resources to construct the roads that they wanted. Before the war, there had been resentment on the part of sections of the political establishment that general taxation and therefore ordinary taxpayers might have to foot the bill for the transport network. It might appear odd now, but it points to the distance between the motorist and what we might term the mass of taxpayers at that moment in time.

In addition to the Road Fund tax, motorists had to pay a petrol tax, which in 1928 was four pence a gallon, and which was also intended to go towards the upkeep of the road system. All of this added a significant additional cost to motoring, though it is still unclear how far such demands on the motorist's pocket had a major effect on the growth of car ownership in the interwar period.

Trade tariffs and taxes

The Britain of the interwar period presented a range of challenges and opportunities for Austin and his fellow motor manufacturers. One of the key challenges was how they were to compete with US and continental competition. While Austin was re-equipping his factories, Ford was ready to take advantage of the post-war boom. One advantage that the home producers had was a 33.3 percent tariff on luxury goods, such as imported cars. This tax had been introduced in 1915 and remained in force until after the Second World War; the McKenna duties, as they became known, were extended in 1926 to commercial vehicles imported into Britain. The tariff was really only of short-term significance as Ford moved from assembling to manufacturing cars in Manchester and later built a plant at Dagenham, just outside London, so avoiding the tax. Despite this, Austin continued to be a very vocal supporter of the tax as an important protection for the British car industry against what he felt was undue foreign competition. Why he should have been so vehement a critic is not clear. However, Source 7, from a report of his speech to a dinner of the Austin Motor Company, suggests he feared that scrapping the tax would result in production being moved overseas, as had been the case in parts of the interwar fashion industry.

SOURCE

From a report of Austin's speech at an Austin Motor Company dinner, which appeared in the company magazine in October 1929. He makes reference to the removal of duties on clothing, which was blamed for a rapid rise in cheap imports that threatened to take market share from home producers.

Sir Herbert Austin, speaking at the dinner of the Austin Motor Company, at the Connaught Rooms last night, said the coming year could not be otherwise than abnormally difficult. Let them take, for instance, the possible refusal of the Government to retain the McKenna Duties. We are all doing our best to prevent such a catastrophe from arising, he said, and, while it might be very consoling for shareholders to say that to say that such a pierce of folly could not possibly arise, we are doing everything we can be prepared for the worst. Designs for the sake of change should be discouraged, Sir Herbert Austin added. They did not want to get the motor industry into the somewhat unhappy state of women's fashions.

The other duty to affect manufacture was the so-called 'horsepower' tax, an annual tax to be paid on motor vehicles, introduced in the 1909 budget to raise revenue for road building. The original formula was devised by the Royal Automobile Club, which was a calculation of piston diameter divided by the number of cylinders in the engine. The problem was that cars of equal engine capacity were taxed more heavily if the pistons' area in the engine was larger. In 1921, it was decided to simplify the tax and the rate was fixed at £1 per horsepower. The change in some ways favoured Austin and his fellow British carmakers, as US cars tended to have greater horsepower capacity. The Model T Ford, the mainstay of the US producer, saw the tax increase from £6.6s to £23 a year, the same as a Rolls Royce Phantom, which appealed to a very different market to the Ford.

ACTIVITY
KNOWLEDGE CHECK

Tax and the motor trade

1 Read the section on trade tariffs and taxes and write down what tariffs and taxes were paid on motor vehicles and the rate at which they are charged. With a partner, consider what you know about the UK car market in the interwar period and reflect on how significant you think the taxes and tariffs were in keeping foreign produced cars out of the home market.

2 Read Source 7. In your opinion why would Austin be so concerned about a reduction in tariffs?

3 Considering the taxes and tariffs on the motor trade and Austin's attitude to them, how important do you think they were to helping shape the development of the business at Longbridge? Set your answer out as a series of bullet points.

The changing landscape

The rapid rise in car ownership after the First World War could be seen in the proliferation of garages and filling stations along the main highways. Before the war, car owners could pick up sealed two-gallon cans, often stocked by bicycle dealers, hotels and even newsagents. The first American-designed petrol pump was erected in Shrewsbury in 1915, but it was not until 1919 that the first roadside filling station, which consisted of a shed and a petrol pump, was built by the Automobile Association (AA) in 1919 at Aldermaston in Berkshire. It was soon followed by thousands of others, some sponsored by oil companies, but many were built by independent entrepreneurs who saw that there was money to be made in the trade. In depressed rural areas, a filling station offered a scarce source of income, with many former servicemen going into the business when work was hard to find. By 1929, there were some 54,000 filling stations throughout the country. It is interesting to note that this massive transformation came about without any central direction and there was no attempt to rationalise the distribution of filling stations. However, the change did not go unnoticed and the Campaign for Rural England, founded after the First World War in response to rapid urban development, was critical of the advertisements and petrol stations that were considered to ruin the traditional nature of rural villages. The magazine *The Motor* ran an article in 1923 drawing attention to the threat posed to beauty spots by the encroachment of the car-owning public. It called for architects to make sure that such things as garages and filling stations were domestic rather than industrial in their design and sympathetic to their surroundings. The growing campaign to preserve the countryside resulted in the **Petroleum (Consolidation) Act 1928**, which gave local authorities the power to limit where filling stations were sited and regulate their appearance.

One further addition to the roadside furniture of the interwar years was the appearance of telephone call boxes. The AA had begun installing them in 1914, and was followed rapidly by the RAC. The motoring organisations began to offer 'get you home' services, utilising a network of approved garages to help the motorist who had broken down. In 1926, the RAC received 7,500 calls from its phone boxes; this rose to 11,000 by 1929, which is again indicative of increasing car use in the years between the wars.

The economic effects of increased car ownership

One of the defining characteristics of interwar motoring was the growth of leisure, with possibly the majority of vehicles being bought for that purpose. This had a significant economic effect as the need to cater for the requirements of motorists offered a host of opportunities. The car was not only a means of transport that permitted large numbers of people to explore the countryside, going wherever the road might take them, it had a physical impact on the fabric of towns and villages. To keep the car owner up to date there rapidly developed a motoring press, the leading interwar journals being *The Motor* and *Autocar*. Petrol and tyre companies such as Dunlop published guides and maps to help the motorist find their way and take note of the places of interest, an example of which was the *Motorist's Guide, Counsellor and Friend*, first printed in 1920. Organisations such as the Caravan Club, formed in 1907, were active in developing facilities for the touring motorist. From the 1920s, there was a growth in day trips to beauty spots and other attractions, one measure of which was an increase in the number of historic houses open to the public, particularly in a time when their owners were facing declining revenues from the land. There was also a steady expansion of roadhouses and cafes to meet the needs of the day-tripper.

KEY TERM

Petroleum (Consolidation) Act 1928
A piece of legislation to regulate the trade in petrol. It required all premises selling petroleum to have a licence, and made local authorities responsible for administering the provisions of the Act.

A Level Exam-Style Question Section B

How far was the building of filling stations and road improvements responsible for the growth in interwar motoring as much as the availability of low-cost cars such as the Austin Seven? (20 marks)

Tip
The question is one that reflects on how widespread car ownership had become by the end of the 1920s. You need to consider whether increasing numbers of motor vehicles on the roads equated with widening social and economic access to them, or if they remained the prerogative of an established middle class.

The seaside towns

More traditional holiday destinations also benefited from the car. Seaside resorts such as Blackpool and Bournemouth had originally developed in the age of steam, with excursion trains ushering in the age of mass tourism. A beach holiday was a mainstay of the interwar period, and increasing numbers of motorists headed to the coast. While the car provided access to more remote bays and inlets, it was the seaside towns, with their pleasure beaches and funfairs, which attracted most holidaymakers. The heady atmosphere of places such as Blackpool also led to incidents where working-class holiday makers would indulge in **joyriding**. In 1932, there were nearly a thousand such incidents in Blackpool alone, the joyriding capital of Lancashire. The architecture of the seaside resort also changed, as places like Bournemouth adopted the new art deco style for their beachfront facilities. The lido, or open-air pool, became a feature of many of these resorts in the interwar years.

Touring holidays

Touring holidays became popular in areas such as the Yorkshire Dales, Lake District and Scotland. The 1925 **Shell** campaign 'See Britain First – on Shell' with its posters of upper-class tourists out and about in the wild landscapes of Britain did much to promote these areas, just as the railway posters had a generation before in encouraging tourists to the seaside and cathedral cities.

However, according to historian Sean O'Connell, the itinerant ways of the motorist created problems for hoteliers, who were used to clients staying a week rather than a couple of nights before moving on to their next destination. It took time for the hotel sector to adjust to these ways and open the business to new entrants. To cater for this kind of motoring, many farmers began to offer bed and breakfast to take advantage of this passing trade. The country holiday offered a chance to generate income in rural communities where the economy in general remained depressed. Touring and the increase in mass motoring also saw a rise in employment in the service sector; with jobs for waiting staff, hotel domestic staff, cooks and petrol pump attendants having a significant impact on areas that had been away from the main centres of population. Roadside restaurants became popular, providing meals for the weary motorist. The increasing demand for 'somewhere to stop' and refresh encouraged a number of the large brewers to build pubs to provide food and a bed for the car driver. An example of this is the massive Black Horse Pub in Northfield, Birmingham, built in the style of a half-timbered mansion, on the main route to the West Country.

Not all drivers took advantage of these new facilities; many families went out for the day armed with a packed lunch and sandwiches. However, the practice of the self-catering day-tripper drew criticism from some. In Yarmouth, the pages of the local press attacked such visitors for spending little money in the town and only leaving litter behind them. The motoring public were equally critical of the problem of parking in seaside towns, with the motoring press full of stories of excessive charges levied by local councils in their car parks. Even in the motoring press, there was a feeling that weekend tourists had a tendency to swamp picturesque villages, overwhelming them with traffic and so destroying the very tranquillity that they travelled to experience. In popular literature, Rudyard Kipling wrote of the destruction of the countryside by the motorist in his short story 'Beauty Spot'.

SOURCE

8 From 'Beauty Spot' by Rudyard Kipling (1932). This short story is an example of the way in which motoring entered the literature of the day. It offers an image of an England that had been debased by the car, which is in sharp contrast to the impression given by the marketing departments of the petrol companies, who offered the motorist the chance to explore an unspoiled rural idyll.

The drivers pulled up by the broken wall, which the publican at the White Hart recommended as a good pitch between drinks. So people used it more and more for picnics and pleasure, and after a Southern Counties private Tour had removed as a trophy the pitiful little sign 'trespassers will be prosecuted', which was Mr Gravell's one protest, the gaps in the wall widened by feet in a week; the rhododendron clumps shrank like water drops on a hot iron and the dell became dotted with coloured streamers, burst balloons, tins, corks, food-bags, old paper, tyre-wrappers, bottles – intact and broken – rags of the foulest, cigarette-cartons, and copious filth.

The Sunday trip out also attracted the disapproval of religious groups. The **National Sunday School Union** blamed cars for diminishing attendance at Sunday schools. The Unitarian and Free Christian Churches blamed a society too immersed in the idea of speed for declining numbers attending on a Sunday. In 1923, a Church of England conference considered the rise in paganism among the young as a product of 'cheap cars'. However, churches in popular day-trip areas, such as Callow with Dewsall near Hereford, and Cirencester, provided evening services to encourage day-trippers to attend. The age of the car was changing the traditional rituals of British society.

The problems of the open road

Motorists faced with the difficulties of planning a trip could look for assistance from the motoring organisations: the Royal Automobile Club, founded in 1897, and the Automobile Association, formed in 1905. These organisations provided both facilities to the motorist and a platform to agitate on their behalf on issues such as taxation and maintenance of the road network. Both provided a network of call boxes for members' use to provide support in case of a breakdown. Lists of approved garages were available, along with the mobile mechanics of the RAC and AA. By the 1920s, they also provided their members with itineraries that included route suggestions, often guiding them from the main roads to avoid the increasing volume of traffic at holiday time. The motoring writer John Prioleau described one such early holiday traffic jam in 1925 on the road to Brighton: 'As a result of those appalling three hours, I decided that nothing but life and death shall drag me, either on my own or someone else's car, to Brighton during the summer.' As well as the growth of traffic on the road, there was concern about the decline in what some considered the manners of motorists and there were calls to create a highway code to help regulate behaviour on the road.

SOURCE

9 From a letter by a motorist to the magazine *Autocar*, 17 September 1926.

> I am on the road a good deal, and in my opinion the driving of the public gets worse and worse, not so much from incompetence as through absolutely wilful caddishness and bad manners. I presume that the class of person who nowadays go about in motor cars and who, ten years ago, were riding in buses like to think themselves gentlemen. I submit that it would be greatly to the public benefit if they went a little further and behaved as such!

Such attitudes are indicative of a middle-class unease about the status of car ownership. The joy of the open road had been the chance to leave the sprawling industrial city behind; now the fear was that its more humble occupants were able to join in the exodus. Contemporary commentators often remarked about the herd instinct of the touring motorist and the growing commercialisation of the most popular destinations. In 1923 *The Motorist* ran an article expressing concern about the impact of mass motoring, fearing that in the future genteel tea gardens would be obliterated by three-storey mass-catering restaurants and thatched cottages hidden behind billboards.

The social effects of increased car ownership

Although a Ministry of Transport survey in 1933 concluded that only 12 percent of driving licences in the UK were held by women, female motorists became more prominent in the interwar years. It is hard to assess how many women drove regularly, but historian Sean O'Connell has suggested that the wife in a middle-class family increasingly used the car to carry out household duties such as shopping. It would appear that few women owned cars by themselves, but were driving partners with their husbands for the family car. A drift to the countryside by those wishing to escape from the suburbs also placed greater emphasis on the car as the key to family transport. An advert for the 'All British Standard' cars portrayed the wife as having the task of driving the husband to the station for his train to work before spending the rest of the day socialising, only to return to the station in the evening to pick him up and take him home. While this was a construction of the imagination of a marketing agency, it still suggests that women were not absent from the narrative of increasing use of the automobile in the 1920s.

While women drivers might have been in a minority, there is evidence that they played an important role in making decisions regarding which car to purchase. Scottish motor manufacturers Arrol-Johnston not only advertised in the trade papers but also took out advertisements in women's magazines. Their explanation for this was the role played by women in selecting cars.

SOURCE

10 From an advertisement for Arrol-Johnston cars in the *Motor Trader* 1919. It is about women as key players in the purchase of the family car and shows a particular gender-based marketing strategy.

The 'Lady of the House' usually has a good deal to say on the choice of a car. And, having the gift of experience, eloquence and the time to think up reasons why, she often wheedles or bullies her poor old husband into buying a car SHE wants. Everyone knows that. The firm of Arrol-Johnston Ltd. recognise the power of women in this matter. They advertise the A.J in several ladies' journals and they never let up on telling the ornamental sex why they ought to have a tame vehicle from Dumfries concealed about the building.

The view that women were the key arbiters regarding choice of vehicle remained throughout the 1920s and 1930s. Vauxhall's advertising department believed that women had tremendous power when it came to car purchase and this was echoed by many motoring manufacturers who attempted to style cars that had particular appeal to women. However, Herbert Austin bemoaned what he saw as women's faddish influence on car design. Despite car companies focusing on women, there remains little hard data on how much influence they exercised, with much evidence being anecdotal.

EXTEND YOUR KNOWLEDGE

Status and customisation

In the late 1920s, a number of companies such as Thrupp and Maberley started customising cars for the motoring community, and these included the less-expensive models such as the Austin Seven. Many manufacturers became interested in design as a key marketing point, which led to annual model changes. *Motor Trader* in 1925 worried that this obsession for fashionable cars would spoil designs by pandering to those who were concerned with image rather than form and function. However, it is far from clear as to what degree this was a result of female power over the purchase of cars or a characteristic of a market that was obsessed with status.

Other evidence of an increase in the visibility of women was a growing number of folk tales about the problems women drivers had in mastering new technology. A favourite myth often seen in the motoring press of the 1920s was that women drivers were unable to use the reverse gear and had to have their cars manually lifted and turned should they need to go in the opposite direction. Such prejudice was indicative of the threat that women were seen to pose to the particularly masculine world of motoring. As with the cycling craze of the 1890s, when the press took against women cyclists, women drivers were constantly stereotyped and patronised.

For a woman, the car could be both liberating and restricting. Where she was a driver, there was the possibility to extend her horizons and she gained a measure of additional independence. Day trips and touring holidays took her beyond the confines of family and home. Yet non-driving women of the middle class might find their mobility restricted by the car. O'Connell argues that the move to the suburbs and beyond, although facilitated by the car, meant that many women experienced confinement to their home and immediate locality if they could not drive and if there was no access to public transport. It also saw women separated from their family support networks. For this group, the car did not bring liberation but rather isolation.

For middle-class families where kinship groups became more dispersed, the car was a means to maintain contact. Family trips to the theatre or cinema were facilitated by the car, which provided a means to transport parents and children from the suburbs into the metropolis. It also became at times a utility vehicle for shopping expeditions and ferrying offspring.

SOURCE
11

Advertisement for Austin Seven from 1928. This is a good example of the focus given by marketing departments to making their products attractive to women, though only about 12 percent of drivers were female.

ACTIVITY
KNOWLEDGE CHECK

Motoring in the 1920s

1 Look at Sources 8 and 9. In what way do the writers believe the behaviour of motorists has changed since the war? What do the sources suggest might have changed in the years since the end of the First World War? Make a list of the changes.

2 Identify with a partner the wider issues raised by the growth in motoring. How did it change the way Britain looked and what people did in their leisure time? Draw a mind map.

3 Looking at your list and mind map, draw up an essay plan in response to the question: 'In what ways did Herbert Austin's idea of promoting mass car ownership change Britain?'

A Level Exam-Style Question Section B

How far was the rise of mass car ownership responsible for reshaping leisure in Britain and the problems that it brings? (20 marks)

Tip

Consider the way in which the car opened up access to parts of the country that were not easy to reach by train. Reflect on the way hotels and cafes catered for the motorist. Also consider the negative consequences of cars related to the effects they had on the countryside.

Conclusion

Herbert Austin saw himself as an innovator. It is true that one could argue that his pre-war designs had a cutting-edge appeal and the post-war Austin Seven set the standard for what might be achieved in the small-car market. However, as a businessman he was probably more astute at adapting to the circumstances in which he found himself, turning them to his advantage. Austin viewed the rapid development of the American motor industry with envy and wanted to emulate its scale and dynamism. Yet this was only possible given a mass market for its products. In Britain, the market was more restricted than in the US, which favoured batch production, and this was given as a reason for the sluggish pace in the adoption of assembly lines that required greater capital investment to create continuous flow of production for mass consumption. Measured against the standards of Ford, Austin's methods and strategy were conservative, but in comparison to other British car manufacturers he emerged as an industry leader. As a manager, he can be seen to have had his weaknesses. The decision to concentrate on a single top-of-the-range model in the immediate post-war period was a mistake that nearly bankrupted his business. A limited market for the product resulted in financial disaster, and it was only the massive success of the Austin Seven that enabled the company to regain its position as a leading car producer.

The little Austin Seven was to become the iconic British car of the 1920s and 1930s, combining utility with style. The design had an advantage over its larger and more expensive challengers, in that it not only cost less to tax and maintain than Ford's Model T, for example, but lighter fuel consumption meant it was cheaper to run, a factor that Bowden has identified as key in shaping the development of interwar British motoring. In developing the small car, Austin was trying to define a new market and develop a design to meet its needs. That the demand for vehicles increased in the decades between the wars is clearly indicated by the rapid rise in domestic production, an indication that car ownership went beyond the small elite of the pre-war world. Yet ownership tended to remain the prerogative of a middle-class market that often saw the car as a leisure vehicle rather than an essential utility. Despite these constraints on growth, there were the beginnings of mass motoring, which led to the development of an essential infrastructure to support the later massive expansion of road transport. The Austin Seven helped open up the world for the day-tripper or touring holidaymaker. Austin's great achievement was then as much adaptation as it was innovation, and he needs to be understood within the context of the market he tried to serve.

The interwar years were to see a steady improvement of the road network as car ownership grew. Within a decade, the countryside experienced a profound change, with the proliferation of petrol stations, garages and cafes. These both altered the physical fabric of village and town life but also provided opportunities to meet the needs of the rising tide of driving public. Motoring became a pastime of many middle-class families taking advantage of the chance to explore beyond the main centres. Organisations such as the National Trust promoted themselves to the motorist, while an extensive range of journals catered to car owners. Motoring organisations not only provided help for the car owner in distress, but also promoted the joys of driving and the places to visit.

As Raphael Samuel suggested, the affordability of the Austin Seven had not only opened up motoring, but had also resulted in a growing anxiety among the middle class over their status. The car had originally established their place in the social hierarchy, but increasing car ownership led to worries that the wrong sort of people were gaining access to the open road. Finally, increasing numbers of women drivers challenged the masculine image of the motorist. While having a driving licence might offer the possibility of greater freedom, the evidence suggests that this was limited to a relatively small number of women who often faced hostility from male road users.

WIDER READING

Austin Memories www.austinmemories.com

Birmingham City Council: A Brief History of Austin and Longbridge www.birmingham.gov.uk/austin

Bowden, S.M. 'Demand and supply constraints in the inter-war UK car industry: Did the manufacturers get it right?' *Business History*, Vol. 33 No. 2 (1991)

Church, R. *Herbert Austin: The British Motorcar Industry to 1941*, Blackwell (1979)

Church, R. *The Rise and Decline of the British Motor Industry*, Macmillan (1994)

Clegg, S. *Organisational Theory and Class Analysis, New Approaches and New Issues*, Holland (1989)

Jeremiah, D. 'Motoring and the British countryside', *Rural History*, Vol. 21 No.2 (2010)

Middleton, V.T.C. and Lickorish, L.J. *British Tourism: The Remarkable Story of Growth*, Elsevier (2005)

O'Connell, S. *The Car and British Society: Class, Gender and Motoring 1896–1939*, Manchester University Press (1998)

Saul, S.B. 'The motor industry in Britain to 1914', *Business History* No. 5 (1962)

ACTIVITY
SUMMARY

Herbert Austin: creating and adapting to market forces, 1905–28

1 What factors made Herbert Austin a successful industrialist? Make a list and then try ranking them in order of importance.

2 Consider Austin's contribution in designing the Austin Seven. To what extent do you think that this car changed the British car industry? What evidence is there that it had a major impact? Present your ideas in the form of a mind map.

3 'Herbert Austin and the Austin Seven brought motoring to the masses.' Using the material you have outlined above, critically assess this statement in the form of a short essay of around 800 words.

4 Consider how interwar motoring changed Britain. Draw up a table with the following headings: 'Government policy', 'Environmental change', 'Economic change' and 'Social change'. List your evidence below each heading.

5 How did the car change society? Use you notes from the activity above to write an 800-word essay.

Preparing for your A Level Paper 3 exam

Advance planning

Draw up a timetable for your revision and try to keep to it. Spend longer on topics that you have found difficult, and revise them several times. Aim to be confident about all aspects of your Paper 3 work, because this will ensure that you have a choice of questions in Sections B and C.

Paper 3 overview

Paper 3	Time: 2 hours 15 minutes	
Section A	Answer 1 compulsory question for the option studied, assessing source analysis and evaluation skills.	20 marks
Section B	Answer 1 question from a choice of 2 on an aspect in depth for the option studied.	20 marks
Section C	Answer 1 question from a choice of 2 on an aspect in breadth for the option studied.	20 marks
	Total marks =	60 marks

Section A questions

There is no choice of question in Section A. You will be referred to a source of about 350 words long, printed in a Sources Booklet. The source will be a primary source or one that is contemporary to the period you have studied, and will relate to one of the key topics in the Aspect of Depth. You will be expected to analyse and evaluate the source in its historical context. The question will ask you to assess the value of the source for revealing something specific about the period, and will expect you to explain your answer, using the source, the information given about its origin and your own knowledge about the historical context.

Section B questions

You will have a choice of one from two questions in Section B. They will aim to assess your understanding of one or more of the key topics in the Aspect of Depth you have studied. Questions may relate to a single, momentous year, but will normally cover longer periods. You will be required to write an essay evaluating an aspect of the period. You may be asked about change and continuity, similarity and difference, consequences, significance or causation, or you may be given a quotation and asked to explain how far you agree with it. All questions will require you to reach a substantiated judgement.

Section C questions

You will have a choice of one from two questions in Section C. Questions will relate to the themes of the Aspects of Breadth you have studied, and will aim to assess your understanding of change over time. They will cover a period of no less than 100 years and will relate either to the factors that brought about change, or the extent of change over the period, or patterns of change as demonstrated by turning points.

Use of time

- Do not write solidly for 45 minutes on each question. For Sections B and C answers, you should spend a few minutes working out what the question is asking you to do, and drawing up a plan of your answer. This is especially important for Section C answers, which cover an extended period of time.

- For Section A, it is essential that you have a clear understanding of the content of the source and its historical context. Pay particular attention to the provenance: was the author in a position to know what he or she was writing about? Read it carefully and underline important points. You might decide to spend up to ten minutes reading the source and drawing up your plan, and 35 minutes writing your answer.

Preparing for your A Level exams

Paper 3: A Level sample answer with comments

Section A

These questions require you to analyse and evaluate source material with respect to its historical context.

For these questions remember to:

- look at the evidence given in the source and consider how the source could be used in differing ways to provide historical understanding
- use your knowledge of the historical context to discuss any limitations the source may have
- use your historical understanding to evaluate the source, considering how much weight you would give to its argument
- come to a judgement on the overall value of the source in respect to the question.

Study Source 4 in Chapter 5 (page 113) before you answer this question.

Assess the value of the source for revealing the difficulties Brunel faced in the building of the Great Western Railway and how far it might be seen as an insight into the shortcomings of Brunel's innovative design.

Explain your answer using the source, the information given about its origin and your own knowledge about the historical context. (20 marks)

Average student answer

The source is very useful in revealing the difficulties Brunel faced in the building of the Great Western Railway because it is a report made to the directors of that railway by Brunel himself. As a result, it is well placed to offer significant commentary about both the issues Brunel had to contend with and any potential shortcomings in his design. Having said that, it also has some limitations in that the directors were Brunel's employers and therefore perhaps he would have to be careful in what he said.

The source is a letter written to the directors of the railway on which Brunel is working and, therefore, it is of considerable utility, offering significant insight into the problems that he may have faced during construction. In particular, it is useful in identifying the nature of the difficulties that needed to be overcome – notably delays and prejudice towards the adapted plans that Brunel employed over more established, traditional engineering designs. Brunel was very much an innovator and was very well known for his modern designs that often flew in the face of convention, and as such he met with opposition from fellow engineers who felt his plans too grand or even unsafe. This had been the case only several years earlier with his winning design for the Clifton Suspension Bridge, which was very different from Thomas Telford's classic design that had been used on the Menai Suspension Bridge in 1826. Since Brunel challenged more established practices, he attracted criticism and opposition to his designs and this is well conveyed within the source.

> A functional introduction that conveys a clear argument and some awareness of the source's provenance. It does not integrate these as effectively as it might have done for a higher-level response.

> This paragraph starts well with a good point being made, however it drifts away from the question demand and only returns fleetingly at the end with a general judgement that could be more developed.

Furthermore, the source is quite reliable because it was written by Brunel himself and therefore offers his own opinion about the difficulties he faced, which were indeed genuine ones. When the source says 'notwithstanding the violent prejudices against us' it is reasonable to accept that this was a real issue which, when considered against his earlier work such as funding the Clifton Suspension Bridge in the early 1830s, would certainly have delayed the railway's construction – another problem that the source mentions. In this sense, therefore, the source is very useful in assessing the problems Brunel had to contend with because it tallies with other projects and comes from the pen of Brunel himself.

This is quite a short paragraph but it has some focus on the question demand and considers the quality of the material. This provenance is used in a general fashion and could have developed a greater sense of judgement if it was explored a little further.

Having said that, however, as good as the source might be, it could be an attempt by Brunel to assure his employers of the progress he was making. In this sense, although it offers some awareness of difficulty, Brunel is quick to be positive about these problems and more particularly how they are now being dealt with. This perhaps undersells the extent of the problems and as such is maybe more limiting than a first look suggests. In this regard, the source might be viewed as a deliberate attempt to explain away real problems for the purpose of retaining employment on Brunel's part. On this point the source should be used with caution. However, in itself this perceived limitation still offers some useful commentary about the pressures upon Brunel, which were regarding his own employment just as much as the railway itself. Therefore, it is still a very useful source for a historian to consider when making their assessment.

This paragraph offers some developed commentary about the provenance of the material and reaches some reasoned judgements about its quality and usefulness.

In conclusion, the source is ultimately quite useful since it presents the opinion of Brunel himself and lays down several clear problems that he had to contend with while building the Great Western Railway. These problems arise from personal interests but also a general sense of prejudice for Brunel's unusual design, which challenged existing convention. In this sense it could be suggested that Brunel created such difficulties through his own designs. The source has limitations but it is still useful in assessing the problems involved during the construction project.

This conclusion is quite clear and presents a consistent argument, albeit fairly general.

Verdict

This is an average answer because:

- it lacks substantive judgement of the question demand
- although the source's provenance is considered, it lacks detailed explanation or development
- it does not come to a strong reasoned judgement.

Use the feedback on this essay to rewrite it, making as many improvements as you can.

Paper 3: A Level sample answer with comments

Section A

These questions require you to analyse and evaluate source material with respect to its historical context.

For these questions remember to:

- look at the evidence given in the source and consider how the source could be used in differing ways to provide historical understanding
- use your knowledge of the historical context to discuss any limitations the source may have
- use your historical understanding to evaluate the source, considering how much weight you would give to its argument
- come to a judgement on the overall value of the source in respect to the question.

Study Source 4 in Chapter 5 (page 113) before you answer this question.

Assess the value of the source for revealing the difficulties Brunel faced in the building of the Great Western Railway and how far it might be seen as an insight into the shortcomings of Brunel's innovative design.

Explain your answer, using the source, the information given about its origin and your own knowledge about the historical context.
(20 marks)

Strong student answer

The source is very useful in assessing the extent of difficulty that Brunel faced – including perhaps his own design flaws – when constructing the Great Western Railway because it is about those themes specifically, and being a document produced by Brunel himself it is of considerable value wherein the limitations it has as a consequence of possible subjectivity are perhaps outweighed by the insight it offers overall.

> An introduction that considers debate and provenance while presenting a clear argument.

Certainly the source has limitations in that it is a letter by Brunel to his employers and this would have a natural subjectivity, especially since, given the tone of the document, it sounds as if Brunel is justifying a particular method of construction. This would imply that there were some doubts as to the manner in which he, as chief engineer, might be conducting the project. If this were the case then the letter might be construed as an attempt to reassure his employers, the directors of the railway under construction. Even despite the natural subjectivity contained within the letter, however, it is still of considerable utility since the fact that Brunel might feel the need to justify his work is itself evidence of the pressures he was facing. In this sense it is not the more obvious ones relating to delays and resourcing, but rather the pressures of project management and especially satisfying those who employ you. Indeed, in this last regard the source is perhaps of particular value since it offers the opportunity to consider the potential attitudes of the directors themselves – their possible scepticism and fears that the project might be under threat.

> There is a clear consideration of provenance that is integrated into the overall discussion of the question focus. The material is analytical and well considered, developing a clear line of argument.

Further, if these men were worried enough for Brunel to have to placate them with reassuring words, as evidenced in the source, then it is also reasonable to suggest that given the magnitude of the project – a railroad from Bristol to London – then it is likely to have garnered considerable public attention that might also be affecting the construction of the project. In this sense the source offers the opportunity to consider the wider problems that a chief engineer such as Brunel might face when managing such a large-scale project. In addition, given that the source was produced during the construction of the railway in 1838, it is also very useful in ascertaining the day-to-day problems that Brunel may have had to deal with – not least the problems of delayed work, but more specifically the 'violent prejudice' against the project. On this last point in

> Here the provenance of the source is used well to develop the argument. Own knowledge is supportive of the overall analytical discussion and argumentation.

particular, the source is quite valuable since it suggests that there was local animosity towards the construction which, given the opportunities it could offer in terms of economic gain, would otherwise have been unimaginable. In this sense the source is of considerable value because it encourages a wider consideration of the project on which Brunel was working and, as such, of the myriad problems he was likely to be contending with.

Reinforcing this idea is also the light the source sheds upon the potential shortcomings of Brunel's own designs. It would be reasonable to suggest that, given his reputation for more 'modern' engineering practices, his plans were therefore more likely to be challenged by the local community and other engineers, who were more used to traditional and established ideas. On this point, although the source does not specifically mention this immediate challenge, the use of the phrase 'prejudice' could reasonably be inferred as such; a dislike of something new and therefore opposing it to the frustration of Brunel himself. The source not only identifies the wider context with regard to local concerns about new building projects, but it also offers an insight into the generally conservative attitudes of Victorian society. Given the need for community support for such projects, it is reasonable to suggest that Brunel failed to fully appreciate this sensibility and therefore increased the likelihood of opposition to himself and his over-ambitious designs.

> The source is used to develop further reasoned inferences that address the question clearly. Appropriate judgements are offered.

Finally, although the source might have limitations in that it is Brunel's own opinion of the situation and perhaps another, more objective, source might yield greater reliability, in actual fact the source is useful for that very reason. Given the nature of the issue, the subjectivity offers a sense of urgency and real significance to the events taking place. This is something that a dispassionate observer might not be able to convey and as a result might not be able to convey a complete picture. This is not to say Brunel succeeds in doing this, but his narrow image is perhaps more useful for being just that – the opinion of a key figure who was orchestrating the overall construction. In this sense the natural limitation might better be considered a strength since it presents the challenges of the project in a truthful, albeit from one perspective, manner.

> Provenance is well considered once more and the overall argument is driven by that same consideration in an effective and analytical way.

Overall, despite some limitations in the quality of the source, it is ultimately very useful to any assessment of the difficulties that faced Brunel during the construction of the Great Western Railway largely because it encourages a much broader awareness of the complexities of the project. By having to justify his approach in the letter, Brunel not only offers the usual problems that engineers may have to face, but also those of the broader community and of his employers. In considering a wider field of interest, the source encourages a more thoughtful consideration of the project and therefore the difficulties it was likely to generate.

> A clear and well-reasoned conclusion that reaches a judgement based on the analytical argument presented in the body.

Verdict

This is a strong answer because:

- it focuses explicitly upon the source when developing an answer
- the provenance of the source is consistently used to develop well-considered points
- it reaches a clearly substantiated judgement that has been justified in the body.

Paper 3: A Level sample answer with comments

Section B

These questions require you to show your understanding of a period in depth. They will ask you about a quite specific period of time and require you to make a substantiated judgement about a specific aspect you have studied.

For these questions remember to:

- organise your essay and communicate it in a manner that is clear and comprehensible
- use historical knowledge to analyse and evaluate the key aspect of the question
- make a balanced argument that weighs up differing opinions
- make a substantiated overall judgement on the question.

'Queen Charlotte's patronage was not necessary for the success of Josiah Wedgwood's pottery business.' How far do you agree with this statement? (20 marks)

Average student answer

To a great extent the patronage of Queen Charlotte was fundamental to the success of Josiah Wedgwood because her interest gave him a reputation that encouraged others to take note of his business. While other factors also added to his success, it was royal support that was undoubtedly the most significant reason.

> A clear introduction that acknowledges a brief debate and presents an argument that has some reasoning applied.

Wedgwood certainly enjoyed great success because of his continual development of good-quality pottery, which he always sought to improve through research and experimentation – conducting over 400 experiments in order to produce an even, translucent glaze for his products. This allowed him to make a very high-quality product that was significantly better than rival creations and which almost certainly placed him on the road to success. The key to this was arguably the improved consistency he was able to create – good pottery was easy to make but it often varied in colour, particularly from batch to batch. This variability often affected the size of orders he received since his products were more consistent and therefore people had a greater degree of confidence in him. It was this confidence that allowed him to be a success.

> This paragraph has some argument but it is a little general and not effectively developed. The evidence in support is appropriate, if a little unspecific.

Wedgwood was also successful because he adopted more thorough working practices that ensured efficient working, and the abandonment of careless methods such as heating the kilns up to too high a temperature or leaving items in too long. If pots were left too long in the kilns then they would become too brittle and often break very easily, wasting both raw materials such as the coal for the kiln and clay, as well as time. Over-baking pots was a common problem in the 18th century largely because the potters themselves, along with their labourers, would usually go to the alehouses while their pots were being fired. Very frequently they would get carried away and not return to the kilns until the pots had been in too long and were consequently ruined. Wedgwood went to great lengths to prevent this kind of behaviour and spent a lot of time in his pottery among the labourers so that they did not end up in the alehouses so frequently. He also spoke to them directly when any problems emerged so that they could be dealt with effectively and quickly,

> This paragraph has some relevant knowledge but the material is quite descriptive and lacks a real focus on the question demand.

thus not wasting any time. It was this dedication to professional working that could be said was the main reason behind his commercial triumphs.

Despite these evident benefits, the real basis of Wedgwood's success was undoubtedly the patronage of George III's wife, Queen Charlotte. This was because before she placed an order for a dinner service, Wedgwood was little-known in the country, or indeed the world. However, once he had been able to present his products to Queen Charlotte and she was favourable towards him, he was able to market himself as 'Potter to Her Majesty' and this encouraged orders from other wealthy families both at court and the country at large, who wanted to dine off royally approved pottery. These new orders included one from the duchess of Argyll and then, perhaps most famously, in 1770 he received a very large order from the Empress of Russia, Catherine II, who paid him several thousand pounds for a vast dinner service with a frog motif. Although this service had cost him only slightly less to actually create and decorate, the profit he made was still substantial and more importantly it helped to enhance his reputation and bring in further orders. Without the initial patronage of Queen Charlotte, access to equally illustrious customers would have been very unlikely and therefore her patronage was of great significance.

> A debate is acknowledged and an argument is developed using some useful, if general, evidence in support. There is some clear reasoning here but it could be more sharply developed in terms of the question demand.

In conclusion, because the patronage of Queen Charlotte created the opportunity for Wedgwood to acquire further large orders from important clients, which both brought in profit and also enhanced his reputation, it was of vital significance to his business.

> This conclusion neatly sums up a consistent argument in a straightforward manner.

Verdict

This is an average response because:

- it is quite narrative throughout
- own knowledge is used in support of the answer, this material could be more precise
- it does not evenly consider a counterargument.

Use the feedback on this essay to rewrite it, making as many improvements as you can.

Paper 3: A Level sample answer with comments

Section B

These questions require you to show your understanding of a period in depth. They will ask you about a quite specific period of time and require you to make a substantiated judgement about a specific aspect you have studied.

For these questions remember to:

- organise your essay and communicate it in a manner that is clear and comprehensible
- use historical knowledge to analyse and evaluate the key aspect of the question
- make a balanced argument that weighs up differing opinions
- make a substantiated overall judgement on the question.

'Queen Charlotte's patronage was not necessary for the success of Josiah Wedgwood's pottery business.' How far do you agree with this statement? (20 marks)

Strong student answer

To a great extent it is unreasonable to suggest royal support was not important because it offered significant opportunities for the potter. Although he adopted modern methods and had a quality product, it was the queen's patronage that enabled him to take full advantage of these attributes and establish the international reputation of his brand, which ultimately made his business the success it was.

It is reasonable to suggest that Wedgwood enjoyed considerable success because he adopted modern methods at his potteries and undertook extensive research to develop effective techniques for getting the best from his raw materials, especially the green and yellow glazes he was able to achieve by the early 1760s. These new techniques enabled him to produce a range of coloured pottery that enjoyed great success and almost certainly promoted his business. Furthermore, his more 'hands-on' approach to the business ensured efficient, effective working, which had been missing in other potteries. Without this direct approach workers often overheated their creations while they spent the firing time in alehouses, ruining the final product and wasting resources. By supervising these men more effectively – banning 'Saint Monday' for example – Wedgwood was able to regulate the quality of his creations. Despite these breakthroughs however, it is reasonable to suggest that they did not entirely make his name, and although he gained several European orders, notably from the Netherlands in 1763, these were neither extensive nor lucrative. In this regard it is perhaps more accurate to suggest that the modern techniques and controls he instituted merely enhanced the products he had rather than promoted the success of the business itself. In developing his products Wedgwood was in one sense ensuring future success, however to ensure it a broader identity was necessary in order to draw the requisite orders.

Given the need to broaden his reputation and get his name known in the interest of growing his business, it is perhaps here that the patronage of Queen Charlotte was more important than anything else. Without doubt the product he sold was of an excellent quality – over 400 experiments had enabled him to develop a fine, even glaze that gave his pottery a beautiful sheen – but this was arguably only of consequence when he was able to present it to the queen, which he did in 1762. This was because by presenting his work to the court the queen became the best person to promote his pottery, and as a marketing opportunity there was none better. The royal court was the centre of English society, determining what was and was not fashionable, and by winning royal approval Wedgwood's reputation would reach a much wider circle. In this sense the favour of Queen Charlotte – given in 1765 when she placed an order for an entire service

> This introduction acknowledges some debate but integrates it into the overall argument, which has some reasoning and clear direction.

> There is a clear discussion here that relates well to the question demand and offers awareness of counterarguments. It successfully integrates counterarguments into the overall argument that was set out in the introduction and uses useful evidence to support these points.

> This paragraph starts to develop a reasoned, analytical, argument about the question's stated factor and it uses some good evidence in support of the points advanced.

– was an introduction to elite society, which in turn could realise substantial orders that would ensure Wedgwood's success.

Indeed, far from being insignificant, the importance of Queen Charlotte's patronage is underlined by the number of orders Wedgwood received after his royal approval; the duchess of Argyll and even the empress of Russia, Catherine II, placed an order for his pottery – the latter eventually paying him £3,500 for a complete dinner service with a personalised frog motif. These orders arguably made Wedgwood an international potter of repute and it would be fair to suggest that without the favour of the British queen this would not have been possible. Furthermore, having established such a reputation he was careful to cultivate it; using it to drive society's tastes himself and thereby being best-positioned to exploit it. This acute business sense was also evidenced in 1773 when he resisted price reductions of his products despite falling market prices. This refusal kept the brand of Wedgwood as an exclusive one, thereby enhancing its reputation and popular desire. Although on this point it is reasonable to suggest that perhaps it was his own character that made his business successful, this came after the royal seal of approval. Had Wedgwood not been in the position he was by the time market prices declined he would not necessarily have been able to take such a decision. On this basis therefore, because Queen Charlotte's patronage had raised the fortunes of his business before the 1770s, Wedgwood was in a much better position to take opportunities that would be further advantageous to him.

Given the advantages that royal patronage therefore afforded to Wedgwood, it is reasonable to suggest that Queen Charlotte was fundamental to the success of his company. Her patronage not only provided an elite client base, but also placed Wedgwood in a strong position not only to dictate fashion but also be able to take advantageous decisions that were not necessarily available to other potters. It was this that set him apart from his rivals and arguably ensured ongoing success beyond everything else he did.

> Another analytical and well-directed paragraph that develops a clear line of argument using well-selected own knowledge. Some debate is considered and related effectively to the argument being made.

Verdict

This is a strong answer because:

- it is clearly analytical and offers a well-defined argument
- the response there is good use of precise and well-selected evidence to support the points made
- it considers a counterargument and includes this as part of the overall evaluation, reaching a reasoned conclusion.

Paper 3: A Level sample answer with comments

Section C

These questions require you to show your understanding of a subject over a considerable period of time. They will ask you to assess a long-term historical topic and its development over a period of at least 100 years, and they require you to make a substantiated judgement in relation to the question.

For these questions remember to:

- organise your essay and communicate it in a manner that is clear and comprehensible
- use historical knowledge to analyse and evaluate the key aspect of the question covering the entire period
- make a balanced argument that weighs up differing opinions
- make a substantiated overall judgement on the question.

How far do you agree that factory reform in 1833 was the most significant event that affected working practices in the years 1759–1928? (20 marks)

Average student answer

The passage of the Factory Act in 1833 was certainly a very significant event that changed working practices during the years 1759–1928 because it was a major piece of legislation that required extensive reforms to the factory system. Despite these wide-ranging changes, however, there were also other factors that were just as important and, therefore, the Factory Act was perhaps only one of many significant events.

In one sense, it is reasonable to suggest that the Factory Act of 1833 was the most significant event in changing the nature of working practices in Britain because it demanded extensive reforms that transformed the way factories managed their workforces. These reforms included no children under the age of nine to be employed, children to not work days longer than 12 hours nor work at night and also to receive basic schooling for two hours each day. These were substantial reforms that greatly affected working practices because they undermined the existing way of conducting work by placing restrictions on a previously uninhibited system. In particular, this was problematic because children were a cheap source of labour and were consequently employed quite extensively throughout Britain, making up an important section of the industrial workforce.

The Factory Act was also important for changing working practices because it forced managers to give children some basic education. This would mean that the factories were not working at optimal capacity, as many of their child employees would be in lessons rather than working at or under their machines. Also, by limiting the number of hours children were allowed to work, the Act began to change working practices. This was because before 1833 managers could make their employees work as long as they wanted – often up to 14 hours a day and even through the night if they required it. This practice was allowed because the government adopted what was called a laissez faire or free trade attitude, which meant they just let owners get on and do what they wanted because they felt that was the best course of action to promote profit. By staying out of the economy, the government let business govern itself and this was effective because it could then be flexible and respond to market forces as and when necessary. Long days were therefore very common before 1833.

This introduction offers a general argument and acknowledges some debate. However, it could be more focused in terms of how the debate relates to the argument presented. This would sharpen the argument and allow for a better sense of direction in the response.

This paragraph offers some good ideas and there is an argument presented that is generally analytical. It does not develop this analysis very far and towards the end there is a useful point being made that is not clearly explained in terms of the question demand.

This paragraph has some focus, but it drifts into narrative quite quickly. Once again the analysis is generally undeveloped beyond a one-sentence comment.

Although the Act was very significant for changing working practices, there were other Acts, such as the Health and Morals of Apprentices Act, passed in 1802, already in existence. This means that maybe the 1833 Act was not entirely the main reason for changing working practices because other legislation had already been produced. In this sense the Act was only one of many attempts by the government to regulate children's working practices. Also, after 1833 there was additional legislation such as the 1847 Factory Act, which limited the working day to ten hours. This was maybe more important than the 1833 Act because a ten-hour working day had been demanded by people like Richard Oastler for many years. Therefore, this Act was of greater significance because it gave the workers what they actually wanted and asked for.

In conclusion, because the 1833 Act was only one of many attempts to legislate for working practices in the 1800s, it is not perhaps the most significant event but rather one of several. More important was probably the 1847 Factory Act, which actually gave the working people what they had been demanding for years.

This paragraph offers some clear debate that is related to the question demand. It also contains some good own knowledge that is used to support the points being made. Once again, however, these points are not really developed very far, which limits the opportunity for evaluation.

This conclusion has a judgement that is generally supported by the main body. It is related to the question demand, but the overall focus could be sharper, which in turn would enhance the evaluation being made.

Verdict

This is an average answer because:

- it is quite narrative throughout and does not cover the breadth of the timeframe asked for
- the points made are developed in a general way, albeit with some good own knowledge
- it does not evenly consider a counterargument.

Use the feedback on this essay to rewrite it, making as many improvements as you can.

Paper 3: A Level sample answer with comments

Section C

These questions require you to show your understanding of a subject over a considerable period of time. They will ask you to assess a long-term historical topic and its development over a period of at least 100 years, and they require you to make a substantiated judgement in relation to the question.

For these questions remember to:

- organise your essay and communicate it in a manner that is clear and comprehensible
- use historical knowledge to analyse and evaluate the key aspect of the question covering the entire period
- make a balanced argument that weighs up differing opinions
- make a substantiated overall judgement on the question.

How far do you agree that factory reform in 1833 was the most significant event that affected working practices in the years 1759–1928? (20 marks)

Strong student answer

To a great extent the 1833 Factory Act was the most significant event affecting working practices because it was not only comprehensive legislation that regulated employment, but also the precursor for additional legislation after that date. In this sense, although other reforms undoubtedly impacted upon the working lives of people, 1833 was the seminal moment that opened the floodgates to further changes.

Throughout the 1759–1928 period, working practices were significantly transformed, but it was the 1833 Act that perhaps did more to alter these practices than any other. This is arguably because that particular legislation introduced more extensive restrictions upon the use of child labour than ever before. By doing this, the Act encouraged working practices to shift since using children was a cheap, and therefore popular, source of labour – costing less than half that of an adult male worker. The consequent restrictions placed on this 'resource', therefore, began a slow but gradual removal of young children from the labour market, as employers increasingly looked to older workers who were not so restricted in their working hours. Although this was a very slow transition – more so since families relied upon the wages of their children and therefore tried to avoid the new legislation – it nonetheless was significant because it began that process which, by the end of the century, was all but complete, with all children under the age of ten excluded from factory working.

Reinforcing the impact of the 1833 Act was the wider influence it also had upon working practices. Certainly the role of children began to be reduced, but this change also motivated a more critical look at practices more generally. Following the legislation, there grew a more determined movement to reduce the number of working hours for adults as well. The most prominent of these was the Ten Hours Movement organised by Richard Oastler, which secured the support of both Michael Sadler and Lord Ashley, both prominent politicians who were interested in factory reform. This movement had originated in 1830, but it was arguably with the legislation of three years later that it became more pronounced, since major reform had already been implemented and therefore the chances of further change were much greater. Having already breached the defensive walls surrounding employers' practices, the demands of the Ten Hours Movement became more achievable and in 1847 they were successful when parliament finally passed legislation to that effect. In this regard, the importance of the 1833 Factory Act lay in the groundwork it had set down for building a pathway for further reforms, and in this manner it was not only influential but also very successful since the 1847 Factory Act itself can be viewed as a landmark reform in the history of British labour.

> In this introduction, there is a clear argument being developed that integrates an awareness of debate and uses this to inform the overall idea being presented.

> This paragraph is clearly analytical and starts to build the argument presented in the introduction. There is some supporting evidence, but to make this even better a little more would be useful.

> Like the previous paragraph, this is nicely analytical and continues to build a clear argument that is consistent and well focused. There is more supporting evidence here that enhances the points being made.

On the point of foundations, it is reasonable to suggest that the 1833 legislation was itself the product of earlier reforms, without which it would not have been likely that 1833 would have been possible. In this analysis, the 1802 Health and Morals of Apprentices Act is perhaps the initial motivator, since this was the first time any thought had been applied to factory conditions. It was legislation that was introduced by Sir Robert Peel, father of the future prime minister Robert Peel, after an outbreak of fever at his mills outside Manchester in 1784, and it sought to introduce a healthier standard of care for young children apprenticed to factories. This was the first piece of factory legislation that was intended to introduce some, albeit limited, regulation, and without this the more substantial reforms of 1833 may not have been possible. This is arguably because the interest of employers was so strong that any attempt to restrict their activities would have been met with opposition. By first introducing limited changes, it softened the blow and made subsequent reforms more palatable. This idea has further validity in the sense that small changes helped to promote a different attitude, and by 1833 it is reasonable to suggest that the earlier changes instituted by, first, the 1802 legislation and then subsequent reforms such as the 1819 Cotton Mills and Factory Act, which further restricted child labour to over nine years old, helped to foster a more sympathetic attitude that allowed for the extensive changes made in 1833. By the same token, it is reasonable to suggest that this Act then gave future reforms the same opportunity – the 1842 Mines Act and 1847 Factory Act in particular. In this sense, although it is fair to say that there were other reforms after 1833 that were just as significant, if not more so, the existence of that legislation is what made all that followed possible.

> This paragraph introduces some debate, but relates it effectively to the overall argument using logical development and a good range of evidence in support.

In conclusion, the 1833 Factory Act can legitimately be celebrated as a substantial influence upon working practices in the period 1759–1928 because it not only set down clear regulations and restrictions for working practices but also paved the way for future reforms that helped to transform the experiences of workers in Britain.

> A clear judgement is made here that is well supported in the body of the response.

Verdict

This is a strong student answer because:

- it is clearly analytical and offers a well-defined argument
- throughout the response, there is good use of precise and well-selected evidence to support the points made
- it considers a counterargument and includes this as part of an overall developed evaluation.

Index

Acknowledgements

The authors and publisher would like to thank the following individuals and organisations for permission to reproduce photographs and text in this book.

(Key: b-bottom; c-centre; l-left; r-right; t-top)

Alamy Images: Classic Image 63, ClassicStock 58, Heritage Image Partnership Ltd 153, Liszt Collection 75, National Geographic Image Collection 6, World History Archive 29; **Birmingham Museums Trust:** 172; **Bridgeman Art Library Ltd:** De Agostini Picture Library/G. Dagli Orti 146, Private Collection 82, Salisbury Museum 67; **Fotolia.com:** Juulijs 93; **Getty Images:** Culture Club 100, Edward Gooch 162, Oxford Science Archive/Print Collector 80, SSPL 112, 132; **Mary Evans Picture Library:** 8, 22, 34, 43, 61, Illustrated London News Ltd 121, 134, 155, Peter Higginbotham Collection 49, Thaliastock 13; **National Trust Images:** 87, Mike Williams 94; **Punch Limited:** 149; **Science Photo Library Ltd:** 127; **The Francis Frith Collection:** 89; **The Wedgwood Museum:** 70; **TopFoto:** 120

Cover image: Getty Images: Science and Society Picture Library

All other images © Pearson Education

Figures

Figure 4.2 from Was technological change in the early Industrial Revolution Schumpeterian? Evidence of cotton textile profitability, *Explorations in Economic History*, vol. 49, pp.516–27 (Knick-Harley, 2012), copyright © 2012, with permission from Elsevier; Figures 7.1, 7.3 adapted from *Herbert Austin: The British Motor Car Industry to 1941*, Europa Publications Ltd (Roy Church 1979) Tab.1, p.19, with permission from Emeritus Professor Roy Church; Figure 7.2 from The motor industry in Britain to 1914, *Business History*, vol. 5 (1), p.25 (S.B. Saul, 1962), copyright © 1962 Routledge, reprinted by permission of Taylor & Francis Ltd, http://www.tandfonline.com; Figure 7.4 after *Herbert Austin: The British Motor Car Industry to 1941*, Europa Publications Ltd (Roy Church 1979) Tab.5 and Tab.6, pp. 82,84, with permission from Emeritus Professor Roy Church; Figure 7.5 from Demand and supply constraints in the inter-war UK car industry: Did the manufacturers get it right?, *Business History*, vol. 33 (2), pp.241–267 (Sue. M. Bowden, 1991), copyright © 1991 Routledge, reprinted by permission of Taylor & Francis Ltd, http://www.tandfonline.com.

Maps

Map 5.1 adapted from Philip Bagwell, *The Transport Revolution from 1770*, Batsford Ltd (1974), reproduced with kind permission of B.T. Batsford, part of Pavilion Books Company Limited.

Text

Extract p.14 from The rise and fall of the factory system: Technology, firms, and households since the Industrial Revolution, *Carnegie-Rochester Conference Series on Public Policy*, vol. 55 (1), pp.1–45 (Joel Mokyr), Dec 2001, copyright © 2001 Elsevier B.V., reprinted with permission from Elsevier; Source 4 p.18 from a speech by Michael Sadler (1829) from *Hansard Parliamentary Debates*, 3rd set, 1830–1891, Contains Parliamentary information licensed under the Open Parliament Licence v3.0; Extract p.42 from *First Report of Commissioners for Inquiring Into the Employment and Condition of Children in Mines and Manufactories* (London: Her Britannic Majesty's Stationery Office, 1842), vol. 16, pp.83–85, Contains public sector information licensed under the Open Government Licence (OGL) v3.0.http://www.nationalarchives.gov.uk/doc/open-government-licence; Extract p.46 from *Poverty: A Study of Town Life*, Macmillan (Benjamin Seebohm Rowntree, 1901) p.137, reproduced with permission; p.52 from The National Education League, *The Spectator*, 23/10/1869, p.13 (J.L.L. Davis), http://archive.spectator.co.uk/article/23rd-october-1869/13/the-national-education-league, copyright © 2013 The Spectator (1828) Ltd. All rights reserved; Extract p.55 from *Hansard*

Education Bill, HC Deb 13 March 1918, vol. 104 cc335–447 www.Parliament.uk © Parliamentary Copyright, Contains Parliamentary information licensed under the Open Parliament Licence v3.0; Extract 1 p.80 from The canal system of England by Hubert Gordon Thompson, 1904, https://en.wikisource.org/wiki/Page%3AThe_Canal_System_of_England.djvu/20, Licenced under the Creative Commons Attribution-ShareAlike License; Extract 2 p.80 from *The Archaeology of the Roman Economy,* University of California Press (Kevin Greene, 1990) p.34, republished with permission of University of California Press, permission conveyed through Copyright Clearance Center, Inc.; Extract 1 p.98 from Legal child abuse by Wendy McElroy (01/04/2001) http://www.independent.org/newsroom/article.asp?id=26, Wendy McElroy is an individualist feminist and fellow of the Independent Institute who has authored several works on feminism; Extract 3 p.80 from The decline of the canals by Mike Clarke, https://canalrivertrust.org.uk/enjoy-the-waterways/canal-history/the-decline-of-the-canals, Canal River Trust, reproduced with permission; Extract 2 p.98 from *Child Workers and Industrial Health in Britain 1780–1850,* Boydell & Brewer (Peter Kirby 2013), reproduced with permission; Extract 3 p.102 from British mercantilist policies and the American colonies in *The Cambridge Economic History of the United States,* Cambridge University Press (John McCusker, eds. Stanley L. Engerman and Robert E. Gallman, 1996) p.339, Copyright © 1996 Cambridge University Press; Extract 4 p.102 from Mercantilism by Laura LaHaye, http://www.econlib.org/library/Enc/Mercantilism.html#abouttheauthor, Copyright © 2008 Liberty Fund, Inc. All Rights Reserved; Extract 5 p.102 from Mercantilism: a lesson for our times? by Murray Rothbard (01/11/1963), Foundation for Economic Education, http://fee.org/articles/mercantilism-a-lesson-for-our-times/, Licensed under Creative Commons Attribution 4.0 International Licence; Extract p.108 from Brunel's obituary, *The Engineer,* 23/09/1859, reproduced with permission; Extract 1 p.128 from *Brunel: The Man Who Built the World,* Phoenix Press (Stephen Brindel and Dan Cruickshank 2006) p.179, copyright © Weidenfeld & Nicolson 2005, reproduced with permission from The Orion Publishing Group London; Extract 3 p.128 from *Brunel: The Life and Times of Isambard Kingdom Brunel,* Hambledon Continuum (R. Angus Buchanan, 2002) p.213, © Angus Buchanan 2002, used by permission of Bloomsbury Publishing Plc; Extract p.142 from *The Wheels of Chance* (H.G. Wells, 1896), reproduced with permission from The United Agents LLP on behalf of The Literary Executors of the Estate of H.G. Wells; Extract 1 p.147 from Representations of the New Woman in the 1890s, unpublished PhD thesis by Clare Mendes, University of Leicester 2013, pp.122–123, reproduced with permission; Extract 1 p.156 from The motor industry in Britain to 1914, *Business History,* vol. 5 (1), p.22 (S.B. Saul, 1962), copyright © 1962 Routledge, reprinted by permission of Taylor & Francis Ltd, http://www.tandfonline.com; Extract 2 p.156 from *The Rise and Decline of the British Motor Industry,* Cambridge University Press (Roy A. Church, 1995) p.6, copyright © 1995 Cambridge University Press; Extract p.157 from re: the Austin Motor Co. *The Times,* p.13, 1914. Copyright © The Times 2016; Extract p.161 from *Austin Motor Company Report,* 1919, Austin Memories, http://www.austinmemories.com/styled-65/index.htm, © British Motor Industry Heritage Trust; Extract p.164 from Notice for Austin Seven, 08/01/1923 by Austin Motor Co., Austin Memories, http://www.austinmemories.com/styled-65/index.htm, © British Motor Industry Heritage Trust; Extract p.170 from Manners on the road, *Autocar,* 17/09/1926, reproduced with permission.